Purchased from
Multnomah County Library
Title Wave Used Bookstore
216 NE Knott St, Portland, OR
503-988-5021

SYRIA
and the NEW
WORLD
ORDER

SYRIA
and the NEW
WORLD
ORDER

 Neil Quilliam

Durham Middle East Monographs Series

ITHACA
PRESS

SYRIA AND THE NEW WORLD ORDER

Ithaca Press is an imprint of Garnet Publishing Limited

Published by
Garnet Publishing Limited
8 Southern Court
South Street
Reading
RG1 4QS
UK

First Edition

ISBN 0 86372 249 0

British Library Cataloguing-in-Publication Data
A catalogue record for this book is available from the British Library

Jacket design by Michael Hinks
Typeset by Samantha Abley

Printed in Lebanon

Contents

Figures

Abbreviations

AA	Air-to-air
ACC	Arab Cooperation Council
ASU	Arab Socialist Union
ATF	Advanced Tactical Fighter
CIA	Central Intelligence Agency
FIS	Front islamique du Salut (Islamic Salvation Front)
GCC	Gulf Cooperation Council
GDP	Gross Domestic Product
GIA	Groupe islamique armé (Armed Islamic Group)
IDF	Israeli Defense Forces
IMF	International Monetary Fund
LF	Lebanese Forces
LNM	Lebanese National Movement
MBT	Main Battle Tank
NATO	North Atlantic Treaty Organization
NICs	Newly Industrialising Countries
NPF	National Progressive Front
NSC	National Security Council
NSF	National Salvation Front
PDFLP	Popular Democratic Front for the Liberation of Palestine
PFLP	Popular Front for the Liberation of Palestine
PFLP-GC	Popular Front for the Liberation of Palestine – General Command
PLA	Palestine Liberation Army
PLO	Palestine Liberation Organisation
PNC	Palestine National Command
SAM	Surface-to-air Missile
SCP	Syrian Communist Party
SEATO	South-East Asia Treaty Organisation

SS	Surface-to-surface
SSNP	Syrian Socialist National Party
TNCs	Transnational Corporations
UAR	United Arab Republic
UN	United Nations

Acknowledgements

I would like to extend my gratitude in particular to Dr Anoushiravan Ehteshami, who supervised this study, and has continued to inspire me through his dynamism, professionalism, and optimism, and to Professor Ray Hinnebusch, whom I was fortunate to work with in 1993-4. I benefited greatly from his experience, insights and intellectual generosity. My first research trip to Syria was enhanced through his extensive knowledge of the country and his network of loyal friends.

Caution deters me from acknowledging specific friends and contacts established in Syria, but I am indebted to those individuals who granted me access to their families, society and political culture.

During those dark days of writing up, the inspiration flowed from Deheisheh camp, and the poetry of Mawgojzeta made the difference.

Neil Quilliam

If a person were to try stripping the disguises from actors while they play a scene upon the stage, showing to the audience their real looks and the faces they were born with, would not such a one spoil the whole play? And would not the spectators think he deserved to be driven out of the theatre with brickbats, as a drunken disturber? . . . Now what else is the whole life of mortals but a sort of comedy, in which the various actors disguised by various costumes and masks, walk on and play each one his part, until the manager waves them off the stage? Moreover, this manager frequently bids the same actor go back in a different costume, so that he who has but lately played the king in scarlet now acts the flunky in patched clothes. Thus all things are presented by shadows.

(**Erasmus,** *The Praise of Folly*)

Introduction

One is faced with two insoluble problems when writing about contemporary politics. The first is the propensity for political change. This alone can challenge the authenticity of one's research or, alternatively, confirm one's own analysis. I have been fortunate with my subject as Syria has enjoyed an unprecedented period of stability for the past twenty-seven years; but I have also lived under the shadow of President Hafiz al-Asad's imminent death. This has contained the seeds of destruction of my hypothesis.

It is my contention that Syria has been prepared for peace since the early 1970s. In contrast with the speculation about Asad's death, the possibility of a breakthrough in the peace talks has held the chance of vindicating my hypothesis. For now, the moment has passed, and I have to wait alongside other Syria watchers to observe history reveal itself.

Secondly, where there is political stability, one is also faced with the prospect of regurgitating existing ideas and analyses. The proliferation of articles and books published since Syria's entry into the Gulf War coalition in 1990, and its participation in the Madrid Peace Conference in 1991, have pre-empted and contributed to my analysis. In order to put these analyses in context, I have attempted to incorporate Syria's adjustment to the New World Order in a theoretical framework.

The contribution of this work, therefore, is its attempt to offer a better understanding of how the structural determinants of the international political system have affected Syria's foreign policy since the advent of the New World Order.

This work is organised in six chapters. Chapter 1 describes the tools of analysis used for the theoretical framework of this study. The components of Syria's power, and the centres of Syrian power, are addressed in Chapters 2 and 3 respectively. Chapter 4 examines Syria's role in the regional balance of power, with particular reference to its struggle with Israel. And the two case studies, of the Gulf War and the Madrid Peace Conference, are scrutinised in Chapters 5 and 6.

Syrian foreign policy

Syrian foreign policy, since independence in 1946, has been shaped and justified by Arab nationalism. After the Ba'th party had seized power in 1963, Syrian foreign policy called for the total liberation of Palestine, and the overthrow of the Arab state system. The military disaster of 1967, however, discredited the cogency of Arab nationalism as a dynamic political force.

Asad's assumption of power in November 1970 heralded a new era in the formulation of foreign policy; since then, a sense of realism has been injected into the process. The role of ideology was relegated, and the new determinants of foreign policy have been shaped primarily by the international political system. Syrian foreign policy has been based on:

(a) The preservation of national security;
(b) The enhancement of its power and prestige within the regional state-system.

The hypothesis of this research is that Syria has managed to adjust to the New World Order by following a rational foreign policy. Syria's adjustment to the New World Order, which represented a transformation in the global redistribution of power, has been consistent with its regional objectives. Syria's participation in the second Gulf War, and its decision to engage in the Madrid Peace Conference, are testaments to its implementation of rational policies. These decisions were founded upon its national interest, national security, and the containment of Israel.

The New World Order

The conclusion of the Cold War was marked by the collapse of the Soviet system and the succession of the US-led world capitalist system. The end of the bipolar world order has produced a period of political unipolarity and economic multipolarity. Wherever Soviet influence has abated, US political, economic, and cultural hegemony have superseded it.

In the absence of the bipolar system, the US has filled the political vacuum and assumed the role of global leader. State and non-state resistance to US hegemony have, in some cases, resulted in punitive measures. The bombing of Libya in 1986 pre-empted the collapse of the old world order, and set a precedent for the flexibility at the core of the changing world order, with the wider foreign policy options available to the US as a result of the change in superpower relations. Without the support of their Soviet patron, the "pariah" states of the Middle East became vulnerable to US foreign policy designs.

The implosion of the Soviet Union in August 1991, and the ensuing transformation of the world order from a bipolar to a unipolar structure, have compelled Syria to adjust to the dominant US hegemonic order. *Inter alia*, the objective of this study is to define the New World Order, especially within the Middle East, and to ascertain how Syria has adjusted, whilst remaining consistent in its foreign policy.

The destruction of Iraq by the US-led coalition, in the liberation of Kuwait, indicated the nature and potency of the New World Order. The unipolar dimension of the Middle East, perpetuated by the presence of Israel, has become a resounding feature of the New World Order.

Perceived as an irrational, irredentist, and ideological opponent of the US throughout the 1980s, Syria appeared to have a most uncertain future. Adjustment without capitulation became a necessity for the Syrian state; the political elite required the opportunity to display its commitment to the changes of the New World Order. Iraq's invasion of Kuwait provided Syria with the prime opportunity to change its strategy, and to adjust to the New World Order.

Case studies

Syria's accommodation of the New World Order will be appraised through an examination of two case studies: Syria's inclusion in the US-led Gulf War coalition in 1990-1; and its decisive entry into the Madrid peace process in 1991.

The Gulf War coalition

With the decline of Soviet influence in world affairs, unipolarity, particularly in the Middle East, has defined the structure of the world order in the post-bipolar era. The absence of Soviet support has accentuated Syria's security dilemma. Its inability to resist the pull of the hegemonic world order has compelled it to abandon its former foreign policy strategies and to adopt a more US-centric approach.

The primary motivation behind Syria's participation in the Gulf War coalition derived from its necessity to realign its global position. Syria's decision was calculated according to a rational set of criteria. The gravity of the decision emanated from Syria's new found regional and international vulnerability. In order to occupy a role in the postwar regional order, Syria joined the US-led coalition.

Its participation afforded it the chance to move closer to the US without capitulating in its foreign policy objectives. The execution of this decision appeared, to some observers, to undermine Syria's Arab credentials. It is the contention of the author, however, that Syria's decision was consistent with its Arab nationalist agenda. The US promise to convene an international peace conference underlay Syria's motive for allying itself with the conservative Gulf Arab states, and the world's hegemonic power.

The Madrid Peace Conference

The transformation in the world order created a *window of opportunity* for Israel and the Arab states to reach a resolution of the Arab–Israeli conflict. The structural determinants, namely, the emergence of the US as the world's superpower, coupled with a weakened Arab world, have produced a political climate conducive to resolving the conflict. International and regional hegemony invested the US with enough power to impose peace upon the region.

The hypothesis of this research proffers that peace for Syria has become a strategic option since the decline of Soviet support and the ascension of US influence in the New World Order. This will be examined with special reference to the Madrid Peace Conference. The period under review runs from the beginning of the Conference, in October 1991, until the election of Benyamin Netanyahu as Prime Minister of Israel in May 1996.

The Madrid Peace Conference has initiated an irreversible process in which Jordan, a Palestinian delegation, Lebanon, Syria, and Israel participated in peace negotiations. Syria's commitment to the peace process has been consistent with its foreign policy goals, namely: (a) the liberation of the Arab territories occupied in 1967; (b) the restoration of Palestinian rights; and (c) the containment of Israel.

Despite popular public perceptions, Syria's participation in the peace process has been compatible with its foreign policy. The achievement of comprehensive peace has been an option for the Syrians since 1974. The term "comprehensive" refers to a coordinated approach by the Arab states to reach a final settlement with Israel. Prior to the Madrid Peace Conference, peace, for the Syrians, included a total Israeli withdrawal from the Arab territories occupied in 1967 and the restoration of Palestinian rights.

Egypt's signing of the Camp David Accords in 1979 had severely weakened Syria's regional standing and increased its vulnerability to Israel's hegemonic ambitions. Israel's invasion of Lebanon in 1982, sanctioned by the US, demonstrated Syria's vulnerability to the conclusion of the separate peace between Egypt and Israel. The Madrid formula gave Syria the chance to place itself at the centre of the peace process and to coordinate the policies of its partners: Lebanon, the Palestine Liberation Organisation (PLO), and Jordan. The agreements between Israel and the PLO, and between Israel and Jordan, however, have circumvented the centrality of Syria to the peace process.

Despite the separate agreements, Syria has resisted capitulation and remained resolute in fulfilling its objectives of preserving security, maximising power, containing Israel, and extending its hegemony throughout the Levant. Adjusting to the New World Order has enabled Syria to attend to its foreign policy objectives.

1

The Tools of Analysis

Introduction

The change in the international political environment during 1989–90, precipitated by the collapse of the Soviet Union and the emerging unipolar distribution of power, held significant implications for Syria. The New World Order contained an implicit threat to Syria and the other "pariah" states of the Middle East, as the US and its allies enjoyed the triumph of a new era in international relations. One result of the New World Order was the diffusion of US hegemony in the Middle East region; the Cold War logic that pitted and restrained direct Israeli–Syrian conflict dissipated overnight, and exposed Syria to both Israeli and US hostility.

The demise of its superpower patron, the Soviet Union, added to Syria's regional and international isolation. Syria's vulnerability to the vagaries of the region's politics challenged both the support of the regime and its role in the region. Without Soviet aid, the Syrians were left to defend their interests in Lebanon, engage in a struggle for the leadership of the Arab world with a newly invigorated Iraq and a rehabilitated Egypt, and maintain a state of confrontation with Israel. The determinants of the new regional and international political systems dictated that Syria had to pursue a different strategy to the one adopted after the signing of the Camp David Accords. Adjusting to the prerequisites of the New World Order was an essential facet of Syria's foreign policy reorientation in the late 1980s and early 1990s.

The Syrians were compelled to reappraise their foreign policy as the search for strategic parity with Israel became a casualty of the New World Order. The Syrian response to the New World Order entailed a more accommodating approach to US-led initiatives without capitulation in its foreign policy objectives. The goal of strategic parity was replaced with the notion of the strategic option for peace. Syria's overtures, however, appeared to Western observers to be empty words. And then Iraq invaded Kuwait.

Syria was able, given the golden opportunity, to realign itself towards a more US-centric position following Iraq's invasion of Kuwait in August 1990. Unwittingly, Saddam Hussein provided his old enemy, Asad, with a bargaining counter which he could use to negotiate Syria's support of the US-led Gulf War coalition. As Saddam challenged the nature of the New World Order, he opened up an opportunity for Asad, who seized it with sagacity, and surged for the starting-blocks of a promised international peace process.

The paradigms of international relations

The paradigms of realism, pluralism, and globalism will provide the foundation-stones for this study. After a summary of the paradigms has been presented, a revised version of Steven David's concept of omnibalancing is offered as the most suitable framework for this study.[1] Omnibalancing will enable us to gain a more comprehensive understanding of Syria's foreign policy, as it addresses some of the issues neglected by the Western-centric paradigms.

Realism

Realism is considered to be a timeless study of power politics; it proffers a universal and conclusive understanding of international relations. Power is central to realism: it exists in the three levels of analysis, the *individual*, the *state*, and the *system*.[2] For the realists, power is accumulated, monopolised, and exercised by the state.

The four main assumptions in the realist paradigm can be summarised as follows:

(a)   The state is the principal actor in international relations;
(b)   The state is unitary;
(c)   The state is a rational actor;
(d)   The state is preoccupied with national security.[3]

Neo-realism

Realism is grounded in a basic understanding of human nature. As a timeless and universal constant, human nature is depicted by realists as *egoistic.* Self-preservation and self-interest motivate human behaviour. Human destiny is, therefore, marked by the struggle for survival through a competition for finite resources.[4] Motivated by competition, individuals have formed themselves into organisational units to maximise their potential. The historical progress of human organisation has led to the complex form of the state.

Neo-realism is based on the same assumptions as realism, but rather than locating human nature as the source of state behaviour, neo-realism places its emphasis on the structure of the international political system. Neo-realism, or structural realism, identifies the natural state of anarchy, within which states exist, as the main determinant of state behaviour. Survival is the primordial reason for the state, where behaviour is governed by self-help in a system of states.[5]

Neo-realism avers that the behaviour of states is dictated by universal laws that emanate from the structure of the system of states. The differentiation among states in terms of size, population, and geopolitics affects the power-ratio of relations; nevertheless, all states function according to the determinants of the international political system. Consequently, the behaviour of states is codified by the system rather than by domestic concerns.

Both realists and neo-realists agree that the internal dynamics of states, such as their domestic political systems, are not relevant to the formulation of foreign policy. Foreign policy should be based upon a rational set of objectives if the state is to survive in the anarchic arena. To protect their sovereignty, states try to achieve a balance of power.

Of the numerous definitions of the balance of power, the most appropriate one to this study is perceived·as *the distribution of power in the international political system.*[6] The balance-of-power theory operates from the assumption that the structure of the international political system is anarchic: "self-help is necessarily the principle of action in an anarchic order."[7] States are motivated by their national interests, and naturally compete with each other for resources both within regional and international contexts.

Pluralism

Pluralism owes its legacy to a combination of idealism and liberalism. In pluralism, unlike in realism, power is not the central theme. Pluralism is more concerned with the notions of *cooperation, coexistence,* and *interdependence.* Cooperation and interdependence in pluralism place the stress not on the state of anarchy but on the notion of peaceful coexistence. Pluralists stress the interdependent nature of the global economy. The success of global capitalism is considered to be an inevitable triumph for the common good.[8]

The pluralist image of international relations is based on four main assumptions:

(a)   Non-state actors are important;
(b)   The state is not a unitary actor;
(c)   The state is not a rational actor;
(d)   The agenda of international politics is extensive.[9]

Globalism

The last paradigm to be used in this study can be termed "globalism". It shares some features with both realism and pluralism, but is distinguished in its perception of the world capitalist system. The essence of globalism can be found in its study of dependency. While pluralists perceive the global economy in terms of *interdependence*, globalists view the global economy in terms of *dependence.*[10]

Globalists contend that the structure of the world capitalist system perpetuates an inequitable relationship between the North and the South.[11] Wallerstein demarcates the organisation of the global economy into *the core* and *the periphery.* In this model, the periphery serves the interests of the core, and the inequitable level of exchange ensures that the core remains the dominant partner in the relationship. He identifies a transition belt between the two poles, known as the *semi-periphery,* that accommodates Newly Industrialising Countries (NICs), such as Taiwan, Singapore, and Hong Kong.[12] Mobility between the poles, however, is strictly limited, and this ensures that the states of the periphery remain dependent upon the states of the core.[13]

Globalists use systems analysis as their mode of enquiry. They perceive the economic relations between the North and the South as dependent. The outcome of the structure and processes of global capitalism represents the next stage of imperialism. Wallerstein approaches the succession of capitalism from a diametrically opposed position to that of the pluralists; he denotes that global capitalism perpetuates dependency and oppression. His work concentrates on identifying anti-systemic forces that will initiate the next systemic phase of global economic and political organisation.[14]

Globalists, in their analysis of international relations, adhere to four main assumptions:

(a)   Economic globalism defines the international system;
(b)   The international system defines the level of analysis;
(c)   Historical analysis is relevant;
(d)   Dependency is perpetuated by mechanisms of economic domination.[15]

Omnibalancing – the way forward?

If it is possible to reduce the above paradigms to their absolute minimum, they can be summarised by the following terms:

(a)   Realism – *power*;
(b)   Pluralism – *interdependence*;
(c)   Globalism – *dependence*.

Omnibalancing manages to incorporate components of each paradigm and presents a multidimensional model that is more appropriate to the Third World. Omnibalancing attempts to bridge the division between the international perspective, which is lodged in systemic or world systems analysis, and the domestic analysis of state behaviour.[16] It provides us with a model that can account for the multiplicity of inputs that affects the behaviour of states. It operates from a realist perspective in the international realm, and integrates pluralist and globalist maxims in the domestic field. Omnibalancing is founded on the following assumptions:

(a)   Power is the focus of international politics;
(b)   Third World states are not unitary;
(c)   The leader of the state is a level of analysis;
(d)   Foreign policy is conducted according to a rational criteria.[17]

Power is the focus of international politics

In keeping with realist thought, omnibalancing stresses the centrality of power to government of relations among states. The balance of power emerges as the most effective mechanism available for regulating international relations. The balance of power, however, is considered to provide an inadequate explanation for Third World states' behaviour. This is because it is confined to international relations and dismisses the relevance of the internal dynamics of states.[18]

Third World states are not unitary

Omnibalancing departs from realist and neo-realist analysis when addressing the issue of the state. Unlike in realism, omnibalancing considers the state in the Third World to be a unitary actor. The state is divided and subject to intense competition among a variety of social, ethnic, confessional, and sectoral groups. Competition deviates from that portrayed by pluralists; because of the turbulence generated by state-building, survival of the regime is dependent upon the subjugation of opponents. In this case, the environment of the domestic arena is perceived as anarchic rather than hierarchical.

Omnibalancing transposes the anarchy present within the international system into the domestic system. Without an indigenous institutionalised political system to channel opposition through a political process, Third World regimes have striven to balance the interests of competing groups in order to limit domestic unrest. For David, then, the balance of power can be used to examine domestic politics, and is an analytical tool for explaining state or regime behaviour.

Regimes of the Third World have tended to be composed of specific ethnic or linguistic groups that benefited from the divide-and-rule policies of previous colonial powers. These ruling minority groups have depended upon authoritarian rule and the creation of patrimonial structures to guarantee their survival. With a narrow base of support and their survival constantly threatened, such ruling groups have conducted policies according to their particular interests rather than national interests. This has been particularly true in the case of state leaders.[19]

The leader of the state

Because of the recent historical experiences of most Third World states, which were created artificially and not according to contiguous precedents, social cohesion has tended to be low. In such cases, state–society relations have often lacked an institutional framework to support the role of civil society and, therefore, a disjunction between regime and society has developed.[20]

David intimates that in the Third World authoritarian rule has been accompanied by the development of personality cults. State leaders have occupied positions that have remained largely uncontested and unaccountable to the public.[21] The decision-making process rotates around the interests of the leader and his closest aides; decisions taken by the regime are supported by the security services and the regime barons to secure regime survival.

Regime survival is the foremost objective of Third World leaders and can be achieved through balancing the interests of domestic groups and forming alliances according to the regional balance of power.[22] This has led David to reassert that state interests, in the Third World, are necessarily subordinate to the requisites of regime survival.

Foreign policy – a rational criterion?
Systemic factors are held partially responsible, by neo-realists, for foreign policies of Third World states, but for David domestic politics play the primary part in shaping the determinants of foreign policy.[23] Despite the importance that David attaches to the role played by domestic politics and the structural forces of the international system in forming foreign policy, omnibalancing recognises that foreign policy is based upon a rational decision-making process. The political elite balances the constraints and the opportunities of the domestic arena against the international system, exercising rational policies to maximise the longevity of the regime. By doing so, it offers the regime a degree of flexibility and autonomy from both domestic and international constraints. David does, however, give greater importance to the role of internal threats than to that of external threats as motivators of foreign policy; in this vein Goode suggests that foreign policy is domestic policy pursued by other means.[24]

Syria's adjustment to the New World Order will be analysed here using a revised omnibalancing model construed from the three paradigms of international relations theory. This study will be based upon the following assumptions:

(a) The state is the principal actor;
(b) National security dominates the concerns of the state;
(c) The state balances international politics against domestic politics;
(d) Power accumulation serves the objectives of the state.

In contrast to other parts of the world, the threats to, opportunities for, and constraints on the states of the Middle East are especially acute. They owe their existence to the continuous presence of international actors in the Middle Eastern state-system. The penetration of the Middle East region by the world's powers has guaranteed that the international political system impinges upon states' foreign policies. In contrast, the lack of institutionalisation in many of the states of the Middle East has made them particularly susceptible to the configurations of power within the domestic realm. Hence, it is important to examine the autonomy of the state.

Autonomy of the state

The political scientist is beset with numerous problems when attempting to quantify the autonomy a state enjoys. It is crucial, however, to appreciate the extent of this autonomy in order to understand the role of the state in international relations.[25]

Before discussing the components of autonomy, four points, suggested by Potter, should be taken into account:

(a) State autonomy and state power are not synonymous. States are autonomous when they are *free* to decide on and pursue their own goals. States are powerful when they also have the *capacity* to achieve these goals despite opposition.[26]

(b) The autonomy of states in relation to the global economy can vary at different levels. States in economically disadvantaged countries can be largely autonomous in relation to domestic groups; meanwhile, they have little autonomy from transnational corporations (TNCs) and internationally dominant groups.[27]

(c) A state is composed of a collection of entities, where one part may be more autonomous in relation to domestic and international forces than another part.

(d) State autonomy is not static; its study, therefore, must be undertaken with respect to the historical moment. Chomsky refers the analyst to the case of the NICs. The autonomy of these states was originally considerable as their propulsion towards the semi-periphery was engineered by the state.[28] However, private capital has strengthened the position of the domestic capitalist class *vis-à-vis* the state, and the autonomy of the state in some cases is diminishing.[29]

Nordlinger identifies four variables which are useful for determining the degree of autonomy a state enjoys. The first two refer to the positive sides of autonomy: insulation and resilience; the second two refer to the challenge to autonomy: malleability and vulnerability.[30] Although the four variables tend to overlap, and some parts seem rather obvious, it is, nevertheless, useful to delineate them for the convenience of this study.

Malleability

Malleability refers to the responsive features of the state. If a state is particularly receptive and sensitive to certain domestic interests, it is deemed malleable. The extent of malleability can be gauged through the cohesion of the state.[31] If the cohesive factor of the state is high, the level of porosity is low, and the state enjoys some autonomy. The level of cohesion depends upon two factors:

(a) **The historical formation of the state**: If the state has emerged from a long struggle with domestic actors, as in a revolutionary struggle, its cohesion tends to be durable. A struggle with an external power, however, might produce cohesion, usually based on nationalism, but the durability of that cohesion is short-lived, due to the disparate and latent forces of the nationalist struggle waiting to re-emerge.[32]

(b) **The role and the function of the bureaucracy**: Where a bureaucracy is highly developed and self-perpetuating, the state is cohesive and less malleable. When a bureaucracy is less developed and based on patrimonialism, the state's cohesion is less and the degree of malleability is high.[33]

Vulnerability

Vulnerability connotes the ability of a state to implement a policy that may run against public opinion and the interests of powerful domestic groups. Nordlinger suggests that public officials realise that some policy goals cannot be realised by offering material incentives, or by simply issuing laws and regulations.[34] Vulnerability is not constrained to the domestic sphere; states are becoming increasingly vulnerable to the vagaries of the global economy. For example, the constraints placed upon developing states to oblige them to conform to the regulations of the International Monetary Fund (IMF), often resulting in the implementation of unpopular economic policies, add to the states' vulnerability.[35]

Insulation

The ultimate source of insulation that ensures autonomy for the state is its ability to exercise monopoly over coercive means. If the autonomy of the state is under direct threat, it may resort to coercive measures. The willingness to use such coercive means is often dependent upon, though not necessarily, the history of the state and the legitimacy of its ruling institutions. If the institutions of the state are not well defined and only tacitly accepted among the domestic population, opposition to the state may take the form of an insurrection.[36]

Resilience

Insulation and resilience are closely interrelated and help develop the concept of autonomy. Insulation is the *protection* of autonomy, and resilience is the *maintenance* of that autonomy. The resilience of the state refers to its capacity to counteract potential and actual opposition, whose aims may range from challenging the administrative rule to the overthrow of the state.[37]

Resilience can exist in the form of coercive means, the transfer of ideas, or a dependency upon national issues.[38] Traditionally, the state's monopoly over information has served the interests of the state, but the growth of information technology has divested the state of such controls. In its more primitive forms,[39] information could be disseminated in conjunction with the objectives of the state. Resilience has been perpetuated by the constant portrayal of internal and/or external threats to the national interest.[40]

The definition of an autonomous state, which seems most appropriate to this study, is a state that prevails when its interests conflict with those of other powerful actors. The autonomy of the state is not only subjected to the configuration of domestic interest, but is also inherently influenced by the diffusion of power within the international political system.

Power

Power is a key concept in understanding the behaviour of states but is extremely difficult to quantify because it has both tangible and intangible forms. Power can exist in a potential or a realised form. The conversion of potential power to realised power, however, is not always proportionate;

this can lead to a situation where a state acts beyond its means and capabilities.

Power can be considered simply as the ability to get others to do what they would otherwise not do.[41] This definition works on the assumption that a state attempts to influence the decisions taken by other states; nevertheless, the structural determinants of the international system can compel the state to take decisions that are not in favour of its perceived interests.[42]

If a state is to impose its preferences on to another state, its power projection should be greater than the projection of its adversary to succeed in a bilateral challenge or exchange.[43] Exchanges rarely include only two actors, as the structure of the international system and the existence of interdependent interests invite third parties to intervene diplomatically or otherwise. To gauge the power projection of a state it is necessary to define the repositories of power and analyse their relative value.

Power inputs

The sources of power available to the state can be identified as:

(a)   Geography;
(b)   Population;
(c)   Natural resources;
(d)   History and nationalism.

Geography

Geography refers to the geopolitical location of a state, and the size of its territory. The location of a state, and the number of boundaries it shares with other states, often determine the level of state vulnerability. The size of the territory can endow a state with abundant indigenous resources.[44] Size, however, has also proven to contain debilitating factors. Before the transportation and communication revolution, large territories, such as Russia and China, were rendered vulnerable to the excesses of Turkish, British, and Japanese imperialism. The utility of geography, as a source of national power, depends on the cohesion and distribution of population.[45]

Population

The size, composition, and distribution of a population can have an important impact on national power. A large population can provide an input into industrialisation, militarisation, and national purpose.[46] It can sustain a long-term war (such as the Iran–Iraq war), and can provide an engine for economic change (as in China).[47] A large population is not, however, sufficient in itself to produce these goals. Algeria and Egypt have substantial populations, but they have not propelled their respective states towards the centre or the semi-periphery of the global economy.[48] For a state to achieve empowerment through its population, the state must enjoy:

(a) Social cohesion;
(b) A high level of universal education;
(c) An adequate distribution, and maintenance, of skills;
(d) A national purpose.[49]

Natural resources

Resources are another tangible form of state power. Natural resources can elevate the position of a state in the international system. If they are successfully converted and realised, natural resources can enhance the influence of a state, both in regional and global terms. The extraction, appropriation, and control of natural resources correspond to the conversion of potential power into realised power. The educated population factor adds at this point to the efficacy of the state's control over its own resources, and concomitantly to its own power.

Being a source of power, natural resources can empower or enslave a state. Many of the Third World states exist in the periphery of the global economy. Through policies of economic imperialism, their natural resources have been appropriated, by the core states, on unfavourable terms. The dependency of the periphery upon the core is perpetuated by an uneven exchange of natural resources in return for expensive consumer products. Natural resources, therefore, have been a double-edged sword for the Third World.

History and nationalism

History is a psychological source of power; it plays a major role in constructing *self-perception* and *national identity*. Common historical experiences, founded in culture, religion, and linguistics, produce cohesion within confessions, communities, states, and civilisations.[50] These historical experiences often feed into another ephemeral base of power – nationalism.[51] Nationalism can be used as an instrument to empower a state by mobilising a population behind a national cause. The relevance of nationalism to state behaviour fluctuates. Nationalism can imbue the state with legitimacy, particularly when the state's security is under threat. Hence, nationalism cannot be described as a static input; it is subject to the changes that take place in the political environment.

The state can transform the power inputs of geography, population, natural resources, history, and nationalism into power outputs. This allows a state to project its capabilities onto the regional and international political system.

Power outputs

The conversion of power inputs into outputs has traditionally been perceived within the context of the military and/or security capabilities of the state. Power outputs have served the interests of high politics, especially in areas such as national security.[52] The outputs of power mainly include:

(a) The military;
(b) The economy;
(c) Information.

The military

The military is the most familiar repository of national power. Military capability, in both quantitative (troops and armaments) and qualitative (high-tech weapons systems, training, morale, and cohesion) terms, is the residual power base of any state; it is the ultimate source of diplomacy.[53] The military capability of a state can act as a deterrent, in real terms and in reputation, to a threatening state. The military is more pervasive in the new states of the Third World. Because of their contemporary role in the formation of states, the leaders of the military often occupy sensitive posts in the regime. The military constitutes the backbone of the regime because of the deficit of legitimacy prevalent in the Third World states. The military in some Third World states has been called upon to support their regimes in the event of insurrection or civil war.

The economy
The economy as an output of the state's power can affect the behaviour of other states without incurring or precipitating war. Trade and commerce form a mutual point of contact among states. A buoyant national economy will allow a state to influence the behaviour of its trading partners, especially those within its regional sub-system.

Information
Information has become an output of state power in its own right, and yet it contains a potential to circumvent the national power of the state. As a source of power, information can be used to control or mobilise the populations. Alternatively, information can subvert the predominant ideology of the state, expose the fallibility of the government, and challenge the state's monopoly of truth. Information has always been open to manipulation by the state to serve its own interests.[54]

The afore-mentioned sources of power available to the state can enable it to provide security within the domestic realm and from the international political system. Survival and security are considered to be the prime objectives of statehood.

Traditionally, national security has focused on the physical security of international boundaries. The preoccupation of decision-makers within the state has been the maintenance of secure borders against external threats. From this perspective, national security is tangible and quantifiable as it is concerned with ensuring the territorial integrity of the state.[55]

National security is a difficult concept to analyse where *state* and *nation* are not synonymous. In the Arab world, for instance, where states are a new creation, the Arab nation encompasses the states of the region, giving rise to the Arab system.[56] National security has often been used to refer to the protection of the Arab nation, rather than of specific states.

In the unconsolidated states of the Third World, identifying the recipient of security adds another complication to the notion. As most of these states were artificially created by the imperial powers, the incumbent states lack legitimacy, and, therefore, their regimes feel insecure. In their attempt to legitimise their existence, these regimes are willing to jeopardise the security of their populations in order to preserve their own survival.

As the states of the Third World, and particularly of the Middle East, attempt to consolidate and legitimise their rule, they are obliged to engage in the international political system.

The international political system

To examine Syria's adjustment to the New World Order, it is necessary to understand the relationship between the Middle Eastern state-system and the present international political system. This relationship can be identified in the structure of the international political system. The relationship between the two systems has undergone a transformation since the advent of the New World Order in 1991. It is therefore necessary to scrutinise the coordinates of the New World Order.

The New World Order

The New World Order is no longer new and the debates and discussions over its nature have been fairly comprehensive and conclusive. It has become evident that the New World Order has not represented a significant change in the medium of international relations. Moreover, the role of arbitrary force, previously balanced by the competition between the superpowers, has become a prevailing instrument of the new order. The liberation of Kuwait, and the subsequent games of brinkmanship between the US and Iraq over the terms and implementation of the cease-fire arrangements, have illustrated how the absence of an alternative superpower has allowed the US to dominate the politics of the Middle Eastern region.

The concept of the New World Order was conceived in pluralist terms and espoused by the Bush administration on the eve of the liberation of Kuwait. The connotations of the term conveyed the idea of a new era in international relations, cast in hope and optimism. The conclusion of the Cold War and the emergence of the New World Order were presented as a progression in international relations.[57] There existed, however, a large gulf between rhetoric and reality. Capitalism, democracy, and liberalism triumphed at the failure of communism. Nevertheless, the actions of the Bush administration during the second Gulf War contradicted the liberal ethic of the New World Order and illustrated the predominant role of force in international relations.

Realists work from the perspective that the balance of power manages global and regional affairs, but that it cannot produce a permanent solution to the competition among states. Motivated by the security dilemma, states are cast into an endless race for security.

Bipolarity is a form of balance of power that polarises the world into two hegemonic camps. The polarisation is based upon the distribution of power between the two main antagonists. It is also a system in which power is distributed in such a way that the two states are so powerful that they can defend themselves against any combination of states.[58] The distribution of power that characterised the world order between the conclusion of World War II and the breakdown of the Soviet Union was bipolar; it is thought to have produced far more stability than the multipolarity of the early twentieth century.[59]

The New World Order for realists represents a reconfiguration of this balance of power. The implosion of the Soviet Union created a significant power vacuum, and the US attempted to accommodate the change. In pluralist language, the dislodging of the Soviet Union from its global role was portrayed as an ideological victory. Realism, avoiding the lexicon of the Cold War, recognised a traditional change in the balance of power brought about through the demise of one hegemonic power and the succession of another. The US became the unipolar power in the 1990s.

Unipolarity is the feature of the existing realist model of international relations but, according to realists, this will be replaced by a more fractious multipolar balance of power. The primary position of the US can only be guaranteed by its military superiority. Without a decisive industrial edge, the US will be challenged by the emerging economic centres of Europe, Japan, and China. The New World Order, cast in this mould, refers to the transition from a bipolar organisation of international relations to a multipolar one.

The multipolar division of the world implies that power is distributed among a variety of major states, each containing different sources of power. Through a coalition of alliances, a balance is struck among the states, thus curbing any hegemonic ambitions of expanding states.[60] Where one state develops its capabilities at the expense of its neighbours, thereby constituting a security threat, a realignment of forces takes place to curtail the power of the aggressor state. Thus, equilibrium governs the anarchic state of affairs that is inherent in international relations.

Globalists were aware of the unipolar position of the US before the announcement of the New World Order. Their conceptualisation of international relations, based on the model of dependency, located the states of the Third World in the periphery of the global economy. The arrival of the New World Order confirmed the supremacy of the US as the economic and military leader in global affairs.

Because of a shift in global affairs, Third World states are confronted with significant political implications, deriving not from the ideological perspective of the New World Order, but from the consideration of the realignment of power. US- and Soviet-favoured regimes were supported throughout the Cold War despite some of their precarious domestic positions. The demise of the Soviet Union has led to an era where this support is no longer guaranteed. Two possible scenarios can arise from this diminution of assistance:

(a) The Third World states will be consumed by their dissatisfied domestic constituencies;
(b) The US and emerging centres of power will try to compensate for the withdrawal of Soviet support through policies of economic assistance.

Globalists believe that the constraints of the global economy will continue to produce discontent within these Third World states and may result in a breakdown of domestic order.

Concluding note

The succession of the US as the unipolar power dictates the momentum of contemporary international relations. A sentence in the "Defense Planning Guidance for the Fiscal Years 1994–1999" captured the substance of the US interpretation of the New World Order when it stated: "We will retain the pre-eminent responsibility for addressing selectively those wrongs which threaten not only our interests, but those of our allies or friends, or which could seriously unsettle international relations."[61] Consequently, the New World Order within which Syria finds itself is a world order that is dominated by the US, its culture, politics, military and economic system – a system where US interests remain paramount and are supported by US military superiority and hegemony.

NOTES

1 S. David, "Explaining Third World Alignment", *World Politics*, vol. 43, no. 2 (January 1991), pp. 233–56.

2 K. Waltz, *Man, the State and War: A Theoretical Analysis* (New York: Columbia University Press, 1968).

3 R. Keohane, "Theory of World Politics: Structural Realism and Beyond" in R. Keohane (ed.), *Neorealism and Its Critics* (New York: Columbia University Press, 1986), pp. 164–5.

4 K. Waltz, *Man, the State and War: A Theoretical Analysis* (New York: Columbia University Press, 1968) pp. 85–6.

5 S. Brown, *International Relations in a Changing Global System: Toward a Theory of the World Polity* (Boulder: Westview Press, 1992).

6 K.Waltz, "Anarchic Order and Balances of Power" in R. Keohane (ed.), *Neorealism and Its Critics*, (New York: Columbia University Press, 1986).

7 K. Waltz, *Theory of International Politics* (Reading, Mass.: Addison-Wesley, 1979), p. 111.

8 R. Little, "International Relations and the Triumph of Capitalism" in K. Booth and S. Smith (eds.), *International Relations Theory Today* (Cambridge: Polity Press, 1995), p. 78.

9 P. Viotti and M. Kauppi, *International Relations Theory: Realism, Pluralism, Globalism* (London: Macmillan, 1987), pp. 192–3.

10 K. Hopkins and I. Wallerstein, "Patterns of Development of the Modern World-System" in K. Hopkins and I. Wallerstein (eds.), *World-System Analysis: Theory and Methodology* (Beverley Hills: Sage, 1982), p. 72.

11 I. Wallerstein, "The Rise and Future Demise of the World Capitalist System: Concepts for Comparative Analysis", *Comparative Studies in Society and History*, vol. 16, no. 4 (Autumn 1974), pp. 387–415.

12 A. Ehteshami, "The Rise and Convergence of the 'Middle' in the World Economy: The Case of the NICs and the Gulf" in C. Davies (ed.), *Global Interests in the Arab Gulf* (Exeter: Exeter University Press, 1992), p. 141.

13 C. Chase-Dunn, *Global Formation: Structures of the World Economy* (Oxford: Blackwell, 1992), p. 238.

14 R. Little, "International Relations and the Triumph of Capitalism" in K. Booth and S. Smith (eds.), *International Relations Theory Today* (Cambridge: Polity Press, 1995), pp. 62–3.

15 P. Viotti and M. Kauppi, *International Relations Theory: Realism, Pluralism, Globalism* (London: Macmillan, 1987), pp. 9–10.

16 See S. David, "Explaining Third World Alignment", *World Politics*, vol. 43, no. 2 (January 1991), pp. 233–56.

17 Ibid., p. 236.

18 Ibid., p. 233.

19 Ibid., p. 236.

20 B. Smith, *Understanding Third World Politics: Theories of Political Change and Development*, (Bloomington: Indiana University Press, 1996), pp. 175–8.

21 S. Huntington, *Political Order in Changing Societies* (New Haven: Yale University Press, 1968), chapter 8.

22 S. David, "Explaining Third World Alignment", *World Politics*, vol. 43, no. 2 (January 1991), p. 236.

23 Ibid., p. 235.

24 R. Goode, "State Building as a Determinant of Foreign Policy in the New States" in L. Martin (ed.), *Neutralism and Non-alignment* (New York: Praeger, 1962).

25 T. Skocpol, "Bringing the State Back in: Strategies of Analysis in Current Research" in P. Evans, D. Rueschemeyer, and T. Skocpol (eds.), *Bringing the State Back in* (Cambridge: Cambridge University Press, 1990), p. 9.

26 D. Potter, "The Autonomy of Third World States within the Global Economy" in A. McGrew and P. G. Lewis *et al.*, *Global Politics: Globalisation and the Nation-State* (Cambridge: Polity Press, 1992), p. 223.

27 T. Niblock, "International and Domestic Factors in the Economic Liberalization Process in Arab Countries" in T. Niblock, and E. Murphy (eds.), *Economic and Political Liberalization in the Middle East* (London: British Academic Press, 1993), p. 17.

28 N. Chomsky, *World Orders, Old and New* (London: Pluto Press, 1994), pp. 146–7.

29 D. Potter, "The Autonomy of Third World States within the Global Economy" in A. McGrew and P. G. Lewis *et al.*, *Global Politics: Globalisation and the Nation-State* (Cambridge: Polity Press, 1992), pp. 223–4.

30 E. Nordlinger, "Taking the State Seriously" in S. Huntington and M. Weiner (eds.), *Understanding Political Development* (London: Little, Brown, 1987), p. 372.

31 Ibid., pp. 373–4.

32 Ibid.

33 Ibid., pp. 374–5.

34 Ibid., p. 383.

35 T. Niblock, "International and Domestic Factors in the Economic Liberalization Process in Arab Countries" in T. Niblock and E. Murphy (eds.), *Economic and Political Liberalization in the Middle East* (London: British Academic Press, 1993), p. 56.

36 C. Clapham, *Third World Politics: An Introduction* (London: Croom Helm, 1985), pp. 138–9.

37 E. Nordlinger, "Taking the State Seriously" in S. Huntington and M. Weiner (eds.), *Understanding Political Development* (London: Little, Brown, 1987), p. 379.

38 Ibid.

39 These forms are national television, radio, newspaper, and party propaganda.

40 S. David, "Explaining Third World Alignment", *World Politics*, vol. 43, no. 2 (January 1991), pp. 233–56.

41 R. Dahl, "Balance of Power and World War I" in J. Nye (ed.), *Understanding International Conflicts: An Introduction to Theory and History* (New York: HarperCollins, 1993), p. 50.

42 See Syria's entry into the Gulf War coalition in chapter 5.

43 T. Couloumbis and J. Wolfe, *Introduction to International Relations: Power and Justice* (Englewood Cliffs: Prentice-Hall, 1987), pp. 63–4.

44 H. Morgenthau, *Politics among Nations: The Struggle for Power and Peace* (New York: Knopf, 1968), pp. 109–10.

45 M. Merle, *The Sociology of International Relations* (Leamington Spa: Berg, 1987), pp. 123–6.

46 H. Morgenthau, *Politics among Nations: The Struggle for Power and Peace* (New York: Knopf, 1968), pp. 118–21.

47 M. Merle, *The Sociology of International Relations* (Leamington Spa: Berg, 1987), p. 127.

48 P. Farques, "Demographic Explosion or Social Upheaval" in G. Salame (ed.), *Democracy Without Democrats? The Renewal of Politics in the Muslim World* (London: I.B. Tauris, 1994), pp. 158–60.

49 M. Merle, *The Sociology of International Relations* (Leamington Spa: Berg, 1987), p. 154.

50 See Halliday's rebuff of Huntington's seminar paper on the clash of civilisations: F. Halliday, "A New World Myth", *New Statesman*, 4 April 1997, p. 42.

51 F. Hinsley, *Nationalism and the International System* (London: Hodder & Stoughton, 1973), pp. 11–24.

52 B. Buzan, *People, States, and Fear: An Agenda for International Security Studies in the Post-Cold War Era* (Boulder: Lynne Rienner, 1991), p. 60.

53 J. Tickner, "Re-visioning Security" in K. Booth and S. Smith (eds.), *International Relations Theory Today* (Cambridge: Polity Press, 1995), p. 176, and E. Carr, *The Twenty Years Crisis: 1919–1939* (London: Macmillan, 1939).

54 D. McQuail, *Mass Communication Theory: An Introduction* (London: Sage, 1989), p. 56. For more details on this subject see A. Gramsci, *Selections from the Prison Notebooks* (London: Lawrence & Wishart, 1971).

55 B. Buzan, *People, States, and Fear: An Agenda for International Security Studies in the Post-Cold War Era* (Boulder: Lynne Rienner, 1991), p. 60.

56 P. Noble, "The Arab System: Pressures, Constraints, and Opportunities" in B. Korany and A. Dessouki (eds.), *The Foreign Policies of Arab States: The Challenge of Change* (Boulder: Westview Press, 1991), pp. 49–102.

57 F. Fukuyama, *The End of History and the Last Man* (London: Penguin, 1992).

58 R. Wagner, "What Was Bipolarity?", *International Organisation*, vol. 47, no. 1 (Winter 1993), p. 89.

59 K. Waltz, "The Stability of a Bipolar World", *Daedalus*, vol. 93, no. 3 (Summer 1964), pp. 881–909.

60 E. Luard, *The Balance of Power: The System of International Relations 1648–1815* (New York: St Martin's Press, 1992), p. 1.

61 A. Kubursi and S. Mansur, "Oil and the Gulf War: An 'American Century' or a 'New World Order'", *Arab Studies Quarterly*, vol. 15, no. 4 (Fall 1993), p. 15.

2

Syria:
The Components of Power

Introduction

Historically, Syria has been a victim of the various regional and international balances of power in the Middle East. In their attempts to extend their hegemony, the empires of the past have battled over Syria as a key to maintaining their political authority, hence producing the protracted "struggle for Syria".[1] Since Asad seized power in November 1970, Syria has extracted itself from this struggle and engaged in a broader struggle for the Middle East.[2]

As discussed in the previous chapter, according to realism, the balance of power is a universal mechanism for regulating international relations within a state-system. Syria's role in the contemporary Middle Eastern state-system has been determined by the balance of power in two regional sub-systems:

(a)   The Arab–Israeli sub-system;
(b)   The Persian Gulf.

The foreign policy of Syria has been guided by the conflicts that have arisen from both sub-systems. In the Arab–Israeli conflict, once Asad came to power, Syria's *raison d'état* became the recovery of the Arab territories lost in the Six-Day War of June 1967, and the restoration of Palestinian rights. With a foreign policy conceived in realist terms, Asad has tried to maximise Syria's power potential in order to balance the power of Israel. Asad has inscrutably aspired to balance Israel's military, political, and economic power before engaging in limited wars or peace negotiations.

In the Persian Gulf, Iraq and Iran constitute the major powers around which the region's states coalesce; they form the poles of the balance of power. The states of the Gulf Cooperation Council (GCC) are geographically encased by both middle powers, and have remained vulnerable to their regional aspirations. Syria's eastern border with Iraq has guaranteed it a role in the politics of the Persian Gulf. Its involvement in the Iran–Iraq War of 1980 to 1988 allowed it to counterbalance the impinging power of Iraq through its support of Iran. Maintaining the balance of power was a key factor in Syria's decision to intervene against its Arab neighbour.

In the above cases, the balance of power defined Syria's self-perception within the region, and the course of its behaviour. Power is the currency of politics; and Syria's position in the Middle Eastern state-system is largely dependent upon its power, and its power projection.[3] Syria's tangible power base is small when compared to those of the region's large powers (Egypt, Iran and Iraq), or compared to Israel's military and economic foundations. In spite of this, Syria, through skilful politicking, has attained a middle-power status greater than that which its natural resources would normally allow.[4]

Despite its small, heterogeneous population, and the lack of substantial natural resources, Syria has been able to exert considerable regional influence since 1970. Syria's disproportionate role in the region can largely be attributed to its unique geographical location, and historical experience. This chapter will examine the factors that have enabled Syria to play a role beyond its capabilities,[5] and will aim to establish a context within which Syria's foreign policy capabilities can be identified.

This chapter will also provide an insight into the components of Syria's tangible and intangible power base. Any analysis of Syria's power or power projection must study the following repositories of power:

(a) Geography;
(b) Natural resources;
(c) History;
(d) Population;
(e) The military;
(f) The economy.

Before we focus upon these elements of Syria's power, however, the term "Syria" requires further definition.

Defining Syria

The term "Syria" entails a number of differing meanings; it has both historical and contemporary connotations. "Historical Syria" refers to the region rather than the modern state, and is commensurate with the land along the Eastern Mediterranean between the Sinai Peninsula and the mountains of Southern Turkey. The Arabs labelled historical Syria "Bilad al-Sham", which included Syria, Lebanon, Palestine and Jordan.[6] The role of Bilad al-Sham was considered to be crucial to the formation and proselytisation of Arab nationalism in the early twentieth century, where Syria represented the *beating heart* of Arabism because of its location as the historical capital of the Umayyad empire.[7]

"Greater Syria" is the concept of Syria used by the Syrian Socialist National Party (SSNP). Greater Syria incorporates the states mentioned above, in addition to Cyprus. As a concept, it is more exclusive than Arab nationalism as it envelops a pan-Syrian nationalism.[8] It is more a regionalist than a pan-Arab idea and should not be confused with the Fertile Crescent (Iraq) or Greater Syria (Trans-Jordan) schemes of the Hashemite families during the struggle for Syria.[9]

The Syria of this book is defined by the term "modern Syria", which refers to the state of the Syrian Arab Republic, so named in 1961. The republic is coextensive, except for Alexandretta, with the League of Nations Mandate of 1923–46.[10]

Geography

Physical geography

The land area of Syria amounts to 185,180 sq. km., and comprises six distinctive natural regions:[11]

(a) The Mediterranean coastal plain extends along the length of the country's sea coast. The plain is agriculturally productive, and includes the base for the main port of Latakia, the oil-export terminal at Baniyas, and the port of Tartous.

(b) To the east of this coastal plain lies the mountain range that characterises Syria. In the northern region, one can find Jabal al-Nusayriyah; in the centre, the Anti-Lebanon range delineates Syria from Lebanon; and in the south, Mount Hermon impinges upon the landscape.

(c) Beyond the mountain ranges, there is an extensive plateau which is divided by a south-west and north-east zone of complex folds and faults associated with the Palmyra Folds.

(d) To the west of the Euphrates and north of Palmyra, there is the steppe land that produces the bulk of the country's grain. Aleppo, Hama, and Homs are situated within this region.

(e) Jabal al-Druze, south-west of Palmyra, is surrounded by the cultivated plain – Hawran.

(f) The north-east of Syria, Deir al-Zor, was empty desert inhabited by nomads; the discovery of oil in the 1970s has transformed the region into Syria's main source of income.

The majority of the population (80 per cent) live in the western 20 per cent of Syria.[12]

Political geography

Syria has been the keystone of the Middle East for over 3,500 years. Lying between the Mediterranean and the Euphrates, it has served as the trade route between the Occident and the Orient. As pointed out by Antoun: "Syria's geographical and strategic position at the eastern end of the Mediterranean Sea and near the convergence of three continents established its political importance long ago."[13] Damascus and Aleppo, the two competing trading centres of the region, have been located on the main trade corridors. The control of these corridors, through the Palmyra oasis and the Turkish mountain wall, gave successive administrations power over their neighbours.

Throughout history, Syria has been subjected to endless invasions and the political machinations of great empires and regional powers. Syria has been part of the Assyrian, Chaldean, Persian, Greek, Roman, Islamic, Seljuk, Mongolian, and Ottoman empires. Egypt and Iraq, the region's major players, have continually competed for influence over Syria in order to extend their hegemony.[14] Because of its strategic location, Syria has continuously played a pivotal role in the regional, and more recently, international dynamics of religious, economic, and political affairs.

The termination of the French mandate, the last period of external rule, in 1946, did not end Syria's subjugation to external powers. The ensuing struggle for Syria was extended during the era of the Cold War, when the US and the Soviet Union were competing to assert their global hegemony through the Middle Eastern state-system. Syria was one of the key pieces for the Soviet Union in the zero-sum game.[15]

Syria's geographic location at the centre of the Levant has helped to shape the orientation of Syrian foreign policy towards the Arab world.[16] Syria's relatively small population and lack of strategic depth have rendered it vulnerable to the contingencies of the region. Its contiguous borders with Jordan, Turkey, Iraq, and Israel have made it inherently vulnerable, as each of these states has, at some stage, posed a threat to Syrian national security. The domination of Syria's regional environment by threats and constraints makes security a prime preoccupation of the Syrian regime and population.[17]

Natural resources

Syria is not endowed with the same large quantities of natural resources, such as land and oil, as its neighbours. One third of Syria's land is agriculturally productive. Of the total cultivable area (six million hectares), 93 per cent was cultivated in 1992.[18] Cyclical variation and seasonal distribution in rainfall are critical factors in the western Fertile Crescent, as they are primarily responsible for producing enormous swings in grain production. Since virtually all of the country's grain crop is subject to such variations, the average yield is low. Consequently, the average income of grain-farming families is also low.[19]

Oil was first discovered in Syria in 1956, by the Menhall Company, at Karachuk-Hamzah oilfield. New fields were later discovered at various locations in the north-eastern region of Syria under the auspices of West German and Soviet guidance. Since Syrian crude contained high levels of sulphur, its value was reduced. It was not until 1986, when the Tayyim field started production, that Syrian oil could be mixed domestically to produce a sweeter more profitable oil. Crude oil output in the 1980s averaged about 9.4 million tons a year, but it increased quite suddenly in 1987 to 11.9 million tons. In 1995, Syrian crude production reached a peak of 610,000 barrels a day (b/d) in the second part of the year. Syria's domestic requirement for oil was around 220,000 b/d in 1993,[20] and its total proven oil reserves are around 2,500 million barrels.[21]

Phosphate extraction started in 1974 at Homs, but the Syrian phosphates are of a lower quality than those of neighbouring states. The value of exports has risen from $19.3 million in 1978, in the early days of production, to a peak of $54.8 million in 1987. It is estimated that phosphate reserves in Syria amount to 1 billion tonnes, but production is set to decline in the coming years.[22]

History

Syria's ancient and modern history has been shaped by its regional location. It has been subject to constant regional and international competition and has for most of its political existence remained under the tutelage of foreign powers. Since achieving independence in 1946, Syria has remained at the centre of regional and international competition. Unlike in the past, however, Syria is no longer the object of external control, as it has consolidated its regional position and asserted its regional hegemony.

Ancient history

The northern and western sections of Syria contain some of the earliest villages discovered with settlements dating back to the ninth millennium BC. Its capital, Damascus, is considered to be the oldest continuously inhabited city in the world. Late in the second millennium BC, the Syrian region was fought over by great empires.

Alexander the Great's conquest of the Persians, in 334–326 BC, was followed by the inclusion of the Syrian realm into the Seleucid empire for 200 years. After the Romans had supplanted the Seleucids and made Syria a Roman province in 64 BC, the evolving Greco-Roman culture became infused with Christianity. The new sect gained its first major urban foothold in Antioch, and flourished under the eastern Roman empire and the successor Byzantine empire. In AD 540, the contest between the Byzantines and the Persians erupted and caused considerable destruction of Syrian society.[23]

The Arab Muslim invasion swept Syria in AD 636, leaving an indelible imprint on both Syria and the entire region. Damascus became the capital of the Umayyad empire during the seventh century – the reign of the first four caliphs, and the Golden Era of Islam. The centre of power shifted to Baghdad in AD 750, when the Abbasid dynasty became the principal family of the Muslim order. For the ensuing 800 years, the region of Syria witnessed contests among the Abbasids, the Ayyubids, the Mamluks, the Seljuks, the Crusaders, and the Mongols.

The Ottomans conquered Syria in 1516, and administered it for the following 400 years until the "Sick Man of Europe" imploded in 1918.[24]

Modern history

Syria's modern history started with the collapse of Ottoman rule in 1918, and the establishment of the French mandate over Bilad al-Sham in 1922. Unlike the British authorities, the French authorities were suspicious of the potency of Arab nationalism; they believed it to be a tool of the British empire:[25]

> The French postulated that Britain encouraged, if not inspired, Arab nationalism and helped to translate it into a political movement in order to weaken French influence in the Arab East and eventually to drive the French out of the region altogether.[26]

In order to inhibit Arab nationalism from developing potency and challenging their administration, the French authorities operated an imperial policy of divide and rule.[27]

The dismemberment of "Historical Syria" into artificial statelets signified a policy that sought to thwart the appeal of Arab nationalism.[28] As the region is full of ethnic, religious, and linguistic minorities, the dismemberment followed a logical pattern that generated structural problems for the future. Mount Lebanon was detached from Syria with the surrounding Muslim environs of Sidon, Tripoli, and Beqa'. The remaining territory was subdivided into four mini-states: Aleppo, Damascus, Latakia, and Jabal al-Druze,[29] thus disrupting the coherence of Arab nationalism within Bilad al-Sham. In 1925, Damascus and Aleppo were united to form what is now known as Syria.[30] But it was not until the end of World War II, on Britain's insistence, that Syria officially became an independent state.[31]

The new leaders of Syria inherited a truncated state without a coherent nation. Modern Syria was a state surrounded by artificial borders; even its constituent parts, namely, Aleppo, Latakia, and Jabal al-Druze, resisted centralisation after France had encouraged regional autonomy. French policy had divided Syria into convenient regional and ethnic compartments. Sub-national loyalties, engendered by the French, formed pockets of resistance to the ambitions of the post-independence leadership.[32] The one point of unity that had pulled the population together was the struggle for independence. Arab nationalism provided the Syrian leadership with the cement to adhere the Syrians to one cause. This cause was pan-Arab in character, and circumvented the issue of the central authority of the Syrian state.

Arab nationalism, with its broad appeal, invested its leaders with social and political leverage over the French and British occupying powers. As a revolutionary force, it cohered the Arab population behind a single cause. The Great Revolt in Syria, between 1925 and 1927, was a manifestation of Arab nationalism, and encapsulated the essence of the Syrian resistance to French rule. It gave the political leaders of the movement a pretext to challenge the authority of their imperial counterparts. The project of national construction was aided by the potential offered by Arab nationalism.

Arab nationalism had been a central doctrine for the disparate communities of Syria and the Arab states of the Middle East. It united the Arab communities of the Mashreq and the Maghreb through common linguistic and cultural bonds. Arab nationalism found its expression, at the turn of the twentieth century, in Bilad al-Sham.[33] It started as a response to the exclusive nationalist policies of the Young Turk movement in the Ottoman empire. It was originally conceived in secular terms, and was guided by the messianic purpose of restoring the dignity and the glory of Arab civilisation.

Through the ambit of Arab nationalism, Syria's national leaders, in the form of the National Bloc and People's Party, started to construct the Syrian state. They attempted to integrate the constituent parts of Syria with Arab nationalism as their legitimising theme. One of the first steps taken by the Syrian government after independence, as part of the trend towards national integration, was to reduce communal representation in parliament. Between 1947 and 1949, the parliamentary representation of the Christian communities was reduced from 19 to 14 delegates, that of the 'Alawi from seven to four, and that of the Druze from five to three.[34] The French policy of divide and rule, however, left a segregated society rife with animosities generated by minority privileges. The ossification of regionalism, and the wider attraction of Arab nationalism, beset the emerging Syrian state with problems of authority. In the midst of establishing its authority, the state received a more direct challenge from the creation of Israel in Palestine.

The creation of Israel

The creation of Israel in May 1948 represented the most immediate threat to the states of the Middle East in general and Syria in particular. After only two years of independence, Syria was confronted with a new form of imperialism, with the creation of a colonial-settler state in its midst. As Israel was carved from Bilad al-Sham, in Palestine, and created under the auspices of the imperial powers, it constituted a double-edged challenge to Syria:

(a)   With the support of the world's imperial powers, the US and the Soviet Union, Israel managed to establish a foothold in the region at the expense of Syria and the indigenous Palestinians.[35]

(b)   The failure of the Syrian bourgeois elite to prevent the creation of Israel and to liberate Palestine gave rise to a generational rift between the radical and conservative Syrian nationalists.[36] This division gave credence to the Arab Socialist Ba'th party, whose ideological foundation rested upon the revitalisation of the Arab world.

The Ba'th party and Israel

The Ba'th party, founded in 1947, represented a more visionary form of Arab nationalism.[37] Its appeal, as a revolutionary movement, far exceeded the chivalrous objectives of the early leaders of Arab nationalism, whose acceptance of the Arab state sub-system, and acquiescence in the creation of Israel, were habitually denounced.[38]

The ideology of the party was expounded in the constitution, which saw the Arab world as a single eternal nation.[39] As an ideology, Ba'thism called for:

(a)   The renaissance of Arabism;
(b)   A regeneration of the great Arab empires;
(c)   The eradication of all occupying powers.[40]

Michel 'Aflaq, one of the founders of the Ba'th party, established the core ideology of the party and wrote: "The ultimate objective of the Party was embodied in its very name, Ba'th, meaning renaissance or rebirth."[41] This term referred to the effecting of a fundamental change in the spirit of the Arab people, which would lead to a reconstruction of the glorious Arab civilisation.

In conjunction with the spiritual element of Ba'thism, *freedom, socialism, and unity* formed the political trinity of the party. The goal of freedom was fundamental to the spiritual renaissance of the Arabs, and it called for the rejection of imperial tyranny. The socialist component of Ba'thism was devised to remove the means of production from the bourgeois class and the landed elite. Regeneration required the levelling of social and economic distinctions within the Arab society. The final encompassing element of Ba'thism espoused by 'Aflaq was unity. Arab unity was the key factor in the realisation of Arab civilisation. Freedom and socialism were dependent upon the fruition that Arab unity would deliver to the Arab world. The trilogy of the party was the essence of Ba'thism, and it offered the Arab world a system for reclaiming its glorious past.

Between 1958 and 1961, Syria embarked on a unity scheme with Egypt, known as the United Arab Republic (UAR). Whereas the union with Egypt served its original purpose of forestalling a communist *coup* in Syria, the hegemonic pretensions of Nasser's Egypt offended the Syrians.[42] After three years of dominance by Egypt, rather than equal partnership, Syria withdrew from the UAR, and has not acceded to any similar relationship since then.[43]

The Syrian Ba'th party seized power in 1963. As part of its rhetorical foundation, the party called for the destruction of Israel, and the breakdown of the Arab state sub-system. At its sixth National Congress, the party revealed its radical political and social agenda.[44] The ideology was composed of Marxist–Leninist thought infused with 'Aflaq's romantic vision of Arab nationalism. Revolution was to emanate from Syria before fulfilling its pan-Arab mission.[45]

Damascus became the revolutionary centre for social and political transformation of the region. Through construction of a Leninist party-state, the Ba'th party mobilised the Syrian rural population in support of its radical programme. The socialist transformation of the state entailed nationalisation and land reforms; the power of the urban and land-owning elite was destroyed as the leaders of the Ba'th started a policy of national integration through social and economic levelling. [46]

The proclaimed enemies of the Ba'th party and their brand of Arab nationalism were Israel and the Western-supported regimes in the region, such as Saudi Arabia and Iran. Conflict between Syria and Israel became an inevitable and enduring feature of the Middle East.[47] Syria's first direct confrontation with Israel, under the leadership of the Ba'th party, exploded on 6 June 1967.

The Six-Day War

The Six-Day War erupted when Israel launched its encompassing offensive against Syria, Egypt, and Jordan in June 1967. Israel occupied Sinai, the Golan Heights, the West Bank, and Gaza. The event represented a watershed in the Middle East, as Israel scored a resounding military victory and established its military superiority over the Arab states. The extent of the Arab defeat changed the face of the region's dynamics. Israel's existence could no longer be denied.[48]

As a consequence of the Six-Day War, Arab nationalism lost much of its resonance as a revolutionary ideal. The revisionist message of Arab nationalism had failed to fulfil its historic requisite; unity had not prevailed and, moreover, Palestine was unequivocally lost to Israel. As a result of the defeat, the Arab state-system became more established. State leaders refuted the efficacy of Arab unity whilst reinforcing the role of the state in the regional environment. Although the high levels of interstate communications and coordination continued, the political differences among the state elites ossified, and their foreign policies became more state-centric.

In Syria, the Ba'th party was held responsible for the disastrous performance in the war. The rhetoric of the revolutionary leadership had not produced results. Despite receiving the military and political support of the Soviet Union, the Ba'th leadership had increased the vulnerability of the state. The repercussions were manifest in the internal challenges posed by the military wing of the Ba'th party against the civilian wing of the party.[49]

The military *coup* of November 1970 saw Asad assume office as the leader of the Ba'th party and the Syrian state.[50] The new regime implemented a set of domestic and foreign policies based upon *realpolitik*, rather than ideological imperatives. The change in the policies of the regime reflected the changing regional environment, and the primacy of the state in conducting regional relations.

From this brief review of Syria's history, it is possible to see that its power potential is inextricably linked with its geopolitical position. Syria has been the focus of numerous regional and international struggles.

Its historical experience has left an indelible scar on the demographic composition of Syria.

Population

Population is another tangible source of a state's power. However, population alone is not enough to embolden a state's power, as a large population can be burdensome to a state with a small resource base. The cohesion of the state determines how effective the population is as a source of power. Cohesion can be brought about through the existence or creation of a national purpose. The national purpose of a state often emanates from the presence of a constant external threat. The potential threat from a hegemonic neighbour serves to heighten the sense of unity. Where traditional rivalries and insecurities exist, between states such as Turkey and Greece, Serbia and Bosnia, Iran and Iraq, and Syria and Israel, national unity is critical.

As described above, Syria's ancient and modern history have militated against the formation of a cohesive population. The policies conducted during the period of the French mandate reinforced the social and ethnic divisions that existed in the artificially created states of the Levant.[51] The complex social and ethnic cleavages that characterised modern Syria presented the central authorities with an insurmountable problem. The regional autonomy granted to the different minorities, during the mandate era, generated a series of confrontations between the state and the regions. The creation of Israel acted as an antidote to Syria's social ailment. It yielded a national mission for the Syrian state and population – notably, to channel their energies towards a national purpose.

According to Tilly, war is the crucible for creating nation-states.[52] The Syrian–Israeli conflict has produced an environment conducive to occasioning a Syrian nation-state. The centralisation of the political process, exacerbated by the conflict with Israel, has engineered a centripetal force that has propelled the population towards unity. Arab nationalism, as a source of regime legitimacy and a broader reference to national identity, nevertheless, has circumvented the evolution of a Syrian nationalism. The impasse between the two competing nationalisms produced a flourishing environment for minorities. Adding to the paradox, the legacy of French rule cultivated a climate in which the 'Alawi and Druze minorities extracted themselves from social degradation, and elevated themselves towards the centres of political and military power.

The conflicting aims of the pursuit of social cohesion in the Syrian state, the fulfilment of Ba'th (Arab nationalist) ideals, and elevation of minorities in the state leadership have led to the Syrian paradox.[53] To appreciate this dynamic nature of Syrian society, it is rudimentary to examine its composition.

The current population of Syria totalled 16.5 million in 1997.[54] The traditional population concentration axis, along the humid steppe belt, Damascus, Homs, Hama, and Aleppo, has more recently extended into the Latakia and Tartous areas. Although Syria's population is small in absolute terms, it doubled between 1963 and 1987, and its current birth rate, 3.4 per cent, is one of the highest in the world. The population is set to rise to 18 million by the year 2000; and the demographic composition of Syria (59 per cent of the population was under the age of 20 in the late 1990s), is likely to undergo a radical transformation.[55] The distribution of the population throughout the provinces of Syria is as follows:

Population of Syrian provinces in 1992 (000s)

Aleppo	2,677	Tartous	644
Damascus	2,824	Latakia	783
Hama	1,046	Suwaida	281
Hassaka	965	Deir al-Zor	565
Homs	1,209	Deraa	568
Idlib	870	Raqqa	485
Quneitra	41		

Source: *Syria – Country Profile 1993/94* (London: The Economist Intelligence Unit, London, 1994).

A heterogeneous society

The Syrian population, despite a measure of cultural uniformity, continues to lack cohesion and a cogent universal identity. The Syrian population was most accurately portrayed by Hourani when he described Syrian society as:

> composed of a large number of groups, local, tribal, linguistic, and religious. On the whole, these groups formed closed communities.

Each was a world, sufficient to its members and exacting their ultimate loyalty. The worlds touched but did not mingle with each other; each looked at the rest with suspicion and even hatred. Almost all were stagnant, unchanging, and limited; but the Sunni world, although torn by every sort of internal dissension, had something universal, a self confidence and sense of responsibility which the others lacked. They were all marginal, shut out from power and historic decision.[56]

The ethnic composition of Syria has become the focus of several academic studies of the region, in which horizontal (class) and vertical (patrimonial) analyses are placed in natural opposition to one another. Van Dam provided one of the most detailed insights into the ethnic composition of Syria.[57] He identified the following factors as contributing to the multi-ethnic fabric of Syrian society:

(a) Syria (Bilad al-Sham) has been the cradle for the three major monotheistic religions, Judaism, Christianity, and Islam.

(b) The Fertile Crescent, as a region, has always been the centre for tribal movements and the focus of empire contests.

(c) Syria has been an area of refuge for displaced peoples.

(d) The differences in tribal and national set-up have become infused with religious diversity leading to a reinforcement of distinct community identity.

(e) The religious, tribal, and linguistic differences have been accentuated by the physical separation of the communities by geographical features.

(f) Due to their physical isolation, the communities have enjoyed substantial autonomy from the central government.[58]

The population can be divided according to language, religion, or ethnic group. Approximately 82.5 per cent of the population speaks Arabic as its first language. The dominant group has, for more than 1,000 years, been Syrian Arabs, who constitute nearly 90 per cent of the population.[59] The great majority of the Syrian Arabs are Sunni Muslims. However, other Arab sub-groups, especially religious confessions, form alternative constellation centres. These sub-groups are: the Christians 14.1 per cent (of whom 4.7 per cent are Greek Orthodox Christians), the 'Alawis 11.5 per cent, the Druze 3 per cent, the Isma'ilis 1.5 per cent,[60] and the Jews 0.78 per cent.[61] The majority of the population (68.7 per cent), are

Sunni Muslims.[62] The ethnic minorities include: Armenians (4 per cent), Kurds (8.5 per cent), and Turcomans (3 per cent). The Kurds and Turcomans, though ethnic minorities, are Sunni Muslims; thus, they belong to the majority of the population.[63]

FIGURE 1
Religious minorities in Syria

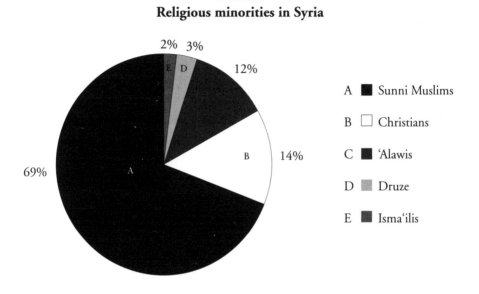

Source: N. Van Dam, *The Struggle for Power in Syria: Politics and Society under Asad and the Ba'th Party* (London: I.B. Tauris, 1996), pp. 1–14.

The Christians
Syrian Christians have a longer tradition than any other Christian group, and their ancestors predated the Muslim Arabs in Syria by 500 years. Syrian Christians subscribed to Arab nationalism at the turn of the century and identified their interests with the Arab world. Christians, apart from the Armenians, all belong to the broader Arab family.[64]

The 'Alawis
Probably the most significant of the confessional groups in Syria is that of the 'Alawis. The 'Alawis originate from the Jabal al-Nusayriyah region of western Syria, they are an offshoot of the Shi'a family of Islam. Their

creed is very secretive, and is reputed to incorporate elements of Islam and Christianity.[65]

Because of their religious deviation from orthodox Islam, they were traditionally persecuted by the Sunni majority, who believe that the 'Alawis "have strayed so far from Sunni (Orthodox) Islam that they are no longer truly Muslims."[66] As they were suppressed for their beliefs, their social status within Syrian society was low; they found employment as agricultural workers and domestic servants to Sunni landlords.[67] Since the mid-1960s, however, the 'Alawis have dominated the political and military apparatus of Syria, and the system of political and social patronage has been inverted. There are concerns within the state, especially from other minorities, that the ruling 'Alawis will be overthrown by the majority of Sunnis. The 'Alawis, however, have showed no fear for their sect as they function according to the broader Syrian national interest.[68]

The Druze

The Druze's faith is based on Isma'iliyya; it emerged at the time of the Fatimid caliph, al-Hakim bi-Amr Allah, whom they expect to return.[69] "Their beliefs are a mystical offshoot of Shi'a Islam combined with features of other religions."[70] They have secret doctrines and they believe in reincarnation. Their community is very closed as they do not accept intermarriage.

The Druze are primarily located around Jabal al-Druze and form 90 per cent of the population in al-Suwaida province.[71] The Druze also benefited from their role in the military. They frequently confronted the authorities during the French Mandate and gained a reputation for their resilience. As a minority they seized the opportunity to rise through the military ranks although they were later to be purged with the succession of the 'Alawi leaders.[72]

The Isma'ilis

The Isma'ilis are an offshoot of the Shi'a branch of Islam. According to Glassé, Isma'ilism is a manifestation, within Islam, of ancient Persian religious systems.[73] Historically, Isma'ilism seemingly began as a splinter group from the Twelver Shi'a sect.[74]

Since the mid-nineteenth century there have been two groups of Isma'ilis in Syria: one located in the Qadmous-Masyaf west of Hama, and the second in Salamiyah. In the ninth and tenth centuries Salamiyah had been the centre of Isma'ili activism.[75] Since the eleventh century, in terms of their access to political power, the fortunes of this group have passed their zenith.[76]

Isma'ili fortunes have slowly improved in Syria since the Ba'th party seized power in 1963. As a vehicle for promoting minorities, the military academies within Syria helped the Isma'ilis to achieve some upward social mobility.

Many Isma'ilis now hold positions in the bureaucracy and the education sector. The traditional rivalry between the Isma'ilis and the 'Alawis in the Latakia region has, however, prevented the descendants of the Assassins from acquiring an independent power base.[77]

The Kurds

The largest ethnolinguistic minority in Syria is that of the Kurds. They have their own distinctive culture, language, and history, which foster their tribal identity. They are located in the northern region of Syria, across the mountains of the north-west and north-east. In addition to the main Kurdish belt in the north, where they are primarily agriculturists, several thousand Kurds live in the cities, especially in Damascus.[78]

The Armenians

The second largest ethnolingusitic minority is the Armenians. They are the least assimilated group in the country because of their strong Armenian identity. They fled Turkish persecution in Armenia during the 1920s and 1930s, and settled in and around Aleppo. They are responsible for many of Aleppo's small industries, as they concentrate on skilled craftwork, especially in gold.[79]

The Jews

The Jews have been present in Syria for over 2,000 years. Under the various Muslim empires, as people of the book (ahl al-kitab), they enjoyed a similar status to that of the Christians. Jews, in a similar fashion to the Armenians, lived and worked in Aleppo and Damascus. They numbered 30,000 before the advent of World War II. The position of the Jews in Syria became ambivalent after the creation of the state of Israel. In 1992, under pressure from the US and as a concession towards confidence-building measures, Syria declared that any of the remaining 4,000 Syrian Jews were free to emigrate. By the end of 1992, 2,600 had received exit visas, and of the 1,400 left, about 400 indicated a desire to stay in Syria.[80]

Irrespective of the ethnic or religious divisions within Syria, the constant threat posed by Israel has been an issue of national unity since 1948. The threat of an external power has congealed the aspirations of Syrian society. The state has been able to channel the insecurities of its citizens into a state-building programme. This programme has sought to develop Syria's military into a formidable counter-threat to Israel.

The preponderance of the armed forces, however, in the state-building programme produced a dialectic between the civil leaders of the state and its military officers. A dichotomy arose where the interests of the military, a minority-dominated institution, clashed with the interests of the Sunni political elite. This led to a period of instability as both groups jostled for power; the army, with coercion as its weapon, managed to seize power in 1949.[81]

The composition of the army was not representative of the ethnic or religious divisions within the state. Whilst Sunni power could be identified in the form of land ownership and mercantile trade, the minorities, especially the 'Alawis and the Druze, started to occupy prominent posts in the military.[82] The military provided the only vehicle through which the minorities could elevate their social status, and improve their standard of living. The combination of domestic and regional insecurities promoted the interests of the minorities as they gravitated towards the pillars of power. The rise of the 'Alawis and the Druze in the Syrian military[83] indicated a shift away from the traditional centres of power in the suqs, towards the military academies throughout Syria.[84]

The centre of power within Syria rests firmly in the hands of the military and the security services. Through its direct access to the state apparatus, the military has gained a crucial role in the state-building process. Instead of the military dislocating the power of the Syrian state, its power has been enhanced by the sectarian nature of society. The population of Syria has constituted a source of potential power for the state.[85] The state has converted this potential, together with the assets of geography, history, and nationalism, into power outputs. These are manifest in the form of the military and the economy. The next section addresses the outputs of the power ratios.

The military

The military provides Syria with its most tangible and quantifiable source of power. By expanding its military, through the auspices of its geopolitical position, Syria has managed to dominate the policies of Lebanon, circumvent the threat of Iraq, and confront, to a limited extent, the ambitions of Israel. Despite the constraints Syria has faced, Asad has successfully managed to transform the Syrian state into a middle power in the region. This has been achieved in two ways:

(a)   By constructing a strong state;
(b)   By enjoining the regional and international balance of power.[86]

Syria's domestic and foreign policies owe their origins to the intervention of the military in political affairs since the early days of independence. Since the first *coup* of 1949, when Zaim seized control of the state apparatus, the military has played an instrumental role in state affairs.[87] The confrontation between Jadid, Syria's ruler,[88] and Asad, minister of defence and commander of the air force, in November 1970, marked the ascendancy of the military in political affairs, and the subordination of the civilian sector in determining state policies.[89]

The efficiency of the military and security apparatus has served to maintain the life of the incumbent regime. Additionally, it has enabled Syria to engage in the regional competition for hegemony because the security of the state has been a preoccupation of the Syrian regime.[90] The domestic and regional vulnerability of the Syrian state has made military intervention a feature of post-independence life.

Since independence in 1946, the Syrian state has been forced to balance the complexities of a truncated and ethnically divided country against the imminent threat posed by the creation of Israel, and by the ambitions of its irredentist neighbours, in the form of the Fertile Crescent and the Greater Syria schemes, as previously mentioned. Domestically, the centrifugal force of the minorities and their semi-autonomous status rendered centralised rule impractical and improbable. Disillusioned with civilian rule and the débâcle of the 1948 war, the army leaders considered themselves as the natural repository of state power.[91]

The military intervened in Syrian politics in 1949, and maintained an intermittent presence in political affairs through a myriad of *coups* and counter-*coups*. The disillusionment of the military with the political leadership of the state took on a new form after the 1967 war. Although both the civilian and military leaderships belonged to the ruling Ba'th regime, the military divested the civilian wing of the party of its power and took full control of the state.[92]

The size of the 1967 defeat rocked the military establishment in Syria as a new era of purges began. The failure of 1948 was revisited, and only a few leading military men escaped without loss of rank or position. The defence minister, Asad, was one of the few who managed to excuse his role in the war, and even enhance his position in the military junta.[93] When he seized control in November 1970, Asad inherited a truncated state, as a result of the loss of the Golan Heights, and a severely defeated army. The new regime set about re-equipping the army to secure its own position at home, and to avenge the humiliation of 1967. From the defeat emerged a new military doctrine based on the accumulation and maximisation of power. Henceforward, realist politics dictated Syria's role in the Middle East.[94]

As a relatively small state with few resources, compared to those of its larger neighbours, Israel, Turkey, and Iraq, Syria's critical power projection can be located in its military. Aware of this, Asad accordingly tried to accumulate military power as this was the only possible route to secure Syria a role in both the regional and international political systems.[95] The energies of the state have been directed towards national security from a domestic, regional, and international perspective.

The military came to be the most visible and dominant output of Syria's power. This can be attributed to the fact that in Syria, the distinction between high and low politics is still pronounced. Although, in general, the economy of a state is a valuable output of power, in Syria, it remains subordinate to the interests of security.[96]

The economy

The Syrian economy is most accurately described as state capitalist, where the state exercises control over strategic industries but allows the private sector to operate in a controlled market.[97] Endowed with limited natural resources, a small population, and an unstable political heritage, Syria has faced many obstacles on the road to economic development. Apparently, economic growth has been constrained by:

(a)   Natural factors;

(b) Government economic policies;

(c) Political instability in the region.[98]

The Ba'th leadership of the 1963–70 era introduced radical economic reforms that transformed the existing liberal economy into a socialism-oriented one. Land reform and nationalisation epitomised the socialist character of the Syrian economy under Ba'th rule. Although the Syrian economy experienced some growth between independence and 1970, mainly in industries controlled by the state, such as textiles, food processing, and tobacco, the pace of this growth was hindered by the socialist orientations of the state.[99] In addition, Syria's recent history has shaped its economic policies, and wherever possible the economy has remained subordinate to foreign policy. In other words, the Syrian economy has been held hostage to the fortunes of the regime and the successes or failures of Asad's foreign policy.

The policies of economic liberalisation, otherwise known as *infitah*, followed by Asad in the 1970s resulted in economic growth and gross domestic product (GDP) grew by more than 150 per cent between 1971 and 1975.[100] *Infitah* served two purposes: firstly, it was used to strengthen the legitimacy of the regime. By attracting the support of the disaffected bourgeoisie, Asad could strengthen the state.[101] Secondly, the incorporation of the business class into the economy could provide an engine and a platform through which Syria could challenge the economic superiority of Israel and balance its economic advantage.[102] The project of national integration, followed by the Syrian Ba'th party, dictated that the economy served the reconstruction of Syrian society, and helped to sustain the Syrian state in its conflict with Israel.

The role of the public sector in the economy has somewhat diminished since the mid-1980s. The state's ability to lead the economy and to determine the course of socio-economic development has receded as a result of the austerity budgets of the 1980s and the rationalisation programme introduced to reduce inefficiency within the bureaucracy.[103]

The private sector experienced new growth between 1986 and 1990. Its share of foreign trade was reduced to 10 per cent in the first half of the 1980s, but rose to 20 per cent in 1986, and 45 per cent in 1990.[104] The manufacturing industries benefited from the incorporation of the private sector into the national economy as they contributed 43–44 per cent of net domestic product in 1990, compared with just 30–35 per cent in the early 1980s.[105] By 1990, the private sector contributed an estimated 55 per cent of Syria's GDP. This sector had employed 60 per cent of the industrial labour force in the 1970s and the 1980s but by 1991 was employing a remarkable 75 per cent.[106]

The introduction of economic liberalisation measures in 1972, 1986, and 1991, expressed a change in economic policy. Though the changes were precipitated by differing circumstances, they indicated a new flexibility within the Syrian political system.[107] They also connoted the impending influence of the global economy and the vulnerability of the Syrian state.

Sources of income

The four main sources of income for the modern Syrian economy are: agriculture; the mining industries; manufacturing, and foreign aid.[108]

Agriculture

Traditionally, agriculture has been a major component of the Syria economy. The development of the Euphrates Dam system has revolutionised Syrian irrigation systems and electricity generation. Like the Aswan High Dam project in Egypt, the scheme was financed by the former Soviet Union. The power station, inaugurated in 1978, generated over 90 per cent of Syria's electrical energy for several years; its significance, however, is decreasing as a result of the introduction of thermal power plants. An equally significant long-range purpose of the Euphrates Dam is the irrigation of 640,000 hectares of land along the Euphrates and its east-bank tributaries. This project is expected to be completed by the year 2000, and will then more than double the area under irrigation in Syria.[109]

The programme of land reform implemented during the brief Syria–Egypt union, between 1958 and 1961, has continued to influence Syrian agricultural production. A large share of the capital invested in economic development, after the late 1960s, went into: land reclamation and land improvement, irrigation schemes and agricultural programmes.[110]

There are currently 20 state collective farms, and a cooperative organisation with 570,000 members.[111] The size of landholdings has changed during the period 1963 to 1995, depending upon the domestic situation. The ideology of the Ba'th party has been diluted over time as the economic needs of the country have taken precedence, and as a result the size of land holdings has increased since 1971 and in particular since the introduction of the Agricultural Law of 1986. Despite state intervention, private-sector farming has remained the dominant force in agricultural production, and between 1987 and 1991 it accounted for two-thirds of the cultivable land.[112]

The liberalisation programme of the 1990s altered the relationship between the farmer and the state and the private sector started to assume greater control over production, pricing, and the marketing of commodities.[113] Despite the agrarian character of the economy, however, Syria has continued to be a net importer of foodstuffs.[114] The economic plan of 1991–5 sought to return agriculture to the core of the economy with the aim of securing long-term self-sufficiency.[115]

As a result of the oil boom, and the stress on industrial production, by the end of the 1970s, the emphasis of the economy had gravitated towards a manufacturing and commercial base. Although the Syrian economy has since become more diversified, a brief look at the country's macro-economic indicators shows that despite efforts to restore agriculture's role a structural transformation from an agrarian to an industrial economy has not taken place.[116]

Mineral industries

Syria's main mineral industries are crude oil production and phosphate rock extraction. Mining and manufacturing contributed 28.1 per cent of Syrian GDP in 1993, with petroleum and its derivatives accounting for 66.7 per cent of Syria's principal exports.[117] From the mid-1970s to the mid-1980s, and again from 1992 onwards, oil exports accounted for 70 per cent, or more, of Syria's total export income, which rendered the country heavily dependent on world oil prices.[118]

Manufacturing

For many centuries, Damascus was famous for its metalwork, fabrics, muslins, linens, silk brocades, tapestries, and carpets. All of these crafts have survived but are inadequate to provide the basis of a national manufacturing complex in the modern technological world. The Third Five-Year Plan (1971–5) was designed to upgrade manufacturing industry and 46.3 per cent of public investment was directed towards strengthening established industries. There was considerable investment in heavy industry and phosphate-processing and fertilizer manufacturing plants as well as chemical and engineering plants.[119]

The main manufacturing industries in Syria are state-owned and include those of: food, sugar, textiles, chemicals, engineering, cement, and building materials. Although mining and utilities have remained under the jurisdiction of the state, the private sector contributed 40 per cent of manufacturing output in 1991. The private sector is most active in the production of textiles, food, leather, paper, chemicals, electrical goods and machinery.[120]

Foreign aid

The country's small natural resource base has been a handicap to Syria's economic development. In contrast, Syria's unique geopolitical position in the Middle Eastern sub-system has enabled it to extract aid and other financial support from its Arab and Iranian neighbours. Syria's support for Iran in the Iran–Iraq War, and its participation in the liberation of Kuwait, proved to be instances in which Syria's political orientations generated disposable income for the regime. This was made possible by its policy of acting like a Bonapartist state. As defined by Marx, the Bonapartist state, is able to conduct a rational and coherent policy conceived away from the constraints of the dominant social forces in the domestic arena.[121] The unique position occupied by the state *vis-à-vis* society has allowed the state to subjugate the domestic necessities of the economy to achieve its political ends both from domestic and regional perspectives.

Foreign aid and finance have contributed substantially to the Syrian economy. The fact that foreign aid, as a source of state revenue, has risen by an estimated 400 per cent since 1991, suggests that a form of *rentierism* has dominated the economy.[122] This financial income can be attributed to the critical role played by the Asad regime in the region's two arenas of conflict: the Arab–Israeli dispute and the Iran–Iraq war.

As a front-line state in the Arab–Israeli conflict, Syria has been the recipient of foreign aid from the Gulf Arab states and foreign aid accounted for 40.9 per cent of state revenues in 1979.[123] Receipt of foreign aid has afforded Syria the opportunity to maximise its limited resources and concomitantly to increase its power projection. It has achieved this in two ways:

(a) Through balancing the interests of the Gulf Arab states with those of Iran, Syria managed to seize the role of regional mediator, hence promoting its own diplomatic and political agenda. Syria's accumulation of diplomatic credit with the GCC states and Iran gave it the pretext to extract rent from both parties, whilst Syria's main Arab rival, Iraq, was engaged in a putative war with Iran. With Iraq effectively removed from the Arab–Israeli conflict, Syria became the central actor and requested further economic aid from the Gulf Arab states;[124]

(b) Through the support of the Gulf Arab states, Iran, and the Soviet Union, Syria was able to embark on its quest for strategic parity.

One could contest that because of Syria's relatively poor resource base it has been necessary for the Syrian regime to utilise its geopolitical position to acquire rent in the form of aid. Sometimes the state has implemented unpopular foreign policies to secure rent.[125] The state's careful balancing of domestic and international interests carries a high risk and cost. As long as there is a margin for political manoeuvring and there is sufficient aid to prop up the Syrian economy, the state can manipulate regional insecurities. A consequence of Syria's *rentierism* is that the economy has, at times, become hostage to the fortunes of Syria's political role.

To recap, the Syrian economy is tied to two factors: the fortunes of the region's major oil producers, and the regional configurations of power. The combination of these factors has guaranteed that Syria could remain economically strong and seek its regional objectives. Syria's economy flourished during the 1970s after the oil boom, and particularly after Syria had become the only front-line state in 1979. The crisis of the 1980s, however, including the foreign exchange crisis of 1986, reflected the extent to which the Syrian economy had become dependent upon the region's economic position.[126] Soviet and Iranian aid did not alleviate Syria's economic ailments; the gradual move towards economic liberalisation appeared to present the most viable option for reviving its economy.[127]

The economy and foreign policy

Despite the structural adjustment programmes that Syria has undertaken, its economy is still dependent upon the security of the regime and the success of its foreign policy. Although domestic industry and agriculture formed part of Syria's economic power base, the largest component of economic strength has appeared to emanate from Syria's ability to extract rent for its military services and alliance potential.

The Syrian state has managed, to date, to insulate itself from the determinants of the global economy. Whereas most of the states on the periphery of the global economy have traded part of their autonomy for aid, loans, and international investment, Syria has, to a large extent, insulated its autonomy. This has been achieved by subjugating economics to power politics and by the extraction of geopolitical rent.

The area of low politics within Syria (which comprises domestic economics), has been consigned to the field of high politics (that which relates to foreign policy).[128] The stability of the state has taken precedence over economic policy. Unlike in most Third World states, prescribed economic policies to cure Syria's ailments have been introduced independently of external pressure. The introduction of piecemeal reforms was designed to alleviate the immediate economic problems whilst maintaining the overstaffed public services. The continuation of these inefficient services offered the state a residual base of legitimacy and support.

Even during the crisis of 1986, Syria did not apply for standby credits or other IMF facilities that could have involved economic reforms. Nor did it conclude any agreements with the World Bank that could have demanded the implementation of structural adjustment programmes.[129] Syria's debt to the World Bank, which amounted to $400 million in 1993, has not forced it to concede to World Bank pressures.[130] The most the World Bank has been able to achieve is the provision of advice – the World Bank, IMF, and the European Union have all conducted economic studies that offer recommendations to revive the economy.[131] The withdrawal of credit facilities has affected Syria's ability to borrow, yet Syria's geopolitical position has enabled it to receive rent or loans from the Gulf Arab states. The Gulf Arab states have not made their loans conditional upon the implementation of economic reform, as their own economies might prove to be susceptible to the destabilising force of regional change.[132]

The pattern of dependency between the peripheral and core states has not been reproduced in the Syrian case. By exploiting its geopolitical position, Syria has resisted the incremental loss of autonomy to the global economy and non-state actors. Pre-empting the policies of perestroika,

Syria administered an ad hoc package of economic reforms that awarded the state some room for political manœuvring.

During the Cold War, the international political system had provided Syria with enough leverage over the Soviet Union to avoid encasing itself in the restrictions of internationally administered debt relief.[133] The demise of the Soviet Union and the advent of the New World Order gave Syria the opportunity to attract Gulf Arab aid and international loans.

Conclusion

Syria's physical resources are the most tangible sources of its power and can be identified as geography, natural resources, and population. However, they have not been sufficient to endow the Syrian state with adequate power in its contention with its neighbours. The intangible sources available to the state, especially nationalism, appear to have offered the most potent form of power.

Syria's geographical location, as the keystone between the Orient and the Occident, has subjected it to endless invasions throughout its history. The history of Syria has been dominated by the rivalries among the region's major powers. Consequently, the Syrian state, inherited by its post-independence leaders, was fractious and lacked credible legitimacy from its society. History had denied the state a coherent nation, and implanted centripetal forces that tore at the very heart of Syrian society.

Geography and history have weakened the Syrian state. The matrix of ethnic and religious communities that compose Syrian society has often undermined the authority of the state. Challenged by several ideologies, such as *Arabism, Ba'thism*, and *socialism*, Syrian society has had to consider its primordial and supranational loyalties. Syrian society has been under pressure since independence to foster the country's Syrian Arab identity above its other religious or ethnic identities. Arab nationalism has proven to be the most effective vehicle for conveying a national purpose for the Syrians. Utilising Arab nationalism, the Syrian state has attempted to convert its population from a *potential* source of power into *realised* power. A growing population, united by a national purpose, provided a resource for development. A cohesive and educated population offered the state a firm foundation on which to build a strong economy. As urbanisation has taken place, the potential for industrial growth has risen.

Arab nationalism, as a source of power, provided the adhesive for Syria's heterogeneous society, and empowered the state to implement a state-building process. The conflict with Israel has intensified Syria's national insecurity, and provided a crucible in which the state could forge a national identity. The state, however, has remained vulnerable to the existence of an external threat, and malleable to the activities of Syria's civilian and military leadership.

The military leadership's succession to the civilian leadership in 1963, when the Military Committee of the Ba'th party seized power, marked a significant change in the vulnerability of the Syrian state. The ensuing struggle between the two wings of the Ba'th party, the military and the civilian, produced the climate for the 1967 war against the Israelis.[134] The defeat of the 1967 war was devastating for the whole Arab world. Not only did it rupture the dream of Arab nationalism, but it also indicated the permanence and pre-eminence of the state of Israel. The qualitative edge of Israeli military hardware and its superior military organisation led to a resounding defeat for the Arabs. After the humiliating defeat, Asad moved to occupy the post of state leader. His emergence as the ruler of Syria in 1970 represented the apex of Syria's arduous climb to stability. Asad initiated a policy of state consolidation, a prerequisite to balancing the power of Israel.

Despite its rupture, Arab nationalism has remained a source of power for the Syrian state. The dream may have lost some of its resonance, but it did not lose its appeal as a mobilising force. Arab nationalism has afforded the state the opportunity to coalesce the interests of the society into a national form. The advent of the October War in 1973 rallied the Syrians behind their state, and the relative success of the war restored some of the dignity lost in the June War of 1967. With an injection of legitimacy, accumulated through the war, Asad embarked on a state-building project that sought to transform the vulnerability of the Syrian state.

As a front-line state in the Arab–Israeli conflict, Syria managed to attract rent from the Gulf Arab states. Being the beating heart of Arabism, Syria became a major recipient of financial aid. In other words, Syria was able to change its main source of weakness, notably, its strategic position as the keystone in the Middle East, into a military, political, and diplomatic advantage. This transformation has enabled the Syrian state to develop a military doctrine based on attaining a balance of power with Israel.

The military has proven to be one area where Syria's geographical position, as a tangible source of power, combined with the potential of its population, has translated itself into a quantifiable output of power. The expansion of the Syrian military owed its roots to the unique position occupied by Syria in the Arab–Israeli conflict and Middle Eastern sub-system of states. Syria's vulnerable location at the heart of the trade routes between the East and the West, between the competing zones of Egypt and Iraq, in a zone of imperial contest between the French and British governments, and where the Soviet Union and the US vie for influence has been transformed into a source of power as the Syrian state has gained in resilience. The policies of Asad have successfully insulated the Syrian state from the domestic, regional, and international interventions of the past. In conclusion, although the endowment in natural resources of the Syrian state is limited, the appeal of Arab nationalism, and the skilful politicking of its political elite, have enabled Syria to assume a regional role greater than its natural assets would normally allow.

NOTES

1 P. Seale, *The Struggle for Syria: A Study of Post-War Arab Politics, 1945–1958* (London: Oxford University Press, 1965).

2 P. Seale, *Asad of Syria: The Struggle for the Middle East* (London: I.B. Tauris, 1988).

3 Z. Ma'oz, "The Evolution of Syrian Power 1948–1984" in M. Ma'oz and A. Yaniv (eds.), *Syria under Assad: Domestic Constraints and Regional Risks* (London: Croom Helm, 1986), p. 69.

4 A. Drysdale and R. Hinnebusch, *Syria and the Middle East Peace Process* (New York: Council on Foreign Relations, 1991), p. 3.

5 Ibid.

6 M. Kessler, *Syria: Fragile Mosaic of Power* (Washington: National Defense University Press, 1987), p. 4.

7 R. Hinnebusch, "Revisionist Dreams, Realist Strategies: The Foreign Policy of Syria" in B. Korany and A. Dessouki (eds.), *The Foreign Policies of Arab States: The Challenge of Change* (Boulder: Westview Press, 1991), p. 377.

8 P. Seale, *The Struggle for Syria: A Study of Post-War Arab Politics, 1945–1958* (London: Oxford University Press, 1965), pp. 64–72.

9 For more details of this period, see P. Seale, *The Struggle for Syria: A Study of Post-War Arab Politics, 1945–1958* (London: Oxford University Press, 1965).

10   Held, C. *Middle East Patterns* (Boulder: Westview Press, 1994), p. 203.

11   *Syria – Country Profile 1993/4* (London: The Economist Intelligence Unit, 1994), p. 2.

12   M. Bannerman, "Syrian Arab Republic" in D. Long and B. Reich (eds.), *The Government and Politics of the Middle East and North Africa* (Boulder: Westview Press, 1995), p. 203.

13   R. Antoun, "Ethnicity, Clientship, and Class: Their Changing Meaning" in R. Antoun and D. Quataert (eds.), *Syria: Society, Culture, and Polity* (Albany: State University of New York Press, 1991), p. 1.

14   M. Kessler, *Syria: Fragile Mosaic of Power* (Washington: National Defense University Press, 1987), pp. 3–14.

15   N. Chomsky, *Deterring Democracy* (London: Vintage, 1992), p. 47.

16   R. Hinnebusch, "Revisionist Dreams, Realist Strategies: The Foreign Policy of Syria" in B. Korany and A. Dessouki (eds.), *The Foreign Policies of Arab States: The Challenge of Change* (Boulder: Westview Press, 1991), p. 377.

17   Ibid., p. 375.

18   *Syria – Country Profile 1994/95* (London: The Economist Intelligence Unit, 1995), p. 25.

19   C. Held, *Middle East Patterns* (Boulder: Westview Press, 1994), p. 212.

20   *Syria – Country Profile 1994/95* (London: The Economist Intelligence Unit, 1995), p. 30.

21   *Syria – Country Profile 1996/97* (London: The Economist Intelligence Unit, 1997), p. 16.

22   C. Held, *Middle East Patterns* (Boulder: Westview Press, 1994), p. 215.

23   Ibid., p. 206.

24   Ibid., p. 207.

25   P. Khoury, "Syrian Political Culture: A Historical Perspective" in R. Antoun and D. Quataert (eds.), *Syria: Society, Culture, and Polity* (Albany: State University of New York Press, 1991), p. 21.

26   P. Khoury, *Syria and the French Mandate: The Politics of Arab Nationalism 1920–1945* (Princeton: Princeton University Press, 1987), p. 53.

27   G. Antonius, *The Arab Awakening: The Story of the Arab National Movement* (London: Hamish Hamilton, 1961), p. 248.

28   P. Khoury, *Syria and the French Mandate: The Politics of Arab Nationalism 1920–1945*, (Princeton: Princeton University Press, 1987), p. 43.

29   Ibid., p. 57.

30   Ibid., p. 59.

31   B. Saunders, *The United States and Arab Nationalism: The Syrian Case, 1953–1960* (London: Praeger, 1996), p. 5.

32   M. Van Dusen, "Political Integration and Regionalism in Syria", *Middle East Journal*, vol. 26, no. 3 (Spring 1972), p. 123.

33   P. Khoury, "Syrian Political Culture: A Historical Perspective," in R. Antoun and D. Quataert (eds.), *Syria: Society, Culture, and Polity* (Albany: State University of New York Press, 1991), p. 19.

34   M. Ma'oz, "The Emergence of Modern Syria" in M. Ma'oz and A. Yaniv (eds.), *Syria under Assad: Domestic Constraints and Regional Risks* (London: Croom Helm, 1986), p. 21.

35   M. Rodinson, *Israel and the Arabs* (Middlesex: Penguin, 1969), pp. 29–40.

36 I. Lapidus, *A History of Islamic Societies* (Cambridge: Cambridge University Press, 1991), p. 647.

37 I. Rabinovich, *Syria under the Ba'th 1963–66: The Army–Party Symbiosis* (Jerusalem: Israel University Press, 1972), p. 6.

38 M. Ma'oz, "The Emergence of Modern Syria" in M. Ma'oz and A. Yaniv (eds.), *Syria under Assad: Domestic Constraints and Regional Risks* (London: Croom Helm, 1986), p. 21.

39 I. Rabinovich, *Syria under the Ba'th 1963–66: The Army–Party Symbiosis* (Jerusalem: Israel University Press, 1972), p. 9.

40 Ibid., pp. 6–11.

41 D. Betz, "Conflict of Principle and Policy: A Case Study of the Arab Baath Socialist Party in Power in Syria, 8 March 1963–23 February 1966" (Ph.D. Thesis, Ann Arbor), (Ann Arbor: Xerox University Microfilms, 1976), p. 4.

42 D. Hopwood, *Egypt: Politics and Society 1945–90* (London: HarperCollins, 1991), p. 60.

43 E. Kienle, *Ba'th v. Ba'th: The Conflict between Syria and Iraq, 1968–1989*, (London: I.B. Tauris, 1990), p. 13.

44 K. Abu Jaber, *The Arab Ba'th Socialist Party: History, Ideology, and Organization* (Syracuse: Syracuse University Press, 1966), pp. 80–1.

45 R. Hinnebusch, *Peasant and Bureaucracy in Ba'thist Syria: The Political Economy of Rural Development* (Boulder: Westview Press, 1989), pp. 19–20.

46 Ibid., p. 20.

47 M. Ma'oz, *Syria and Israel: From War to Peace-making* (Oxford: Clarendon Press, 1995), pp. 82–4.

48 Ibid., p. 103.

49 E. Kienle, *Ba'th v. Ba'th: The Conflict between Syria and Iraq, 1968–1989* (London: I.B. Tauris, 1990), pp. 51–8.

50 N. Van Dam, *The Struggle for Power in Syria: Politics and Society under Asad and the Ba'th Party* (London: I.B. Tauris, 1996), pp. 65–6.

51 M. Ma'oz, "The Emergence of Modern Syria" in M. Ma'oz and A. Yaniv (eds.), *Syria under Assad: Domestic Constraints and Regional Risks* (London: Croom Helm, 1986), p. 15.

52 C. Tilly, "War Making and State Making as Organised Crime" in P. Evans, D. Rueschemeyer and T. Skocpol (eds.), *Bringing the State Back in* (Cambridge: Cambridge University Press, 1990), pp. 169–90.

53 M. Ma'oz and A. Yaniv (eds.), "The Syrian Paradox" in *Syria under Assad: Domestic Constraints and Regional Risks* (London: Croom Helm, 1986), pp. 254–5.

54 D. Butter, "Special Report: Syria", *Middle East Economic Digest*, vol. 39, no. 39, 29 September 1995, p. 9.

55 *Syria – Country Profile 1993/94* (London: The Economist Intelligence Unit, 1994), p. 12.

56 A. Hourani, *Minorities in the Arab World* (London: Oxford University Press, 1947), p. 22.

57 N. Van Dam, *The Struggle for Power in Syria: Politics and Society under Asad and the Ba'th Party* (London: I.B. Tauris, 1996).

58 Ibid., p. 1.

59 M. Kessler, *Syria: Fragile Mosaic of Power* (Washington: National Defense University Press, 1987), p. 30.

60 N. Van Dam, *The Struggle for Power in Syria: Politics and Society under Asad and the Ba'th Party* (London: I.B. Tauris, 1996), p. 1.

61 F. Khuri, "The 'Alawis of Syria: Religious Ideology and Organisation" in R. Antoun and D. Quataert (eds.), *Syria: Society, Culture, and Policy* (Albany: State University of New York Press, 1991), p. 49.

62 N. Van Dam, *The Struggle for Power in Syria: Politics and Society under Asad and the Ba'th Party* (London: I.B. Tauris, 1996), p. 1.

63 Ibid.

64 C. Held, *Middle East Patterns* (Boulder: Westview Press, 1994), p. 209.

65 F. Khuri, "The 'Alawis of Syria: Religious Ideology and Organisation" in R. Antoun and D. Quataert (eds.), *Syria: Society, Culture, and Policy* (Albany: State University of New York Press, 1991), pp. 49–61.

66 M. Bannerman, "Syrian Arab Republic" in D. Long and B. Reich (eds.), *The Government and Politics of the Middle East and North Africa* (Boulder: Westview Press, 1995), p. 204.

67 For a good analysis of the 'Alawi community and its rise to power see: A. Drysdale, "The 'Alawis of Syria" in G. Ashworth (ed.), *World Minorities* (London: Quartermaine House/Minority Rights Group, 1978), vol. II, pp. 1–5; A. Drysdale, "The Syrian Armed Forces in National Politics: The Role of the Geographic and Ethnic Periphery" in R. Kolkowicz and A. Korbonski (eds.), *Soldiers, Peasants and Bureaucrats* (London: Allen & Unwin, 1982), pp. 52–76, and M. Faksh, "The 'Alawi Community of Syria: A New Dominant Political Force", *Middle Eastern Studies*, vol. 20, no. 2 (April 1984), pp. 133–53.

68 M. Bannerman, "Syrian Arab Republic" in D. Long and B. Reich (eds.), *The Government and Politics of the Middle East and North Africa* (Boulder: Westview Press, 1995), p. 206.

69 "Druzes" in *Islamic Desk Reference Compiled from the Encyclopaedia of Islam by E. Van Donzel*, (Leiden: E.J. Brill, 1994), p. 89.

70 D. Butter, "Lebanon" in *The Cambridge Encyclopaedia of the Middle East and North Africa* (Cambridge: Cambridge University Press, 1988), p. 369.

71 N. Van Dam, *The Struggle for Power in Syria: Politics and Society under Asad and the Ba'th Party* (London: I.B. Tauris, 1996), p. 10.

72 Ibid., pp. 48–61.

73 C. Glassé, "Isma'ilis" in *The Concise Encyclopaedia of Islam* (London: Glassé, 1989), p. 194.

74 Ibid., p. 196.

75 N. Lewis, "The Isma'ilis of Syria Today", *Royal Central Asian Society Journal*, vol. 39, no. 1 (January 1952), pp. 69–77.

76 N. Van Dam, *The Struggle for Power in Syria: Politics and Society under Asad and the Ba'th Party* (London: I.B. Tauris, 1996), pp. 11–12.

77 Ibid. The Assassins were a religio-political Islamic sect existing between the eleventh and thirteenth centuries who considered resisting the Crusader Kingdoms to be a religious duty.

78 M. Bannerman, "Syrian Arab Republic" in D. Long, and B. Reich (eds.), *The Government and Politics of the Middle East and North Africa* (Boulder: Westview Press, 1995), p. 204.

79 C. Held, *Middle East Patterns* (Boulder: Westview Press, 1994), p. 209.
80 Ibid., p. 210.
81 J. Nevo, "Syria and Jordan: The Politics of Subversion" in M. Maʻoz and A. Yaniv (eds.), *Syria under Assad: Domestic Constraints and Regional Risks* (London: Croom Helm, 1986), p. 142.
82 N. Van Dam, *The Struggle for Power in Syria: Politics and Society under Asad and the Baʻth Party* (London: I.B. Tauris, 1996), pp. 34–47.
83 For a comprehensive study of the minorities in Syria see: N. Van Dam, *The Struggle for Power in Syria: Politics and Society under Asad and the Baʻth Party* (London: I.B. Tauris, 1996); H. Batatu, "Some Observations on the Social Roots of Syria's Ruling Military Group and the Causes of its Dominance", *Middle East Journal*, vol. 35, no. 3 (Summer 1981), pp. 331–44, and N. Van Dam, "Middle Eastern Political Clichés: 'Takriti' and 'Sunni' Rule in Iraq; 'Alawi' Rule in Syria, a Critical Appraisal", *Orient*, vol. 21, no. 1 (January 1980), pp. 42–57.
84 N. Van Dam, *The Struggle for Power in Syria: Politics and Society under Asad and the Baʻth Party* (London: I.B. Tauris, 1996), pp. 34–47.
85 The process of state-building is addressed in chapter 4.
86 See chapters 4, 5 and 6.
87 M. Maʻoz, *Syria and Israel: From War to Peace-making* (Oxford: Clarendon Press, 1995), pp. 20–5.
88 As leader of the secret Military Committee, Jadid was Syria's ephemeral ruler from 1966 to 1970. See P. Seale, *Asad of Syria: The Struggle for the Middle East* (London: I.B. Tauris, 1988), p. 105.
89 M. Maʻoz, *Syria and Israel: From War to Peace-making* (Oxford: Clarendon Press, 1995), pp. 116–19.
90 R. Hinnebusch, "Revisionist Dreams, Realist Strategies: The Foreign Policy of Syria" in B. Korany and A. Dessouki (eds.), *The Foreign Policies of Arab States: The Challenge of Change*, (Boulder: Westview Press, 1991), p. 375.
91 G. Torrey, *Syrian Politics and the Military* (Columbus: Ohio State University Press, 1964), p. 104.
92 R. Hinnebusch, "Political Recruitment and Socialization in Syria: The Case of the Revolutionary Youth Federation", *International Journal of Middle Eastern Studies*, vol. 11, no. 2 (1980), pp. 143–74.
93 P. Seale, *Asad of Syria: The Struggle for the Middle East* (London: I.B. Tauris, 1988), p. 148.
94 A. Khalidi and H. Agha, "The Syrian Doctrine of Strategic Parity" in J. Kipper and H. Saunders (eds.), *The Middle East in Global Perspective* (Boulder: Westview Press, 1991).
95 See chapter 5.
96 V. Perthes, *The Political Economy of Syria under Asad* (London: I.B. Tauris, 1995), p. 292.
97 L. Robinson, "Rentierism and Foreign Policy in Syria", *Arab Studies Journal*, vol. iv, no. 1 (Spring 1996), p. 38.
98 M. Bannerman, "Syrian Arab Republic" in D. Long and B. Reich (eds.), *The Government and Politics of the Middle East and North Africa* (Boulder: Westview Press, 1995), p. 206.

99 Ibid., pp. 206–7.

100 Ibid., p. 207.

101 The relationship between the state and the bourgeoisie had been disrupted through the radical policies of the Ba'th party after 1966. See chapter 4.

102 M. Bannerman, "Syrian Arab Republic" in D. Long and B. Reich (eds.), *The Government and Politics of the Middle East and North Africa* (Boulder: Westview Press, 1995), p. 207.

103 V. Perthes, "Stages of Economic and Political Liberalization" in E. Kienle (ed.), *Contemporary Syria: Liberalization between Cold War and Cold Peace* (London: British Academic Press, 1994), p. 62.

104 Ibid., p. 61.

105 Ibid.

106 Ibid.

107 The liberalising measures of 1972–7 were introduced to broaden the base of the regime and to mobilise the capital of the estranged business community to the national effort. In 1986 another set of liberalising measures was induced by the foreign exchange crisis (because of the precipitous drop in the price of oil), and the diminishing rent from the Gulf Arab states. The most recent measures, such as Investment Law 10 of 1991, were adopted to help Syria acclimatise to the changes in the world order. For more information on this topic consult E. Kienle (ed.), *Contemporary Syria: Liberalization between Cold War and Cold Peace* (London: British Academic Press, 1994), and V. Perthes, *The Political Economy of Syria under Asad* (London: I.B. Tauris, 1995).

108 *Syria – Country Report 2nd Quarter* (London: The Economist Intelligence Unit, 1996), p. 23.

109 C. Held, *Middle East Patterns* (Boulder: Westview Press, 1994), p. 213.

110 *Syria – Country Report 2nd Quarter* (London: The Economist Intelligence Unit, 1996), p. 23.

111 Ibid.

112 C. Held, *Middle East Patterns* (Boulder: Westview Press, 1994), p. 212.

113 V. Perthes, *The Political Economy of Syria under Asad* (London: I.B. Tauris, 1995), p. 91.

114 Ibid., p. 29.

115 *Syria – Country Report 2nd Quarter* (London: The Economist Intelligence Unit, 1996), p. 18.

116 V. Perthes, *The Political Economy of Syria under Asad* (London: I.B. Tauris, 1995), p. 29.

117 *Syria – Country Profile 1994/95* (London: The Economist Intelligence Unit, 1995), p. 31.

118 M. Bannerman, "Syrian Arab Republic" in D. Long and B. Reich (eds.), *The Government and Politics of the Middle East and North Africa* (Boulder: Westview Press, 1995), p. 207.

119 *Syria – Country Report 2nd Quarter* (London: The Economist Intelligence Unit, 1995), p. 37.

120 Ibid.

121 R. Magraw, *France 1815–1914: The Bourgeoisie Century* (London: Fontana Press, 1987), p. 165.

122 L. Robinson, "Rentierism and Foreign Policy in Syria", *Arab Studies Journal,* vol. iv, no. 1 (Spring 1996), p. 36.

123 Ibid.

124 A. Ehteshami and R. Hinnebusch, *Syria and Iran: Middle Powers in a Penetrated Regional System* (London: Routledge, 1997), p. 91.

125 The second Gulf War, which will be discussed in chapter 6, provides a clear-cut example of this.

126 N. Sukkar, "The Crisis of 1986 and Syria's Plan for Reform" in E. Kienle (ed.), *Contemporary Syria: Liberalization between Cold War and Cold Peace* (London: British Academic Press, 1994), pp. 27–8.

127 Ibid., p. 31.

128 D. Waldner, "More than Meets the Eye: Economic Influence on Contemporary Syrian Foreign Policy", *Middle East Insight,* vol. xi, no. 4 (May/June 1995), p. 35.

129 N. Sukkar, "The Crisis of 1986 and Syria's Plan for Reform" in E. Kienle (ed.), *Contemporary Syria: Liberalization between Cold War and Cold Peace* (London: British Academic Press, 1994), pp. 26–43.

130 V. Perthes, *The Political Economy of Syria under Asad* (London: I.B. Tauris, 1995), p. 204.

131 Interview with a Syrian economist, 26 June 1994.

132 V. Perthes, *The Political Economy of Syria under Asad* (London: I.B. Tauris, 1995), p. 205.

133 Syria's estimated debt of $10,000 million in 1991 has been largely written off by the Soviets, but on the condition that new acquisitions are paid for in hard currency and that they are given access to the Aleppine markets.

134 F. Lawson, *Why Syria Goes to War? Thirty Years of Confrontation* (London: Cornell University Press, 1996), pp. 34–50.

3
Syria:
The Centres of Power

Introduction

The hypothesis of this book acknowledges the primacy of the international political system in affecting state behaviour; meanwhile, it endorses the role played by domestic factors in foreign policy formulation of Third World states. Syria's adjustment to the New World Order, which has amounted to a change of strategy in foreign policy, has been facilitated by the structure of its domestic political process. The state in Syria is sufficiently insulated from domestic social forces to orchestrate a radical change in foreign policy. Its resilience to domestic challenges has been incorporated into the structures of the state and the political process. Under Asad, the orientation of the state changed decisively from an instrument of class revolution to a machinery of power in the service of *raison d'état*.[1]

Since he came to power, President Asad has instituted a process of state consolidation which has enabled Syria to engage in a protracted regional struggle with Israel. The pursuit of regional hegemony, manifested through its competition with Israel, particularly in Lebanon, has been Syria's *raison d'état* since 1970.[2]

The national interest, in other words the regional competition with Israel, has been central to the consolidation of the state. Asad has consolidated the Syrian state into a quasi-corporatist state that serves the national interest. He has constructed a state that is construed from a patrimonial system and an institutional form of government. Without a cohesive social and political entity, the consolidation of the state has been governed through the balancing of interests within Syria. One can identify three main centres of interest within Syrian society: the Ba'th party; the armed forces and security services, and the bourgeoisie.

These centres of interest have become centres of power in Syria; they command their own constituencies through the allocation of patronage. The Ba'th party and the armed forces have dominated the state apparatus and the decision-making process since Asad's ascent to power, whilst a reconstructed bourgeoisie has remained subordinate to the state.[3]

In more recent times, the permutation of power among the three centres of interest has reconfigured. Set within the context of the global reconfiguration of power, and the succession of capitalism, the bourgeoisie has started to gain in stature at the expense of the Ba'th party. Before charting the rise of the bourgeoisie and the decline of the Ba'th party, however, I intend to examine the structures of the state and illustrate their impact upon the decision-making process within Syria.

Realism and the decision-making process

Power in Syria is personalised through the politics of Asad; his stamp on Syrian politics and his omnipresence in the life of Syrians cannot be ignored. Asad's portrait adorns the buildings of Damascus; his statues remind the citizens of each province of his paternal leadership, and the press serves to reinforce his persona upon the public psyche. Despite these symbols of Asad's primary role in Syria's decision-making process, there is a danger of oversimplifying the chain of command within the Syrian political system. Beneath the role of the president lies a state built upon corporations of interest which constitute agencies of communication and support between the president and the populace.[4]

The forging of the state, through balancing the interests of the dominant social actors, has produced a unitary state that is responsible for the conception and implementation of domestic and foreign policies. Existing above the dominant social forces, Asad has conducted policies based upon rational considerations. The president has not been held hostage to the dominant social actors; moreover, he has placed a layer of insulation around the decision-making process. This insulation, protected by the state's resilience, the means of coercion, has produced an environment for autonomous decision-making. From the domestic perspective, the state is the principal actor in Syria's foreign relations.

This coincides with the realist paradigm, which suggests that the state is unitary and the principal actor in international relations. Realism is the most apposite paradigm to understanding international relations when the state is a consolidated and legitimate feature of its own political environment. In neo-realist thinking, the state is governed by the structures of the international political system. The adoption of neo-realism's emphasis upon the international political system makes realism a model more appropriate to this study. Realism is a universal paradigm, but its weakness lies in its Western-centric perceptions. In its universality, it fails to address the peculiarities of the Third World.[5] Realism is suitable for the study of the First World, where states have evolved through a protracted historical struggle. We can charge realism with being too Eurocentric in its approach to international relations. Its utility to this study is limited as it does not address the issue of the unconsolidated states in the Third World.[6]

Many new states were created as the era of imperialism receded after the major world wars of the twentieth century. The new states belonged to the pole of the Third World, which represented a constellation of modern independent states. Although these states enjoyed their new found independence, the legacy of imperialism left a pattern of economic dependency and ethnically fractured societies. Many of these states were created across ethnic, cultural, religious, and linguistic boundaries; each factor deprived the new states of common legitimacy.[7]

Without a historical legacy of their own, many of the states of the Third World were unable to consolidate their positions *vis-à-vis* their societies. Imported political systems were used to govern state–society relations, but the absence of a legitimate framework caused the states to depend upon the military to maintain social order. The use of coercion has remained an instrument of control in many Third World states.[8]

After 1945, neo-realism asserts, the international political system continued to govern the behaviour of the world's states. The bipolar division of the world incorporated the states of the First, Second, and Third Worlds. Third World states, such as Syria, were drawn into the competition for international hegemony between the superpowers. The Soviet Union built its alliance with Syria through the transfer of arms in an attempt to counter the imperial designs of the US. Syria's behaviour, in other words, was guided by the structure of the international political system.[9] This structure, and its sub-systems, have continued to shape the formulation of states' foreign policies. In the newly independent states of the Third World, however, the evolutionary phases of state consolidation have thrown up domestic anomalies that affect the formulation and implementation of these policies.

If one is to assess the determinants that influence the foreign relations of Syria, it would be negligent to omit the internal dynamics within the Syrian state. The Syrian state followed the pattern described above; with its fractious past, it was open to the influences of the imperial powers and the dominant domestic actors. The state was shackled to the interests of international forces and the ethnic and religious cleavages present within society.[10]

Between 1946 and 1970, the Syrian state lacked legitimacy and was exposed to a period of social and political instability. Because of the complex ethnic composition of Syrian society, the state was unable to compel allegiance from the populace to the new Syrian state. A combination of the distrust between the ethnic cleavages among the states of Bilad al-Sham, and the autonomous enclaves of Jabal al-Druze, Latakia, Homs, Hama, and Aleppo, undermined the national function of the state and the central rule of Damascus. This effectively invited the military to intervene in state affairs in 1949.[11] Its involvement in Syrian politics has continued to define the nature of the relationship between the state and the society.

Military intervention has proven to be an endemic feature of Third World states. Where states have not been able to assert their authority, through an institutional political process, they have often depended upon the military for support; alternatively, they have been subordinated to the authority of the military.[12] In both cases, domestic politics has tended to impinge upon the autonomy of the state. The decision-making process has been subjected to the competition that has arisen among the dominant actors within the state.

With its emphasis on the unitary nature of the state, realism fails to capture the impact of domestic actors upon the Third World state. The lack of consolidation in many states of the Third World has rendered them malleable to the influences of dominant ethnic and/or religious groups. We are obliged, therefore, to adopt the features of another paradigm that can account for the effect of the international political system and is more sensitive to the impact of domestic politics.

Omnibalancing

The concept of omnibalancing allows us to bridge the difference between the domestic politics' model and the rational actor model, and to gauge their respective effects upon the state. The key to omnibalancing is the degree to which a state enjoys autonomy from the structural determinants of the international political system, and from the constraints present within the domestic system.[13]

In modern Syria, the state has been said to be semi-autonomous from the interests of one group.[14] Asad has successfully constructed a Bonapartist state, that is one balanced between the interests of competing social forces, namely, the Ba'th party, the armed forces and security services, the bureaucracy and the bourgeoisie. Hinnebusch has suggested that Asad sits above the corporate agencies and balances their demands and interests.[15]

Asad's programme of state building sought to free the state from the undue influence of domestic forces, and to elevate the decision-makers of the state above those forces. From this position, the coterie of the regime could enact policies which were unpopular but deemed to be taken in the national interest. This degree of autonomy in decision-making has been achieved through the creation of a quasi-corporatist state whose origins lie in the aftermath of the June War of 1967.

State-building in Syria

The June War of 1967 significantly altered the regional order of the Middle East. The Arab regimes were faced with a resounding defeat in their contest with Israel and the extent of the loss was far-reaching as Israel extended its regional hegemony through the occupation of Sinai, the West Bank, the Gaza Strip, and the Golan Heights.[16]

Post-independent Syria had been enfeebled by numerous military *coups* and counter-*coups* which ultimately resulted in the humiliation of the 1967 war.[17] Against this background, Asad, as the minister of defence, seized power through an internal *coup* from within the existing Ba'th regime on 14 November 1970.[18] The new leadership faced an immediate task, notably, ensuring the survival of the new regime. Security of the regime and the state, from both the domestic and external perspectives, thenceforth took precedence over all policies of the state and has since been pursued through the maximisation of power. The survival strategy of the regime was built upon three tiers:

(a) Coercion;
(b) The struggle with Israel;
(c) A state-building programme.

Coercion has provided the backbone of the regime; it has sustained the regime, especially during the late 1970s and early 1980s when Syria was engulfed in internal dissension. Without the intervention of the security services, namely the Defence Companies of the president's brother, Rif'at Asad, civil war would have enflamed Syria and threatened the leadership of the state.[19]

The state's legitimacy has been built upon insecure foundations. As the cement of Arab nationalism has fallen away, the state's legitimacy has dissipated. Economic shortfalls have served to weaken the state's allocative abilities, and exposed the vulnerability of the state's institutions. Lacking sufficient legitimacy, the state has depended upon coercion to maintain its authority and implement unpopular policies, especially in its taciturn struggle with Israel.[20]

The struggle with Israel has been the primary concern of the new regime and regional competition with Israel took the form of a balance-of-power contest. The balance of power between Israel and the collective Arab states unduly impinged upon Syria's foreign policy. Syria was encouraged by the oil monarchies to desist from the Arab Cold War and engage in new alliances. In doing so, Syria accrued significant economic benefits from the oil monarchies, which assisted its struggle with Israel.[21]

Asad sought to consolidate the gains and losses of the June War, and pursue a more realist path in foreign policy.[22] The grand goals of pan-Arabism were tailored to the realities of Arab capabilities. In effect, Syrian aspirations were curtailed to: the recovery of the Arab territories lost in 1967; the restoration of Palestinian rights; and the incorporation of Lebanon into Syria's sphere of influence.[23]

To achieve these ambitions, Syria had to counterbalance the military potential of Israel. This could be achieved through the expansion of regional alliances, especially with the oil-rich Gulf Arab states, or through the consolidation of the Syrian state, and the cultivation of a Syria-centric base of power. In a new state, without a definitive national identity, the prospect of war proved to be a crucible for state-building. The perpetual threat posed by Israel invoked a preoccupation with security and superimposed, albeit temporarily, a national Syrian consciousness.

State-building was inextricably linked to securing Syria's regional status. The conflict with Israel provided justification for the regime's departure from the political and economic policies of the radical wing of the Ba'th party[24] which had believed in "the primary need to replace the old guard's reformist socialism with a radical social transformation to improve socio-economic conditions in Syria".[25] On the other hand, the policies of Asad's regime were motivated by Arab nationalism, but the regime's perception was less exclusive than that of the radical wing of the Ba'th party, as it included all sectors of society. The regime sought to mobilise the energies and assets of the Ba'th constituency and the merchant class. The struggle with Israel required a united effort, and Asad's task was to engender a sense of loyalty to the Syrian state.[26] Evidently, there was a distinct break with the ideological policies of the 1966–70 period: conflict with Israel was still a central feature of Syrian foreign policy, but the new strategy was based on maintaining the balance of power rather than ideology. State-building was the first step towards the realisation of this goal. This required broadening the base of the regime through an appeal not only to the traditional followers of Ba'thism, but also to those sectors of society who had opposed Ba'th rule and had suffered under it. The socialist content of Ba'thism was diluted as elements of the Syrian bourgeoisie were brought into the state-building project.[27]

Asad's most immediate concern was to construct a durable state in order that Syria might fulfil its regional ambitions. The new Syrian regime thus put priority on domestic matters which required a restructuring of state–society relations imbued with a national agenda, and was attained through the creation of a new governing system.

The governing system

The contemporary Syrian political system was implemented soon after Asad had seized power in 1970. It has been construed from two forms of governance: an institutional system[28] and a neo-patrimonial system.[29] The decision-making process in Syria has existed somewhere between these two competing systems.[30]

The institutional model assumes that state structures are organised according to a society's norms, values, rules, and functions.[31] Hinnebusch suggests that the institutional system exists beyond the exigencies of personal or primordial motives. He comments that "authority of office;

routinized ideology; political skills and procedures and votes in assemblies and bureaus become crucial resources in the political process, subordinating or at least channelling and checking the role of societal resources such as wealth and kinship."[32]

The institutional policy-making model can be seen to operate in the states of the First World, where the political process has been institutionalised through a long historical process. A rational policy, according to Huntington, derives from an institutional decision-making system that contains a series of checks and balances.[33]

On the other hand, patrimonialism (the use of patronage, perpetuated through the male line, at the state level) is incapable of delivering consistent policies based upon a rational set of objectives, as there are often more pressing concerns emerging from the domestic arena. Where patrimonialisation deepens, the coherence, rationality, and popular base of the state are all increasingly at risk. A rational decision in Syria, as well as in many Third World states, must include a calculation of regime survival. The relationship between the state and the regime in the Third World is often ambiguous, especially where the primordial interests of a ruling minority coincide, or conflict, with the national interest.[34]

With the advent of oil wealth in the Middle East, the patrimonial state, founded upon traditional forms of patronage, has been replaced with the neo-patrimonial state.[35] In the neo-patrimonial state, the distribution of favours, in return for support, has been exchanged for the allocation of economic rewards. Hence, the patrimonial state has been transformed into a neo-patrimonial state as the state has gained a more allocative role.[36]

The neo-patrimonial system allows the state to finance a network of support, usually built upon ethnic, cultural, social, or religious ties. It fosters patterns of patronage and "cronyism" throughout society, in return for rent, thereupon stabilising the support of the state. In the Middle East, where states have assumed control over considerable natural resources, the state plays an allocative role which acts as a source of empowerment, as the allocation of contracts entails building layers of support and allegiance. The Gulf Arab states have successfully transformed their patrimonial states into neo-patrimonial states through the auspices of oil.

Syria has been less successful in cementing patronage through the allocation of state contracts and favours based upon oil rent. The ideology of the Ba'th party has acted as a substitute for money in oiling the political system, and the Ba'th party's extensive network in the rural districts has ensured the longevity of the Asad regime. Counterpoised to the efficacy of the institutional model is the loyalty paid to the Asad regime by the system of neo-patrimonialism: "The Ba'ath recruited from all those who were outside the system of connections, patronage or kin on which the old regime was built: the educated sons of peasants, the minorities, the rural lower middle class, the 'black sheep' from lesser branches of great families."[37]

Functioning between institutionalism and neo-patrimonialism, the resulting system of governance has been based upon three overlapping structures:

(a)   The political system;
(b)   The Ba'th party and its corporate bodies;
(c)   The armed forces and the security services that constitute the shield of the regime.

This system of governance can be conceptualised as a quasi-corporatist structure.[38]

The political system

Asad sought to stabilise and consolidate the state through a carefully designed political system which has remained unchanged in character since 1970, despite the limited alterations of 1990.[39] The political system includes a presidency, parliamentary chamber, formal political parties, and a constitution. Its two main national institutions are the Presidency and the People's Council. The president resides above the political system and oversees its functions; all of the political bodies of the state are subordinate to the president. The location of the presidential palace, set high above Damascus and isolated from the social contagion of Syria's capital city, is symbolic of Asad's relationship with the Syrian state and people: the presidential monarch rests above the domestic forces of Syria.

The presidential monarchy is instrumental in the foreign policy decision-making process, but it would be folly to ignore the role of the state institutions and their impact on this process. It is very tempting to oversimplify the influence of the president because the modern state of Syria is in part a creation of Asad. As Asad claims to be a man of institutions, he has set out to endorse the institutional foundation of the Syrian state.[40] There is, however, a contradiction between Asad's proclamations and his actions. A closer examination of the president's powers will enable us to perceive this contradiction and the prevailing chain of command in Syria.

The Presidency

At the apex of the political system, the bureaucracy, the Ba'th Regional Command, the armed forces and the security services stands the president who has the right to:

(a)   Appoint the prime minister;
(b)   Appoint the speaker of the People's Council;
(c)   Make laws when the Council is not in session;
(d)   Legislate without the Council's consent,[41]
(e)   Veto parliamentary laws;
(f)   Dismiss the People's Council.[42]

On 31 January 1973, the People's Council approved a new constitution which limited the president's term of office to seven years, but bestowed upon him (Asad) the rank of commander-in-chief of the armed forces, the power to declare war, to instigate a state of emergency, and to legislate when the parliament is in recess.[43] The powers of the president are thus constitutionally absolute. This constitution was ratified by a referendum on 12 March 1973.[44]

Despite being approved by 88.9 per cent of the electorate, the constitution provoked a series of riots in Homs and Hama whose traditional Islamic communities rejected the secular disposition of the constitution, especially as it described Syria as a democratic, popular, and socialist state.[45] It did not stipulate that the head of state had to be Muslim. Although the military was the regime's tool for exercising social control, it did not prevent the riots in Homs and Hama. Consequently, the constitution was amended to include a provision that the head of state had to be Muslim.

As an 'Alawi, Asad existed outside the community of the Sunni majority. The 'Alawis were not recognised by Sunnis or Shi'as, and, moreover, were maligned as heretics.[46] For Asad to be head of state, he had to belong to an official branch of Islam. He thus tried to satisfy the religious establishment by persuading Musr Sadr, the spokesman for the Shi'a community in Lebanon, to issue a *fatwa* in 1973 declaring 'Alawis to be Shi'as.[47]

The amendment of the constitution and the issue of the *fatwa* demonstrated two points:

(a) The resonance of religion in the traditional sectors of Syria and its resistance to secular rule;
(b) Asad's pragmatic approach to state-building.

By adapting the constitution to incorporate the Islamic essence of Syrian and Arab culture, Asad sought to defuse a potential crisis and appease the religious sector of the population.

Asad has clearly concentrated power in the presidency; the institutions of state, such as the People's Council and the National Progressive Front (NPF), were created to conduct the more mundane business of state. These institutions allowed the regime to divest itself of some of its daily responsibilities and were designed to broaden the base of the regime without soliciting power.

The People's Council
After taking the final step in seizing power, in mid-November 1970, Asad enforced the authority of the military wing of the Ba'th over that of the civilian wing. On 21 November, Asad formed a cabinet, which included fifteen Ba'thists, six Nasserists, two Communists, two Independents, and supporters of Akram Hourani.[48] Asad assumed the portfolios of prime minister and defence minister.

In February 1971 Asad established a parliament, the People's Council, whose members were originally appointed but after 1973 were elected by universal mandate.[49] The Syrian parliament was composed of 195 members until May 1990 when the number of obtainable seats was increased to 250.[50] The People's Council most closely resembles a majlis al-shura, in the traditional Islamic sense; it does not possess sufficient power to preside over high politics, or legislate without the permission of the president.[51] Parliamentary discussion has been confined to the non-political issues of state, such as government performance in the fields of economy and services.[52] It is a discussion chamber that serves as a forum for functional groups within Syrian society.

The main function of this assembly is to represent the different interest groups, rather than constitute a sovereign body that generates and implements policies.[53] The president is responsible for submitting bills to the parliament and promulgates laws that the parliament has passed, but he has the right to veto these laws. Technically, the parliament is invested with the power to overrule his veto by a two-thirds' majority, but this situation has never arisen.[54]

The People's Council is not an autonomous component of a democratic political system. In its current form, it owes its legacy and allegiance to the president, who has granted it nominal powers. The creation of the People's Council was not a derivative of class consciousness or of a demand for greater democratisation; rather, it was an imposition from above.[55] The establishment of the political system served the interests of the elite by broadening the base of support and incorporating members perceived to be outside the immediate boundaries of the Ba'th party, but it did not necessarily serve the interests of democracy. As a consultative, quasi-corporatist body, the People's Council is an integral part of the process that governs the relationship between state and society.[56]

The local government

There are fourteen provinces in Syria. Each province is subdivided into administrative areas, districts, and municipalities. At the head of this local structure is the governor, who consults with a local council of one hundred members elected every five years.[57]

The local governments are invested with powers to attend to local affairs. They are responsible for the everyday running of provincial affairs, and need only to defer to Damascus when seeking project approval or the acquisition of budgets.[58] It is at the local level that we can see the three institutions of the state interacting. In each province there is a close liaison among the governor, the security chief, and the Ba'th party secretary. Each officer observes the policy decisions and actions of their counterpart, as a mechanism for regulating provincial affairs and for engendering loyalty and accountability to the state.[59]

The balance of power among the three provincial leaders is often dependent upon the political environment of the province. Seale alludes to the primacy of the security chief in a province such as Deir al-Zor, because of its proximity to Iraq, whereas in Raqqa', where industry takes priority, the governor would take pre-eminence.[60]

The interplay among the various governing structures allows the state to incorporate the interests of its constituencies, both within the provinces and the urban centres. The policy of incorporation has been a distinctive feature of Asad's rule. In the People's Council, the creation of the NPF allowed the state to envelop the diverse sentiments of the left-wing parties.

The National Progressive Front

In the provincial elections, which took place on 3 and 4 March 1971, the Ba'th party suffered a number of unexpected set-backs. In a series of public speeches, Asad promised to restore some of the public liberties abolished by the previous regime. This reinforced the necessity to develop a wider base of support.[61] On 7 March 1971, the president divested the Ba'th party of some of its nominal powers by establishing the NPF with an 18-member central leadership consisting of President Asad, nine other Ba'thists, and two members from each of the four non-Ba'thist parties, including the Syrian Communist Party (SCP) and the Arab Socialist Union (ASU).[62]

The formation of the NPF signified a change in direction for the inclusion of the left-wing and Nasserist groups' coalition in the governing establishment incorporated a level of opposition in the state apparatus.[63] Including the above-mentioned political parties, the NPF represented the only official channel of opposition. However, its role was dominated by the Ba'th party, whose programme and conference resolutions, according to the NPF charter, provided the political direction of the NPF. The NPF's charter also disqualified all parties, except the Ba'th, from recruiting among students and from the armed forces.[64] The parties themselves, by accepting the conditions of admission, were divested of their powers as centres of criticism.[65] The agenda was firmly set from a top–down perspective. Accordingly, constitutional power-sharing did not result from the creation of the NPF. It provided the regime with an inflated sense of legitimacy, and hence further increased its exercise of central power.

The NPF provided a forum for formal parties, recognised by the regime, to participate in selected matters of state, and under these circumstances the Ba'th party controlled and orchestrated the agenda. Besides members of the NPF, independent candidates were allowed to stand for election, but only after ratification of their legality had been granted by the regime.[66] There was no significant competition among the political parties operating in the system; they formed a joint list for each province and issued a common election manifesto.[67]

The functions of the People's Council and the actions of the NPF have been largely cosmetic. Although a coalition of interests is represented through the parties, the NPF, according to Hinnebusch, has "never constituted more than a transparent attempt, by the regime, to disguise the Ba'th's monopolisation of power".[68] The inclusion of legal parties was only an attempt to legitimise Ba'th rule through the co-option of small but compatible interest groups.

The Ba'th party

The Ba'th party is one of the foundations of the Syrian state. It was originally built as a party of opposition during the period of the French mandate through the inspiration of Michel 'Aflaq and the organisational skills of Salah al-Bitar.[69] Although the Ba'th party was formed as an opposition movement, after it had taken power in 1963 it became a party of government.

Before addressing the dynamic between the Ba'th party and the state, the organisation of the party should be reviewed. The ideological component of the party has been referred to in chapter 3, but its organisation requires further definition.

The organisation of the Ba'th party

The organisation of the party is very distinct and pervades all sectors of Syrian society. The National Command is the party's highest authority and is an inter-Arab and trans-state body. The Regional Command is responsible for the party in each state. It is composed of 21 members and meets once a week.[70] The organisational aspect of the party was construed after the Communist model of the Soviet Union which resembles a pyramidal structure. The party cell is the smallest unit of the party structure. Between four and seven members belong to each cell, and are most operative in the workplace or among friends. There are five levels between the party cell and the National Command which include: cell; company; division; branch and Regional Command.[71]

The structure of the party was carefully designed so that communication flowed from the junior body to the parent body (for example, from the company to the division – see Figure 2). The system of authority within the Ba'th party was originally based on democratic socialism, but since Asad took power, the flow of information has been displaced and flows from the top down.[72] The revolution from above has ensured that policy decisions emanate from the Regional Command, and then radiate throughout the Ba'th party organisation. High politics remains in

FIGURE 2
Ba'th party organisation chart

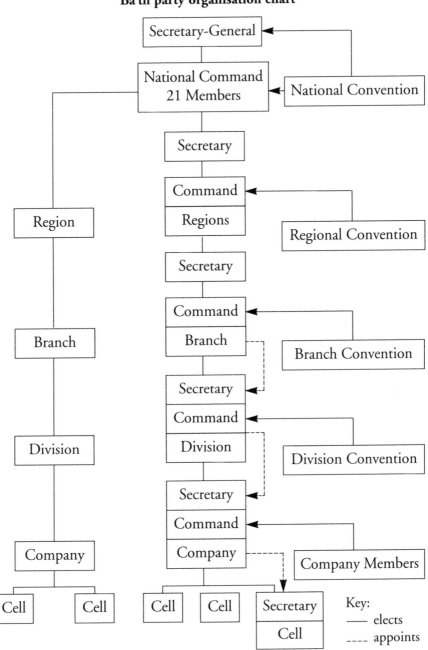

Source: K. Abu Jaber, *The Arab Ba'th Socialist Party: History, Ideology, and Organization* (Syracuse: Syracuse University Press, 1966), p. 145.

the domain of the Regional Command and the president's close advisers. The party, therefore, approves the decisions taken by the party elite, rather than proposes or challenges the leadership.

Adjacent to the hierarchy of levels in the Ba'th party are the corporatist bodies. These are organised according to sectoral interests within Syria and comprise the Peasants', Students', Workers', Women's, and Youth unions. These syndicate agencies were constructed to articulate the interests of each group. As corporate bodies they are granted access to the decision-making process via representation on policy issues. Seale suggests that the secretary of each sectoral body acts as the conduit between leadership and membership. The secretary can voice the concerns of the membership on policy matters, hence transmitting some form of party sentiment, but policy initiatives transcend from the party leadership to the designated corporate body. The influence of the syndicate bodies is, however, limited. For instance, when a faction of the trade union proposed to pull out of the Ba'th system because of the regime's economic policies, the president warned that freedom had to be understood within the framework of responsibility and not contradiction and fragmentation.[73]

Populist corporatism, as a system of state management, has been effective since Asad's rise to power. It includes the incorporation of political elite groups, popular organisations and organised business.[74] The corporations are "divided into compulsory, non-competitive, functionally differentiated, hierarchic associations which are considered to be representative for their members and the membership of the functional groups within society".[75] Each group enjoys some access to the decision-making process, but these privileges are dependent upon the political and economic environment.[76] In this form then, the corporate bodies of the Ba'th party serve two purposes:

(a)   They are conductors of party opinion and thereby indicate levels of legitimacy within the party;
(b)   They act as agents of socialisation for the party.

The relationship between the bodies and the party leadership remains somewhat ambiguous, depending on the directional flow of information and decisions.

Dynamism between the Ba'th party and the state
The Ba'th party is one of the state's principal sources of power. It has

been responsible for political recruitment, indoctrination, education, and mobilisation of the population. More recently, the party has become a ladder of upward mobility providing access to positions of influence. In this sense, it has become more of a bureaucracy, a power broker, and a source patronage than a revolutionary movement.[77] Sadowski writes:

> Twenty-two years in power have changed the Ba'th from a revolutionary movement into a virtual appendage of the state. But this transformation did not destroy the party's influence. Along with the army and the bureaucracy, it remains one of the foundations of the Asad regime.[78]

The state and the Ba'th party are ultimately linked in the governing of Syria through their parallel structures. The president, the prime minister, the speaker, and the officers of the state are all members of the Syrian Regional Command of the Ba'th party. The party is also dominant in the People's Council and the state bureaucracy; additionally, it operates alongside the provincial assemblies.[79]

The Ba'th party has also provided the state with a supply of legitimacy. It has appealed to those groups previously omitted from access to the state, such as: unionised workers, public employees, agricultural workers, and peasants. These groups have remained loyal to the Ba'th and provided some legitimacy for the regime.[80] In trying to establish and maintain legitimacy, the party has "redistributed income, promoted growth, spread literacy, and in general improved the economic lot of their citizens".[81]

The Ba'th party established its credentials with the peasantry, the minorities, and the urban youth as a national party with a radical agenda for change.[82] The socialist and nationalist aspects of the party attracted the disenchanted minorities which had suffered from the urban politics of the political elite. The party offered the opportunity of advancement in a system otherwise determined by the patronage of the notable families of Damascus, Homs, Hama, and Aleppo.[83] The families of the political elite were less inclined to join the party as it challenged the foundations of their heritage and wealth. This produced an environment where peasants and minorities could rise through the ranks of the party, and influence the direction of its politics. The Ba'th party also represented a political and national alternative to the enervated struggles of the National Bloc and the People's Party.[84]

The status of the relationship between the Ba'th party and the state has become less certain since 1985. There has been a qualitative downgrading of the party's influence in the decision-making process. A transition may be taking place in the balance of interests in Syria's domestic arena, as is suggested by:

(a) Syria's admission into the US-led coalition during the second Gulf War without prior consultation with the Regional Command;
(b) The pressure placed upon the political and economic interests of the party by the economic liberalising measures introduced in 1986;
(c) The failure to convene a Regional Congress, which should take place every five years, since 1985.

These factors indicate a change in the substance of the relationship between the party and the state.[85] According to Hinnebusch, the Ba'th party has been "downgraded, de-ideologised and turned into a patronage machine with little capacity for independent action".[86]

The Ba'th party and Syrian society

The distinctive pyramidal chain of command gave the Ba'th leadership access to a class-based clientele that had been excluded from influencing the policies of the traditional Syrian leadership. The Ba'th party invested the inhabitants of the provinces with the power of organisation, and the chance to mobilise their support in exchange for legitimacy.

Although it penetrated Syrian society, the Ba'th party never became a mass party. The emphasis of the party between 1940 and 1966 was on recruiting an active membership. Despite its popularity in the provinces and among the poorer sections of Syrian society, the leadership of the Ba'th party came from the Syrian middle classes. The philosophy of 'Aflaq was encased in the moderate language of the middle classes, which proved to be a cause of antagonism between the 'Aflaq mind-set and the more radical peasantry.

The division within the Ba'th party between the peasantry and the middle class manifested itself through the two wings of the party. The peasants and the minorities captured the military wing of the party whilst the urban middle class retained leadership through the civilian wing of the party.[87] The leaders of the rural and urban centres were polarised whilst the civilian leadership and the middle class were opposed to the nascent leadership of the radicals within the Ba'th party.

A contest for leadership erupted on 23 February 1966 when the military wing, under the guidance of Jadid and the Military Committee, usurped the civilian wing of the party.[88] Their social and political agendas were more radical than those of their successors, as they sought to base the Ba'th party on a Leninist model of organisation. This regime could well have been described as a dictatorship of the petite bourgeoisie. Land reforms, nationalisations, and government control over the market struck at the bases of the bourgeoisie.[89]

The radical regime transformed the class composition of the state. The Ba'thisation of the army replaced the Sunni upper-class and middle-class officers with others of plebeian, rural, and minority origin. The Ba'thists had seized power by military *coup*, but not at the head of a broad cross-classed movement. Their road to power dictated the omnipresence of the military in political affairs and culminated in the overthrow of the civilian wing. Asad's ultimate manœuvre into position from minister of defence to secretary-general of the Regional Command signified a permanent role for the military through the Ba'th party.

The armed forces and security services

The armed forces and the security services have remained the most durable repositories of state power and have been responsible for projecting Syria's power in its conflict with Israel as well as guaranteeing the survival of the regime.

These corporate bodies have become distinct centres of power. Their access to the state and the regime is underwritten by their indispensability to state and regime security. They are directly accountable to the president. Unlike the People's Council, and the NPF, the military centres of power are not subordinate to the president. Both sides are mutually dependent upon each other for their existence. The president requires a pervasive network of security services to guarantee his rule against insurrection whilst the security services need the authority of the president to maintain their power.[90]

The intimate marriage between the military and the regime took place prior to the action of the Corrective Movement in November 1970. As a student leader, with a successful career in the air force, and as the minister of defence for the Jadid regime, Asad had cultivated a bedrock of support within the military establishment. The disproportionate number of 'Alawis in the military and the Ba'th party enabled Asad to cement his ties through the system of patronage.[91]

Systems of patronage are most apparent in the appointments to sensitive posts in the armed and security services. As commander-in-chief of the armed forces, the president is responsible for making the key appointments within the military establishment, which is the main guarantor of the regime.[92] Appointments have traditionally been made in the interests of alliance building. Neo-patrimonialism, instead of merito-cracy, has governed the advancement of officers. The levers of control rest firmly in the hands of Asad's loyal commanders, known as *regime barons*, most of whom derive from the 'Alawi community. The following officers are all 'Alawis and hold critical posts in the armed services:

Shafiq Fayyad	Division commander
Ibrahim Safi	Division commander
'Ali Aslan	Deputy chief of staff
'Ali al-Salih	Missile corps
'Ali Duba	Head of military intelligence (until 1993)
'Ali Haydar	Special forces
'Adnan Makhluf	Presidential guard

It has not been in Asad's interest to alienate the Sunni officers within the armed forces and security services. He has thus balanced their interests against those of the 'Alawis. Asad's selection of senior Sunni military officers has been effective in preserving a semblance of non-sectarianism within the regime elite.[93] The presence of key Sunni officers, such as Hikmat al-Shihabi, the chief of staff, and Mustafa Tlas, the minister of defence, has served to strengthen the regime, thereby reducing the likelihood of a Sunni-led *coup*.[94]

The armed forces, security services and the state
The armed forces and the security services are the least accountable cor-porate bodies of the Syrian state; there are no constitutional mechanisms to govern their activities. Whereas there are institutional processes that govern the functions of the constitutional political system and the Ba'th party, the omniscient security services exist above institutional reproof, and the commanders of each security service exercise some autonomy

from the state. One result of this has been the growth of military fiefdoms that exercise influence over security, the bureaucracy, and social affairs. The power base of these fiefdoms emanates from their access to the regime and through their independent accumulation of capital in the parallel economy.[95]

Syria's continuous role in Lebanese affairs since 1976 has created an environment for a flourishing parallel economy. The army's role in Lebanon has enabled many officers and regular soldiers to amass small fortunes through practices of corruption involving smuggling and drug-trafficking.[96] Working as the coordinators and agents of the black market, the regime barons have been free to trade in consumables, which are otherwise unavailable, irrespective of the harsh penalties of the law. The operation of protection rackets in the suqs, and the military warehouse sales in Damascus, are clear demonstrations of the independent power bases of the regime barons.

In return for guaranteeing the survival of the Asad regime, the regime barons enjoy special privileges. These privileges represent negative manifestations for the state as they form a major obstacle to institutionalising the political system. When the regime barons live outside the confines of the law, they can circumvent the domestic policies of the state. In conjunction, they can contribute to the de-legitimisation of the regime by contradicting state policy without penalty. Such a case occurred in 1977, when the Islamists openly rebelled against the state's policy in Lebanon, and the illicit accumulation of wealth by the 'Alawi regime barons who were extorting monies in smuggled trade from Lebanon and rackets worked within the state bureaucracy.[97] After June 1977 Syria had been plagued with assassinations, riots, and public executions. Public figures from the 'Alawi sect became targets for the Islamic opposition. In order to appease the public, Asad ordered a crack-down on corruption in October 1977. The anti-corruption drive aimed at improving the efficiency of the state machinery, and satisfying public demand that the state would work for the national good. Asad criticised the bureaucracy for ineptitude and inefficiency, and appointed the Committee for the Investigation of Illicit Gains.[98]

This Committee was granted wide-ranging powers, including the powers of attorney, arrest, detention, and sequestration of money. To eliminate the corruption, however, the Committee would have had to penalise the regime barons, in other words challenge the backbone of the regime, the security and military interests, including the Defence Companies of the president's brother, Rif'at Asad.[99] The de facto power of the Committee, therefore, was very limited. Evidently it had been designed to produce nominal figureheads to relieve the regime of responsibility.

Asad's dependence upon the regime barons has set a constraint upon his freedom of action. They are a source of support but at the same time represent an obstacle to reform. It is in the interests of the regime barons, with entrenched positions in the armed forces and security services, to maintain the domestic and regional status quo. The prospect of change in the domestic arena (for instance, the upgrading of the People's Council), or of a transition in the regional environment (such as the conclusion of a peace deal with Israel), could threaten the fiefdoms of the regime barons. In consequence, Asad's leverage over the barons has been constrained; this has not prevented him from emasculating them when necessary, however. By rotating military positions, for example, Asad has prevented the barons from congealing their fiefdoms into independent bodies. For instance in 1993 'Ali Duba is believed to have been removed from his office of military intelligence. After an internal dispute with his coequals, he was "kicked upstairs" as one of three assistant chiefs of staff.[100] His fiefdom was disbanded as his clients were displaced by new recruits, although some of the clients dismissed (such as Muhammad Nassef and General 'Abboud) were appointed by Rif'at Asad, and were also powerful people in their own right. Nevertheless, the fiefdom of 'Ali Duba was not able to reconstitute itself into an independent centre of power.[101]

In an earlier case, Asad effected a reshuffle in the Syrian Military High Command. In August 1974, General Yussef Shakur, the chief of staff during the October War, was forced to retire. Despite Shakur's popularity and considerable power base, the president dispersed his foundations of support and appointed a new chief of staff, thereby removing the potential threat of Shakur's centre of power.[102]

The patrimonial appointment of commanders in the armed forces and the security services has ensured that the state is caught between the two forms of governance, patrimonialism and institutionalism. Although Asad continues to reside above the Bonapartist state, balancing the interests of the competing structures, he cannot afford to alienate the support of the regime barons. He has thus become caught between the demands of the state and his dependence upon his traditional support base.

The New World Order presented Asad with more room for manoeuvre between the patrimonial and institutional systems. The advent of *perestroika, glasnost,* and "new thinking" in Soviet foreign policy precipitated change in the world order. Because of the failure of state-led economic policies, the foreign exchange crisis of 1986, and the monumental changes that took place in Eastern Europe in 1989, the Syrian state altered the course of its domestic policies. Asad was presented with the opportunity of counterbalancing the primacy of the regime barons through the cultivation of the bourgeoisie. Although the role of Syria's bourgeoisie has never been institutionalised beyond the chamber of commerce, the succession of global capitalism increased its influence.[103]

The lack of an institutionalised process in Syria has meant that decision-making is governed by the balance of power. As in all such balances, the flow of power among the main actors is not constant and the flux in the system allows some actors to gain at the expense of others. A zero-sum game can exist among various domestic actors, who are perceived in the polarised forms of the public and private sectors. In Syria, the bourgeoisie has, until recently, been a subordinate partner in the state. The dominance of the Ba'th party, the armed forces, and security services throughout the political system and the corporate structures of the state has ensured that the power of the bourgeoisie has stayed negligible.[104]

The bourgeoisie

During Ottoman rule and the French mandate, Syrian society was classified according to the interlocking features of vertical and horizontal stratification. As Syrian society became increasingly urbanised, the land-owning class, which formed the political elite, cohered into a bourgeoisie. The nationalist struggle against the Ottomans and the French helped to reinforce the bourgeoisie's class identity and further defined its relationship with the rural peasants and the urban proletariat. The policies of the state were conducted through the auspices of the Syrian notables who acted as intermediaries between the foreign administration and the Syrian population.[105] The dominance of the bourgeoisie in Syrian politics ended abruptly with the Ba'thist *coup* in 1963. As described above, the power of the bourgeoisie was destroyed by the policies of land reform and nationalisation. The policies of social levelling removed the threat

[85]

posed by the bourgeoisie to the new state and allowed the state to free itself from the constraints of the old class, and to pursue an autonomous path. The bourgeoisie was the declared enemy of the Ba'th party and the Syrian state.[106]

Asad's overthrow of the Jadid regime and his ascent to power was welcomed by the surviving elements of the bourgeoisie.[107] Throughout his term as president, Asad has tried to balance the interests of the various groups in Syria and has tentatively reversed the alienation of the bourgeoisie by the Ba'th.

On assuming power, Asad's priority became national development and development of the state became synonymous with national strength. All aspects of the national economy, wherever possible, were harnessed to boost the power projection of Syria: "Defence of the homeland, steadfastness, and victory, Asad time and again told his compatriots, were impossible without development."[108] He wished to circumvent the harmful policies of his predecessors who had restricted the activities of private enterprise. Accordingly, Syria embarked on a path of more mixed economic development. In order to combat economic stagnation, the flight of capital, and the ensuing brain drain, Asad in 1971 introduced a number of liberalising measures:[109] import restrictions on certain goods were lifted, and registered importers became entitled to import certain quantities of goods which had been effectively banned from importation.[110] In 1972, imports without foreign exchange transfers were permitted, thus enabling merchants to repatriate some of their wealth. An amnesty on capital flight was declared to facilitate the return of capital, and other economic laws were altered to accommodate the new situation.[111]

Asad recognised the potential of allying the state with components of the bourgeoisie. Such an alliance would not harm the regime's strategic interests, and would enable the entrepreneurial skills of the bourgeoisie to energise the economy under the auspices of the regime.[112] The bourgeoisie represented a useful engine for developing the national economy as long as it refrained from making political demands. Realising this, he dispensed with the levelling philosophy and policies of the Ba'th, and implemented a strategy of limited incorporation.[113]

The demise of the Soviet Union, the collapse of the East European regimes, and the termination of the socialist economic systems have had a resounding effect upon the domestic balance of power within Syria. The reconfiguration of the international political system and the succession of global capitalism have produced a shift in the interplay among Syria's corporate actors.[114] Until now, the state is still dominated by the Ba'th party and the security apparatus, but a visible downgrading of their importance has been identifiable since 1990. The recipients of the political advantage belong to the bourgeois class. This does not, however, represent a simple transition of power from the public sector of the state to the private sector. The zero-sum game analysis bears little fruit, as the interests of the new bourgeoisie are synonymous with the interests of the regime elite.[115] Before examining the dynamics of the military–mercantile complex, it is necessary to identify the groups which constitute the bourgeoisie.

Constituents of the bourgeoisie

Bahout advises against using the term "bourgeoisie", for it connotes that this group has developed into class-for-itself. He acknowledges that there are splinters of the old bourgeoisie and a newly emerging business class in existence, but they have not coalesced to constitute a class. Their interests have remained separated from each other and tied to those of the state. The state has fostered a dependency between the various parts of the business community and itself.[116] Bahout identifies four main groups that make up the business community in Syria: the old bourgeoisie; the *infitahi*; the *nouveaux riches*; the state bourgeoisie. A brief description of these four groups will enable us to understand their relationship with the state, and their role in the balance of power.

The old bourgeoisie

The old bourgeoisie is that element of the landed class which managed to survive the policies of the Ba'th party. They come from the notable families of the Syrian cities of Damascus, Homs, Hama, and Aleppo. They carry the values of the Syrian upper classes and perceive themselves as the natural heirs of Syrian leadership. Through their enduring influence, they have been able to recycle their economic surplus through trade and medium-scale industry.[117]

The infitahi

The *infitahi* resemble the *petite bourgeoisie* in economic activity and political culture, although they are not organised into a political or social unit. They are a group of actors responsible for light industry, manufacturing, commerce, and services. The *infitahi* have grown from the early policies of the Asad regime, and therefore owe their allegiance to the Syrian state. Articulating political or economic demands has not developed as part of their repertoire or political culture.[118]

The nouveaux riches

The most immediate beneficiaries of the 1973 oil price rises, and the subsequent economic development, have been the *nouveaux riches*. Since then, they have played an important role in the national economy. They differ from the old bourgeoisie and *infitahi* in being intimately connected to the state. Their relationship with the state has cultivated a mutually constitutive alliance expressed in the allocation of contracts.

The award of contracts (financed by external funds received from the Gulf Arab states) to the *nouveaux riches* has engendered an intractable loyalty between the *contractors' bourgeoisie* and the state. One result of this has been the penetration of this group into the privileged areas of real estate, construction, tourism, and transportation, which were the exclusive preserve of the state's dependent business sector.[119]

The state bourgeoisie

The state bourgeoisie refers to the select club that guides the implementation of state policies. This group has been able to use its privileged access to the state to proffer favours to selected contractors. Their ties with the children of the leaders of the regime have proved to be particularly lucrative and instrumental in forging links between the state and business classes.[120]

The children of the leaders of the present regime are reputed to have entered business instead of following their fathers' footsteps into the military or security apparatus. They are playing a conciliatory role in binding the fortunes of the state to the interests of the indigenous business class. This shift in orientation has many consequences as the children of the regime, many of whom are 'Alawis, are undergoing the experience of *embourgeoisement*. The transition in the social class of the new political elite from peasant, to soldier, to bourgeois, has started to cement the future of the state to the old and new bourgeoisie.[121]

The bourgeoisie and the state

Having identified the four components of the Syrian business class, we can now recognise each group's dependency on the state. Asad's regime has successfully incorporated the energies of the business class, and tailored their demands for political expression through a relationship based upon patronage and subordination.

After 1970, power accumulation replaced ideology as the motivator of the regime. As part of the struggle with Israel, Asad attempted to construct a national economy that channelled the energies of both the private and public sectors into a national project. The rehabilitation of a compliant business class, operating alongside the public sector, was essential to the achievement of the national purpose. The role of the business community, however, was secondary to those of the Ba'th party, the armed forces and the security services.[122]

The interests of the bourgeoisie have not been recognised at the corporate level. Its role has been very limited because of the ideological disposition of the Ba'th party and the origins of the regime. The relationship between the bourgeoisie and state has thus remained volatile and unreliable since Asad's advent to power. The state granted the bourgeoisie a role in the national economy by implementing economic liberalising measures, and state policies have taken heed of capital accumulation and the specific role played by the bourgeoisie in generating it. The bourgeoisie's role, however, has not been protected by the rule of the law; it has been governed by the rule of the domestic and regional climate.[123]

Politics has dominated the economic realm since 1970. Decisions determined according to political preferences have allowed the regime to protect its autonomy in decision-making, but prevented it from creating a viable, dependable, and sustainable economy. Because of the precarious nature of the regime's legitimacy, society needed to be insulated from the failures of economic policy. Because of diminishing support from the populace, the regime has had to cushion the impact of these failures through the provision of services.

The self-imposed economic reforms of the first *infitah*, in 1971, were designed to broaden the base of the regime and to extend its legitimacy.[124] The state's economic policies were instrumental in harnessing the support of the urban population, among whom the Ba'th party had traditionally failed to establish a stronghold. The first *infitah* ended in 1977 when the state started to reverse some of its liberal policies for political and economic reasons. The *infitah* had led to widespread corruption: for example, importing without foreign exchange transfers had encouraged illegal currency exports. Economic security courts were established to erase the culture of corruption that sought to circumvent the policies of the state. Both the private sector and the regime barons had seemingly abused the liberalising measures. As the growth and independence of the private sector were deemed to be a threat to the state, the privileges granted through liberalisation were removed.[125]

Syria's Lebanon policy also proved to be problematic for the state. The disillusionment with the secular activities of the Syrian state, and the predominant 'Alawi composition of the regime, fuelled an environment sensitive to Syria's policies in Lebanon. The response of the traditional sectors of Syrian society, and the disaffected youth, found its expression in a series of attacks against high-ranking members of the government and the Ba'th party. The 'Alawis were deliberately targeted by the Muslim Brotherhood. The domestic repercussions of Syria's role in Lebanon caused the pace of economic reform to stall and, eventually, policy retracted towards state-led socialism. The focus of the regime turned away from economics and towards the maintenance of the state against an assault from the Muslim Brotherhood.[126]

With the failings of the socialist model of development, the dramatic fall in the price of oil, and the ensuing foreign exchange crisis of 1986,[127] Asad reinstituted the programme of economic liberalisation. This move did not allow the former bourgeoisie to reconstruct itself or institutionalise its relationship with the state; nevertheless, some entrepreneurs were granted informal admission to the decision-making process.[128]

The private sector was granted controlled access to the economic decision-making process[129] and the appointment of Muhammad al-Imady to the post of minister of the economy, in 1987, signified a new economic direction for the state. Imady's ability to reform the structure of the economic system was limited because of the entrenched interests of the regime in the existing state apparatus. He did, however, have the approval of the president to test the waters and proceed at an incremental pace.[130]

The Syrian economy was steered between those domestic forces which supported a more socialist-oriented policy, and those forces that promoted a more progressive programme of economic liberalisation. The economic policies that emerged from these two opposing factions were carefully selected and applied in accordance with the variety of interests balanced by the regime.

In an economy where the state purchases part of its legitimacy, the loss of state revenues inflicts a severe handicap upon the state in servicing its loyalists. The elite that steers the state, therefore, is not insulated from economic failures. Although the state may be resilient and flexible in the political realm, it is nevertheless vulnerable if it fails to fulfil the aims of its basic economic agenda. In this instance, the state turns to the bourgeoisie to compensate for the economic gap. Once this occurs, Heydemann observes:

> economic reform no longer represents the leading political threat. Increasingly, the continued erosion of domestic production, of capital accumulation, and thus of prospects for extraction, undermine the regime's ability to reproduce its system of rule. Under these conditions, the logic of politics becomes, in some measure, the logic of reform.[131]

This time, the economic measures were more far-reaching than in the earlier period, and have been deemed to be irreversible. In return, the state had to undertake to offer concessions to the business community; semi-institutional access to the economic policy process assuaged the interests of the growing private sector. Hinnebusch remarks:

> The door of liberalization was thus opened, but liberalization cannot go very far without the reconstruction of an entrepreneurial bourgeoisie which, being willing to invest, can provide a viable alternative to the public sector.[132]

To reconstruct and rehabilitate the business community, the state created several openings to the economic decision-making process which took the form of independent representation in the People's Council and the creation of a quasi-corporate body, the Prime Minister's Committee for the Guidance of Imports, Exports, and Consumption.[133]

In 1990, one-third of the seats in the People's Council was reserved for independent candidates, who essentially emanated from the private sector.[134] The independents have not formed a bloc to thwart the dominance of the Ba'th party, but their relevance to the institutional process is gaining importance. In May 1990, a member of the Aleppo Chamber of Commerce, and two members from the Damascus Chamber of Commerce, were elected to the People's Council. They were the first agents of the private sector to serve a term in parliament since 1963.[135]

In the election of 1994, the tone of the election address of Ihsan Sankar – an independent candidate openly representing the interests of business – indicated the new respectability accorded to private enterprise and the business community. Ihsan Sankar campaigned on the election platform for the repeal of populist measures, such as land reform ceilings, and progressive taxation.[136] Understood against the background of Ba'th ideology, the call for these measures illustrated the flexibility of the state and the increasing role of the business community in Syrian economic life. This was also a sign that the Ba'th party, though still a patronage-generating entity, was beginning to lose its ideological leadership and its pivotal role in the policy process.[137]

The business community has gained through the policies of economic liberalisation but one should not conceive of the state as losing out in a zero-sum game. The state, managed by Asad, has existed above the various social forces in Syrian society. As Heydemann points out, the state must

> simultaneously persuade the private sector of its sincerity and commitment to reform, without which it would abstain from investing, while persuading its clients and beneficiaries that their positions are secure, that they will be protected from the demands of stabilization, and that economic reform will not interrupt their privileges and benefits.[138]

By selecting a programme of economic restructuring the state has stood to benefit from economic reform. As an economic system, state-led socialism had failed to maximise the limited resources of the Syrian economy. The state remained partially dependent upon a diminishing flow of aid funds, and the cessation of soft loans from the Soviet Union served to exacerbate Syria's ailing economic condition. Through a carefully managed process, the state began to incorporate a reconstructed business class into the economic realm. This class has yet to develop an appetite for political power. Maintaining political stability and state protection from the external markets continues to be the main preoccupation of this group, as shown in this revealing comment by a prominent industrialist and trader from Damascus: "All we want is economic freedom and political stability; for us, democracy often means a *coup d'état* every two years."[139]

The emerging mutuality of interests between the state and the business class has meant a zero-sum loss to the Ba'th party and its loyalists working in the public sector. The regime's natural constituency looks set to lose out in the domestic realignment of social forces. Balancing the interests of the two groups has produced competition between the Ba'th party and the business class.

This competition has started to manifest itself in the dialogue between Muhammad al-Imady, the minister of the economy, and 'Izz al-Din Nasser, who is a member of the Ba'th party Regional Command and head of the Trade Union Confederation. Both figures represent the interests of ideologically opposed groups. The minister's remit to liberalise the economy according to the needs of the state has been challenged by Nasser's attempted reforms of the public sector.[140]

Power-sharing between the public and private sectors has become a feature of Syrian politics. The recent change in the economic direction of the state can be traced to the Eighth Ba'th party Regional Congress, in 1985, when Asad bestowed honour upon the private sector and called for a wider but responsible role for this group. The balance between the Ba'th party and the business community has not altered radically because the Ba'th party has remained the more institutionalised of the two, but the elevation of the private sector has indicated a shift in the internal balance of power.[141]

Whilst the state has been balancing the forces of the Ba'th party and the private sector, the relationship between the state and its corporations has been changing. The formerly populist-dominated corporatist system, where workers and peasants had access to the decision-making process, has been opened to the private sector through the offices of the chambers of commerce and industry. Consequently, the business class and the new political elite have started to tie their fortunes and futures together in a new alliance referred to as the military–mercantile complex.[142]

The military–mercantile complex

The forging of a new bourgeoisie is taking place in Syria. The new alliance between the state elite[143] and the rising business community is transforming the social order of the country. The state is still the dominant partner in this relationship, and resides above all social forces in Syria, but the incremental transfer of its loyalties towards a capital-generating class is in evidence.[144] The children of the political elite have facilitated this transfer by entering the business world and engaging their interests with the business community.

The children of the regime have also taken a leading role in the civilianisation of the state elite. The new 'Alawi generation, raised in a privileged environment, considers itself to be part of Syria's upper class.[145] The incessant fear of the Sunni majority and the threat of revenge is starting to lose credence as the binding of economic interests holds them together. The sons of high-ranking officers have started to establish flourishing businesses. For instance, the sons of 'Ali Duba and Khaddam (Vice President and *Wali* of Lebanon) belong more to the business association than to the officers' club,[146] thus congealing the alliance of the state to the new class.

The pace of economic globalisation is proving to be an irresistible force for the young generation of Syria. The extensive network of global communications has put Syrian youth in touch with a global youth culture.[147] The arrival of satellite television, the significant improvement of the telephone system, and the legalisation of fax machines have helped to free young people from their ideological isolation.[148] The universal youth culture, a hegemonic force radiating from the US, is changing Syrian self-perceptions and attitudes towards the West. The ideology of the past is being superseded by the culture of the lowest common denominator – global American culture.[149]

The global emphasis upon the primacy of capitalism as the dominant economic system sits easily with the new elite. Having received their university education in the US and Europe, the children of the political elite are more disposed to the philosophy of capitalism than that of socialism. Seduced by the excesses of Western consumerism, the young generation has started to adopt a new lifestyle. Music, fashion, and cuisine are unduly influenced by the West, indicating a rejection of indigenous culture and the austerity measures imposed by Ba'thism.[150]

The former antagonism between the state and the private bourgeoisie is being bridged as the political elite acquires a stake in the new economic system. This finds expression in the intermarriage between the political elite and the new bourgeoisie.[151] The business community and the political elite are reaching a *modus vivendi*. Their interests are beginning to coincide, but the terms of their cooperation remain firmly in the hands of the political elite. Neither social actor is interested in comprehensive economic liberalisation. Such a move would hurt the state's original constituency. The state cannot afford to alienate its public sector support, for the latter credits the state with legitimacy. Extensive economic liberalisation would create widespread dissatisfaction among the Syrian population. The state's ability to insulate itself from unpopular sentiment would be severely restricted as unemployment, the removal of basic food subsidies, and a diminution of welfare services would erode legitimacy. On the other hand, comprehensive economic liberalisation would not benefit the bourgeoisie as it would expose it to intense competition. Incremental liberalisation protects the bourgeoisie from domestic, regional, and international competition. Sharing the spoils, therefore, with the political elite is a minimal cost for establishing flourishing businesses and quasi-monopolies.[152]

As Hinnebusch has suggested: "A *modus vivendi* may be shaping up between a state which needs a wealth generating, conservative social force, and a bourgeoisie which needs the economic opportunities and political protection provided by the state."[153] The bourgeoisie looks set to inherit the privilege once enjoyed by the Ba'th party as the balance of interest swings towards the private sector.

The swing in the business community's favour, at the expense of the Ba'th party, was symbolised by Asad's endorsement of independent candidates during the 1994 elections. His appearance at the Damascus Chamber of Commerce received wide coverage in the state-controlled press and further reinforced his support of the business community. The autonomy enjoyed by the state has enabled it to nurture the economic potential of a reconstructed bourgeoisie whilst ensuring that its political aspirations are minimal and its future inextricably linked to the fortunes of the state.

The state: balancing the interests

The dependence of the Ba'th party and the bourgeoisie upon the state has given the latter a large degree of autonomy in the decision-making process. Asad has been able to balance the interests of each group against those of the other, according to the demands of their constituency. The regime barons, who control the armed forces and the security services, underscore the autonomy of the regime. Their role has yet to be institutionalised.

The state's relative autonomy from domestic social forces enhances its freedom of action. The decision-making process exists above the centres of power; the Ba'th party, the bourgeoisie, or the security services, cannot impose their interests upon the state. Foreign policy decisions, in particular, are essentially insulated from overt domestic influences. Chapters 6 and 7 provide two noteworthy examples where the state has pursued policies otherwise considered inimical to domestic interests.

It would be incorrect, of course, to suggest that the centres of power do not exert influence, but the degree of influence is the crucial factor. More recently, we have witnessed a decline in the Ba'th party's role in the decision-making process, and the elevation of the bourgeoisie in the economic field. The state's preoccupation with security naturally gives precedence to the armed forces and security services.[154]

Although the Asad regime has proved to be the most durable one in Syria's modern history, the flux between institutional and patrimonial rule serves as a flashpoint of instability for Syria. The state's dependence upon the security services to preserve civil order, and on the armed forces to counter Israel's military threat has militated against social cohesion and the prominence of civilian rule. Security still dominates the political realm, and Asad's dependence upon the 'Alawi generals and commanders to guarantee the survival of the regime and state prevents the institutional process from ossifying.[155] As the security services are called upon to contain potential domestic instability, it is difficult to determine the level of opposition to the state. Nevertheless, opposition does exist and the following three examples illustrate the potential for domestic instability within Syria.

The Islamic uprising

During the period between 1979 and 1982, Syria experienced serious domestic repercussions from its policy in Lebanon, and was on the brink of falling into civil war. Throughout this period, the future of Asad's regime looked precarious. Syria's regional isolation, resulting from its support of Iran in the Iran–Iraq War, added to the insecurity of the state.

On 16 June 1979, over 60 cadets at the Aleppo artillery school were massacred by adherents of the Muslim Brotherhood.[156] The majority of those killed belonged to the 'Alawi sect and the massacre seemed to be part of an anti-'Alawi campaign. The most worrying aspect of this event for the regime was the role played by Ibrahim Yussef, who was a captain and a high-ranking member of the ruling Ba'th party. He was implicated in the plot, and was thought to have facilitated the operation. As a result, 300 dissidents, including a number of high-ranking officers, were rounded up and executed.[157]

A proliferation of car bomb attacks on government and Soviet buildings marked the return of civil confrontation. The most significant attacks took place in August, September, and November 1981. In August, three members of the prime minister's team were killed in their offices; in September, a car bomb exploded outside the air force command headquarters in Damascus, killing 20 people; and in November another car bomb exploded outside a school, killing a further 90 people.[158]

The institutions of the political process had failed to contain the dissension expressed by the Muslim Brotherhood. The regime relied upon coercion to quell the riots. The repressive tactics against the opposition elicited an equally violent response from the Muslim Brotherhood, pushing the country towards a violent civil war. Homs and Hama remained the centres of anti-regime activities, and the regime engaged in the first of a series of massacres in Hama in April 1981. The defence units, operating under the leadership of Rif'at Asad, were responding to attacks against an 'Alawi village, where attendants at a wedding were killed.[159] The sectarian nature of the violence demonstrated the acrimonious tensions existing beneath the surface of Syrian society. The regime's ruthless massacre of the civilian population at Hama throughout February 1982 has left an indelible mark on Syria's modern history. The town of Hama lived through a month of outright civil war which culminated in the destruction of the town and the eradication of the Muslim Brotherhood's opposition to the regime.[160]

Asad imposed his rule through coercive means, exposing where the strength and ultimate source of his power truly lie. The political process was unable to accommodate the discontent of the Muslim Brotherhood. Opposition, according to this model of governance, requires incorporation and management. The post-Hama domestic policies of the state sought to eliminate the radical voices of the Brotherhood whilst assimilating the interests of the less combative elements of the Muslim opposition.[161]

With the memory of the Iranian Revolution fresh in its mind, the Syrian regime routed the opposition through a relentless massacre in Hama that reverberated throughout the region. This massacre indicated the president's determination to remain in office, and maintain control of the levers of power. The next significant threat to the regime, however, emerged from within the regime elite in the form of Rif'at Asad and his defence units.

The intra-elite struggle

President Asad's heart attack in November 1983 provided the pretext for another assault on the Syrian state. This time it arose from within the regime's political elite in the form of a struggle between the president's chosen coterie and the president's brother, Rif'at, and his allies.

From his hospital bed, Asad instructed the following men to form a committee of command: defence minister Mustafa Tlas; chief of staff Hikmat al-Shihabi; foreign minister Khaddam; prime minister Kasm; the assistant secretary-general of the Ba'th Regional Command, Abdallah al-Ahmar.[162] Rif'at Asad was excluded from the ruling committee.

As an entrenched baron of the regime, with his interests ultimately tied to the health of the Defence Companies and the 'Alawi generals of the regime, Rif'at was persuaded to jockey for a leading position in the succession. A full meeting of the Regional Command was then convened without the president or the information minister, Ahmed Iskandar Ahmed.[163] The Regional Command voted to replace the six-man committee appointed by Asad with Rif'at Asad. A showdown between the president, who was then recovering, and his ambitious younger brother determined the fate of Syria. The political elite looked intent on pursuing a course of self-destruction.[164]

Asad's full recovery led to a muted military confrontation among the forces loyal to both brothers. The president, in a personal showdown with Rif'at, asserted his authority over his younger brother. As a result, the Defence Companies were reduced in size and importance. The appointment of three vice-presidents: Foreign Minister Khaddam, the assistant regional secretary of the Ba'th party, Zuhair Masharqa, and Rif'at Asad, constituted a new chain of command designed to accommodate the succession problem. Rif'at Asad and his rivals, 'Ali Aslan, the commander of the Special Forces, and Shafiq Fayyad, the commander of the Third Division, were part of a delegation sent to the Soviet Union to cool off.[165]

Asad's appointment of the six-man committee displayed two features:

(a) The absence of an institutional process to accommodate the death of the president;
(b) The extent of praetorianism within the state.

Although the Ba'th party constitution provides the Regional Command with forty days to select a new president, who in turn must be elected through universal franchise, this incident illustrated the fragility of the institutional process. The institutions of the state have not been invested with sufficient authority to sustain a transition of presidency. If Asad's institutions cannot command respect from his closest aides, it is unlikely that they have taken root within Syrian society.[166]

The true nature of power in Syria was revealed through the succession crisis. The patrimonial system of government, reinforced by the creation of military units loyal to regime barons, removed the pretensions of the institutional process, and exposed the military authority of the regime. The ensuing struggle among the political elite indicated the divergence of opinions, and the potential for conflict between the interested parties of the regime. The political process, in this instance, was underpinned by the various military divisions and their cross-cutting loyalties to the barons of the regime.

International pressures and political change

The advent of "new thinking" in Soviet foreign policy wrought more changes in Syria's domestic political situation. Its impact was not felt until the fall of the regime of the Romanian president, Ceaucescu, in the final days of 1989. Graffiti appeared on the walls of Damascus drawing comparisons between Asad and Ceaucescu.[167] The regime was forced to take action as the sweeping reforms and silent revolutions of Eastern Europe did not bode well for the regime. Syria thus embarked on a process of political decompression.[168] This was introduced to accommodate the rising tensions within the state, provoked by the change of political systems throughout the Soviet bloc. The structural changes within the Soviet bloc could not have gone unnoticed by Asad's regime. The Syrian state had illustrated its resilience to the Islamist uprisings of the 1980s, but its corporatist structures were modified to coalesce the more moderate critics of the regime, and to isolate the radical elements within society.[169]

Asad expanded the People's Council and gave the bourgeoisie a semi-institutional role. As previously mentioned, the number of members voted to the People's Council in 1990 was increased from 195 to 250. One-third of these seats was reserved for independent candidates, who essentially came from the bourgeoisie, hence guaranteeing them a significant voice in the parliament.[170] Although the Ba'th party still held the majority in the People's Council, the presence of independent candidates signified a labefaction in the role of the Ba'th party, and the elevation of businessmen in the low politics of state.[171]

The expansion of the People's Council in May 1990, and the creation of the prime minister's Committee for the Guidance of Commerce and Industry, were political concessions to the regime-friendly bourgeoisie. These moves, however, did not imply that a power-sharing programme had been adopted, as the power relationship between the political elite of the regime and the bourgeoisie remained unambiguous. The desire of the bourgeoisie to engage in the political process, as a subordinate partner but with access to the economic decision-making process, meant that a *modus vivendi* was arrived at with the state.[172]

Conclusion

To conclude, this book recognises the primacy of the international political system in determining state behaviour. State behaviour is governed by the inherent anarchy that characterises the international political system. The absence of hierarchy within the international political system means that states are preoccupied with the issue of national security. As a result, states are conditioned to act according to a set of rational criteria.

Omnibalancing refers to the balance, attained by the state, between domestic interests and the determinants of the international political system. The author's reservation concerning omnibalancing lies in the priority it gives to the domestic arena over the international political system. Working from the assumption that the international political system provides the prime motivation for state behaviour suggests that states must attain a degree of relative autonomy from domestic forces to pursue a rational policy.

Following a policy of balancing domestic forces within Syria, the state has been able to acquire relative autonomy from society. Between 1966 and 1970, the Ba'th state destroyed the economic and social base of the bourgeoisie. This gave it the possibility to free the state from interests of dominant social actors. The Syrian state, therefore, was able to elevate itself above the social classes in society.

Autonomy from the bourgeoisie has enabled the state to engage in a regional struggle with Israel in accordance with a set of rational principles. The accumulation of power, pursued in its competition for regional hegemony, has remained a priority of the state since 1970. In order to counterbalance the power of Israel, Syria needed to consolidate and develop its power base. This process required the incorporation of the domestic centres of power into a state-building project. Asad initiated a process of state-building after assuming power; this project set out to restructure state–society relations in the service of the national interest. The resulting quasi-corporatist state was built upon three pillars: the armed forces and security services; the Ba'th party, and the institutional political system. Because of the transitory nature of state–society relations, the state was governed by two systems, namely, neo-patrimonialism and institutionalism.

The Syrian president has forged a state around the issue of national security and the national interest. The struggle with Israel has formed the basis of Syria's national interest, and invested it with a historical mission. The responsibility assumed by the Syrian state towards Palestine has helped to legitimise the authoritarian nature of the state. Furthermore, it has granted the state a chance to rise above the competition among domestic forces, and to preserve exclusive rights to the area of high politics.

The decisions of high politics are formulated within the Regional Command of the Ba'th party, and among Asad's closest advisers. Policies are then justified *downstream* through the party apparatus.[173] Relative autonomy from domestic forces has allowed the Syrian state to exercise a foreign policy based upon rational considerations, rather than class or sectarian interests.

The Syrian state, lacking comprehensive legitimacy, has remained dependent upon the gel of patrimonialism to sustain its longevity. To date, the Syrian state has managed to circumvent the overt influence of dominant social forces. The pre-eminence of the corporate structures of the state has prevented the political process from being fully institu-tionalised. The state's autonomy has been supported by its extensive patronage networks. Its vulnerability, one could contend, lies in its dependence upon patronage, and its reluctance to empower the political institutions of the state.

The armed forces and the security services have constituted the backbone of the Ba'th state and have guaranteed the longevity of the regime, in particular when the state was threatened with civil war between 1979 and 1982. The rebellion in Hama posed a serious threat to the security of the state. The state's resilience to this challenge was underwritten by its monopoly over the means of coercion. The reliance upon the armed forces and the security services illustrated the failure of the state's political institutions to pre-empt or contain the grievances of the Muslim Brotherhood.

Balancing the interests within the state, Asad has provided the state with a degree of autonomy that has enabled it to make decisions based on a rational set of principles. The decision to join the US-led coalition against Iraq in 1990 represents one incident where the state's action was founded upon a rational criteria, whilst appearing to contradict the common Arab interest. The state enjoyed enough autonomy to disregard public opinion and follow a policy determined by national interest. Syria's decision was portentous, as it elevated its national interest over the Arab interest, and risked its own legitimacy.

The risk to the domestic legitimacy of the Syrian state in this case was subjugated to the demands of the international political system. The change in the distribution of global power compelled Syria to adjust to the New World Order. Residing above the domestic arena, the Syrian state was insulated enough to adjust to the New World Order without precipitating domestic unrest, and without having to legitimise its decision beforehand.

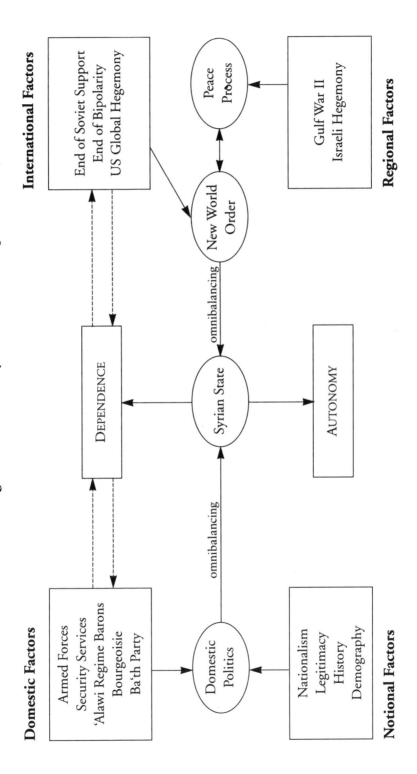

FIGURE 3
Omnibalancing: the international system and domestic politics

NOTES

1 A. Ehteshami and R. Hinnebusch, *Syria and Iran: Middle Powers in a Penetrated Regional System* (London: Routledge, 1997), p. 15.
2 P. Seale, "Asad's Regional Strategy and the Challenge from Netanyahu", *Journal of Palestine Studies*, vol. XXVI, no. 1 (Autumn 1996), p. 28.
3 R. Hinnebusch, "Does Syria Want Peace? Syrian Policy in the Syrian–Israeli Peace Negotiations", *Journal of Palestine Studies*, vol. XXVI, no. 1 (Autumn 1996), pp. 45–8.
4 V. Perthes, *The Political Economy of Syria under Asad* (London: I.B. Tauris, 1995), pp. 223–6.
5 M. Nicholson, *Causes and Consequences in International Relations: A Conceptual Study* (London: Pinter, 1996), pp. 173–6.
6 S. David, "Explaining Third World Alignment", *World Politics*, vol. 43, no. 2 (January 1991), p. 235.
7 S. Huntington, *Political Order in Changing Societies* (New Haven: Yale University Press, 1968), p. 117.
8 B. Smith, *Understanding Third World Politics: Theories of Political Change and Development*, (Bloomington: Indiana University Press, 1996), pp. 246–7.
9 E. Karsh, *The Soviet Union and Syria: The Asad Years* (London: Routledge, 1988), p. 3–4.
10 S. Longrigg, *Syria and Lebanon under French Mandate* (London: Oxford University Press, 1958), p. 117.
11 T. Petran, *Syria* (New York: Praeger, 1972), pp. 96–7.
12 C. Clapham, *Third World Politics: An Introduction* (London: Croom Helm, 1985), pp. 137–9.
13 S. David, "Explaining Third World Alignment", *World Politics*, vol. 43, no. 2 (January 1991), pp. 233–56.
14 I. Daneels, R. Hinnebusch and N. Quilliam, "Omni-balancing Revisited: Syrian Foreign Policy between Rational Actor and Regime Legitimacy", British Society for Middle Eastern Studies (*BRISMES*) conference, 1995, unpublished manuscript.
15 R. Hinnebusch, "Syria under the Ba'th: State Formation in a Fragmented Society", *Arab Studies Quarterly*, vol. 4, no. 3 (Summer 1982), p. 184.
16 M. Diab, "Have Syria and Israel Opted for Peace?", *Middle East Policy*, vol. iii, no. 2 (1994), pp. 79–81.
17 For more details of Syria's tumultuous past see: P. Seale, *The Struggle for Syria: A Study of Post-War Arab Politics 1945–1958* (London: Oxford University Press, 1965), and A. Rathmell, *Secret War in the Middle East: The Covert Struggle for Syria, 1949–1961* (London: I.B. Tauris, 1995).
18 R. Hinnebusch, *Peasant and Bureaucracy in Ba'thist Syria: The Political Economy of Rural Development* (Boulder: Westview Press, 1989), p. 23. See also: V. Yorke, *Domestic Politics and Regional Security: Jordan, Syria, and Israel. The End of an Era?* (Aldershot: Gower, 1988), p. 103.
19 See the Hama massacre below.
20 V. Perthes, *The Political Economy of Syria under Asad* (London: I.B. Tauris, 1995), pp. 151–2.

21 See M. Kerr, *The Arab Cold War 1958–1964: A Study of Ideology in Politics* (London: Oxford University Press, 1965).

22 R. Hinnebusch, "Revisionist Dreams, Realist Strategies: The Foreign Policy of Syria" in B. Korany and A. Dessouki (eds.), *The Foreign Policies of Arab States: The Challenge of Change* (Boulder: Westview Press, 1991), p. 380.

23 R. Hinnebusch, *Authoritarian Power and State Formation in Ba'thist Syria: Army, Party, and Peasant* (Boulder: Westview Press, 1990), p. 145.

24 V. Yorke, *Domestic Politics and Regional Security: Jordan, Syria, and Israel. The End of an Era?* (Aldershot: Gower, 1988), p. 103.

25 Ibid.

26 R. Hinnebusch, "The Political Economy of Economic Liberalization in Syria", *International Journal of Middle East Studies*, vol. 27 (August 1995), p. 306.

27 V. Yorke, *Domestic Politics and Regional Security: Jordan, Syria, and Israel. The End of an Era?* (Aldershot: Gower, 1988), p. 111.

28 Weber refers to the institutional system as the *legal authority*. See M. Weber, *The Theory of Social and Economic Organization* (New York: The Free Press, 1968), pp. 329–41.

29 Ibid., pp. 346–58.

30 P. Seale, "Asad: Between Institutions and Autocracy" in R. Antoun and D. Quataert (eds.), *Syria: Society, Culture, and Polity* (New York: State University of New York Press, 1991), p. 98.

31 R. Hinnebusch, *Peasant and Bureaucracy in Ba'thist Syria: The Political Economy of Rural Development* (Boulder: Westview Press, 1989), p. 4.

32 Ibid., p. 5.

33 S. Huntington, *Political Order in Changing Societies* (New Haven: Yale University Press, 1968), p. 160.

34 S. David, "Explaining Third World Alignment", *World Politics*, vol. 43, no. 2 (January 1991), p. 236.

35 J. Leca, "Social Structure and Political Stability: Comparative Evidence from the Algerian, Syrian, and Iraqi Cases" in A. Dawisha and W. Zartman (eds.), *Beyond Coercion: The Durability of the Arab State* (London: Croom Helm, 1988), pp. 164–202.

36 A. Richards and J. Waterbury, *A Political Economy of the Middle East: State, Class, and Economic Development* (Boulder: Westview Press, 1990), p. 321.

37 Ibid., p. 313.

38 V. Perthes, "Stages of Economic and Political Liberalisation in Syria" in E. Kienle (ed.), *Contemporary Syria: Liberalization between Cold War and Cold Peace* (London: British Academic Press, 1994), p. 9.

39 V. Perthes, "Syria's Parliamentary Elections: Remodelling Asad's Political Base", *Middle East Report (MERIP)* (January/February 1992), p. 18.

40 P. Seale, "Asad: Between Institutions and Autocracy" in R. Antoun and D. Quataert (eds.), *Syria: Society, Culture, and Polity* (New York: State University of New York Press, 1991), p. 99.

41 A. Drysdale and R. Hinnebusch, *Syria and the Middle East Peace Process* (New York: Council on Foreign Relations, 1991), p. 23.

42 V. Perthes, "The Private Sector, Economic Liberalization, and the Prospects of Democratization: The Case of Syria and Some Other Arab Countries" in G.

Salame (ed.), *Democracy without Democrats? The Renewal of Politics in the Muslim World* (London: I.B. Tauris, 1994), p. 252.

43 *Syria – Country Profile* (London: The Economist Intelligence Unit, February 1973), no. 1, p. 3.

44 *Syria – Country Profile* (London: The Economist Intelligence Unit, May 1973), no. 2, p. 2.

45 Ibid.

46 H. Agha and A. Khalidi, *Syria and Iran: Rivalry and Cooperation* (London: Pinter, 1995), pp. 3–4.

47 M. Kramer, (ed.), "Syria's 'Alawis and Shi'ism" in *Shi'ism, Resistance, and Revolution* (Boulder: Westview Press, 1987), pp. 245–9.

48 *Syria – Country Profile* (London: Economist Intelligence Unit, February 1971), no. 1, p. 2.

49 V. Perthes, "Stages of Economic and Political Liberalization" in E. Kienle (ed.), *Contemporary Syria: Liberalization between Cold War and Cold Peace* (London: British Academic Press, 1994), p. 50.

50 V. Perthes, "Syria's Parliamentary Elections: Remodelling Asad's Political Base", *Middle East Report (MERIP)* (January/February 1992), p. 15.

51 V. Perthes, "The Private Sector, Economic Liberalization, and the Prospects of Democratization: The Case of Syria and Some Other Arab Countries" in G. Salame (ed.), *Democracy without Democrats? The Renewal of Politics in the Muslim World* (London: I.B. Tauris, 1994), p. 253.

52 Ibid., pp. 252–3.

53 V. Perthes, "Syria's Parliamentary Elections: Remodelling Asad's Political Base", *Middle East Report (MERIP)* (January/February 1992), p. 18.

54 V. Perthes, *The Political Economy of Syria under Asad* (London: I.B. Tauris, 1995), p. 139.

55 R. Hinnebusch, *Peasant and Bureaucracy in Ba'thist Syria: The Political Economy of Rural Development* (Boulder: Westview Press, 1989), p. 19.

56 R. Hinnebusch, "The Political Economy of Economic Liberalization in Syria", *International Journal of Middle East Studies*, vol. 27 (August 1995), p. 306.

57 P. Seale, "Asad: Between Institutions and Autocracy" in R. Antoun, and D. Quataert (eds.), *Syria: Society, Culture, and Polity* (New York: State University of New York Press, 1991), p. 102.

58 Ibid.

59 Ibid., p. 103.

60 Ibid.

61 *Syria – Country Profile* (London: The Economist Intelligence Unit, May 1972), no. 2, p. 2.

62 Ibid.

63 Ibid.

64 A. Drysdale and R. Hinnebusch, *Syria and the Middle East Peace Process* (New York: Council on Foreign Relations, 1991), p. 27.

65 V. Perthes, "Syria's Parliamentary Elections: Remodelling Asad's Political Base", *Middle East Report (MERIP)* (January/February 1992), p. 16.

66 A. Drysdale and R. Hinnebusch, *Syria and the Middle East Peace Process* (New York: Council on Foreign Relations, 1991), p. 27.

67 V. Perthes, "Syria's Parliamentary Elections: Remodelling Asad's Political Base", *Middle East Report (MERIP)* (January/February 1992), p. 16.

68 A. Drysdale and R. Hinnebusch, *Syria and the Middle East Peace Process* (New York: Council on Foreign Relations, 1991), p. 27.

69 K. Abu Jaber, *The Arab Ba'th Socialist Party: History, Ideology, and Organization* (Syracuse: Syracuse University Press, 1966), p. 143.

70 P. Seale, "Asad: Between Institutions and Autocracy" in R. Antoun and D. Quataert (eds.), *Syria: Society, Culture, and Polity* (New York: State University of New York Press, 1991), p. 99.

71 K. Abu Jaber, *The Arab Ba'th Socialist Party: History, Ideology, and Organization* (Syracuse: Syracuse University Press, 1966), p. 140.

72 Ibid., p. 143.

73 F. Lawson, "Domestic Pressures and the Peace Process: Fillip or Hindrance?" in E. Kienle (ed.), *Contemporary Syria: Liberalization between Cold War and Cold Peace* (London: British Academic Press, 1994), p. 148.

74 The function of organised business has tended to be arbitrary in Syria; its role, however, has become increasingly enhanced since the economic reforms of 1991.

75 V. Perthes, "Syria's Parliamentary Elections: Remodelling Asad's Political Base", *Middle East Report (MERIP)* (January/February 1992), p. 18.

76 R. Hinnebusch, *Authoritarian Power and State Formation in Ba'thist Syria: Army, Party, and Peasant* (Boulder: Westview Press, 1990), p. 197.

77 P. Seale, "Asad: Between Institutions and Autocracy" in R. Antoun, and D. Quataert (eds.), *Syria: Society, Culture, and Polity* (New York: State University of New York Press, 1991), p. 99.

78 Y. Sadowski, "Cadres, Guns and Money: The Eighth Regional Congress of the Syrian Ba'th", *Middle East Report (MERIP)*, no. 134 (July/August 1985), p. 3.

79 P. Seale, "Asad: Between Institutions and Autocracy" in R. Antoun and D. Quataert (eds.), *Syria: Society, Culture, and Polity* (New York: State University of New York Press, 1991), p. 100.

80 R. Hinnebusch, "Liberalization in Syria: The Struggle of Economic and Political Rationality" in E. Kienle (ed.), *Contemporary Syria: Liberalization between Cold War and Cold Peace* (London: British Academic Press, 1994), p. 99.

81 A. Richards and J. Waterbury, *A Political Economy of the Middle East: State, Class, and Economic Development* (Boulder: Westview Press, 1990), p. 314.

82 H. Batatu, "Some Observations on the Social Roots of Syria's Ruling Military Group and the Causes for Its Dominance", *Middle East Journal*, vol. 35, no. 3 (Summer 1981), p. 339.

83 Ibid., pp. 339–40.

84 P. Khoury, *Syria and the French Mandate: The Politics of Arab Nationalism 1920–1945* (Princeton: Princeton University Press, 1987), pp. 605–6.

85 Interview with a Syrian academic, 10 September 1995.

86 R. Hinnebusch, "Syria: The Politics of Peace and Regime Survival", *Middle East Policy*, vol. iii, no. 4 (April 1995), p. 78.

87 I. Rabinovich, *Syria under the Ba'th 1963–66: The Army–Party Symbiosis* (Jerusalem: Israel University Press, 1972), p. 182.

88 Ibid., p. 204.

89 R. Hinnebusch, "Class and State in Ba'thist Syria" in R. Antoun and D. Quataert (eds.), *Syria: Society, Culture, and Polity* (New York: State University of New York Press, 1991), p. 35.
90 Interview with a Syrian businessman, 2 July 1994.
91 The 'Alawis occupy key positions in both the military and the security services, such as those of security chiefs, party bosses, divisional commanders, and have links to the business community.
92 A. Drysdale and R. Hinnebusch, *Syria and the Middle East Peace Process* (New York: Council on Foreign Relations, 1991), p. 23.
93 H. Batatu, "Some Observations on the Social Roots of Syria's Ruling Military Group and the Causes for Its Dominance", *Middle East Journal*, vol. 35, no. 3 (Summer 1981), p. 343.
94 R. Hinnebusch, *Authoritarian Power and State Formation in Ba'thist Syria: Army, Party, and Peasant* (Boulder: Westview Press, 1990), pp. 146.
95 R. Hinnebusch, "Class and State in Ba'thist Syria" in R. Antoun and D. Quataert (eds.), *Syria: Society, Culture, and Polity* (New York: State University of New York Press, 1991), p. 43.
96 *Syria – Country Profile* (London: The Economist Intelligence Unit, January 1977), no. 1, p. 9.
97 Y. Sadowski, "Cadres, Guns and Money: The Eighth Regional Congress of the Syrian Ba'th", *Middle East Report (MERIP)*, no. 134 (July/August 1985), p. 7.
98 *Syria – Country Profile* (London: The Economist Intelligence Unit, November 1977), no. 4, p. 7.
99 Ibid.
100 Interview with a Damascene, 4 July 1994.
101 Interview with a Damascene, 4 July 1994.
102 Interview with a Syrian journalist, 26 September 1995.
103 Interview with a Damascene, 28 June 1994.
104 S. Longrigg, *Syria and Lebanon under French Mandate* (London: Oxford University Press, 1958), p. 117, and T. Petran, *Syria* (New York: Praeger, 1972), pp. 68–73.
105 D. Betz, "Conflict of Principle and Policy: A Case Study of the Arab Baath Socialist Party in Power in Syria" (Ph.D. thesis, Ann Arbor) (Ann Arbor: Xerox University Microfilms, 1976).
106 Interview with a Syrian bureaucrat, 1 October 1995.
107 G. Kanaan, "Syria and the Peace Plan: Assad's Balancing Act", *Middle East Report (MERIP)*, no. 65 (March 1978), pp. 10–11.
108 V. Perthes, *The Political Economy of Syria under Asad* (London: I.B. Tauris, 1995), p. 41.
109 Ibid., p. 49.
110 V. Perthes, "Stages of Economic and Political Liberalization" in E. Kienle (ed.), *Contemporary Syria: Liberalization between Cold War and Cold Peace* (London: British Academic Press, 1994), p. 47.
111 V. Perthes, *The Political Economy of Syria under Asad* (London: I.B. Tauris, 1995), p. 50.
112 R. Hinnebusch, "Liberalization in Syria: The Struggle of Economic and Political Rationality" in E. Kienle (ed.), *Contemporary Syria: Liberalization between Cold War and Cold Peace* (London: British Academic Press, 1994), p. 106.

113 J. Bahout, "The Syrian Business Community, Its Politics and Prospects" in E. Kienle (ed.), *Contemporary Syria: Liberalization between Cold War and Cold Peace* (London: British Academic Press, 1994), pp. 74–5.

114 R. Hinnebusch, "Asad's Syria and the New World Order: The Struggle for Regime Survival", *Middle East Policy*, vol. ii, no. 1 (May/June 1993), p. 14.

115 Ibid., p. 7.

116 J. Bahout, "The Syrian Business Community, Its Politics and Prospects" in E. Kienle (ed.), *Contemporary Syria: Liberalization between Cold War and Cold Peace* (London: British Academic Press, 1994), pp. 72 and 79–81.

117 Ibid., p. 73.

118 Ibid., pp. 73–4.

119 Ibid., p. 74.

120 Ibid., p. 75.

121 Ibid., p. 77.

122 Ibid., p. 75.

123 Ibid.

124 For a more detailed analysis of Syria's first *infitah*, see: Perthes, V. "Stages of Economic and Political Liberalization" in E. Kienle (ed.), *Contemporary Syria: Liberalization between Cold War and Cold Peace* (London: British Academic Press, 1994), and V. Perthes, *The Political Economy of Syria Under Asad* (London: I.B. Tauris, 1995).

125 V. Perthes, *The Political Economy of Syria under Asad* (London: I.B. Tauris, 1995), p. 53.

126 H. Batatu, "Syria's Muslim Brethren", *Middle East Report (MERIP)*, no. 110 (November/December 1982), pp. 12–23.

127 V. Perthes, "The Private Sector, Economic Liberalization, and the Prospects of Democratization: The Case of Syria and Some Other Arab Countries" in G. Salame (ed.), *Democracy without Democrats? The Renewal of Politics in the Muslim World* (London: I.B. Tauris, 1994), p. 245.

128 D. Butter, "Syrian Business Makes a Comeback", *Middle East Economic Digest*, vol. 38, no. 20, 20 May 1994, pp. 2–3.

129 R. Hinnebusch, "Liberalization in Syria: The Struggle of Economic and Political Rationality" in E. Kienle (ed.), *Contemporary Syria: Liberalization between Cold War and Cold Peace* (London: British Academic Press, 1994), p. 102.

130 Interview with the minister of the economy, Muhammad al-Imady, 4 July 1994.

131 S. Heydemann, "The Political Logic of Economic Rationality: Selective Stabilization in Syria" in H. Barkey (ed.), *The Politics of Economic Reform in the Middle East* (New York: St Martin's Press, 1992), p. 15.

132 R. Hinnebusch, "Liberalization in Syria: The Struggle of Economic and Political Rationality" in E. Kienle (ed.), *Contemporary Syria: Liberalization between Cold War and Cold Peace* (London: British Academic Press, 1994), p. 101.

133 Ibid., p. 108.

134 D. Gold, "The Syrian–Israeli Track – Taking the Final Step: What Sacrifices Will Assad Make to Get Back the Golan?", *Middle East Insight*, vol. x, no. 6 (September/October 1994), p. 15.

135 S. Heydemann, "The Political Logic of Economic Rationality: Selective Stabilization in Syria" in H. Barkey (ed.), *The Politics of Economic Reform in the Middle East* (New York: St Martin's Press, 1992), p. 20.

136 R. Hinnebusch, "Syria: The Politics of Peace and Regime Survival", *Middle East Policy*, vol. iii, no. 4 (April 1995), p. 82.

137 V. Perthes, "The Private Sector, Economic Liberalization, and the Prospects of Democratization: The Case of Syria and Some Other Arab Countries" in G. Salame (ed.), *Democracy without Democrats? The Renewal of Politics in the Muslim World* (London: I.B. Tauris, 1994), p. 253.

138 S. Heydemann, "The Political Logic of Economic Rationality: Selective Stabilization in Syria" in H. Barkey (ed.), *The Politics of Economic Reform in the Middle East* (New York: St Martin's Press, 1992), p. 21.

139 J. Bahout, "The Syrian Business Community, Its Politics and Prospects" in E. Kienle (ed.), *Contemporary Syria: Liberalization between Cold War and Cold Peace* (London: British Academic Press, 1994), p. 80.

140 Interview with the minister of the economy, Muhammad al-Imady, 4 July 1994.

141 An indication of this shift has been the incorporation of the al-Shallah family, led by patriarch Badr al-Din Shallah, head of the Damascus chamber of commerce, who is perceived by the Sunni community as incorruptible. See R. Hinnebusch, "Asad's Syria and the New World Order: The Struggle for Regime Survival", *Middle East Policy*, vol. ii, no. 1 (May/June 1993), p. 6.

142 E. Picard, "Espace de référence et espace d'intervention du mouvement rectificatif au pouvoir en Syrie 1970–1982", Université de Sorbonne (Thèse de III Cycle Paris, 1985).

143 The state elite includes the bureaucracy, the armed forces, and the security services.

144 Interview with an economic officer in the US embassy in Syria, 28 June 1994.

145 R. Hinnebusch, "Liberalization in Syria: The Struggle of Economic and Political Rationality" in E. Kienle (ed.), *Contemporary Syria: Liberalization between Cold War and Cold Peace* (London: British Academic Press, 1994), p. 104.

146 Interview with a Syrian businessman, 30 June 1994.

147 Interview with the first secretary of the British embassy in Syria, 28 September 1995.

148 Interview with a Syrian artist, 29 September 1995.

149 Interview with a Syrian businessman, 30 September 1995.

150 Interview the first secretary of the British embassy in Syria, 28 September 1995.

151 J. Bahout, "The Syrian Business Community, Its Politics and Prospects" in E. Kienle (ed.), *Contemporary Syria: Liberalization between Cold War and Cold Peace* (London: British Academic Press, 1994), p. 77.

152 Interview with a Syrian bureaucrat, 1 October 1995.

153 R. Hinnebusch, "Liberalization in Syria: The Struggle of Economic and Political Rationality" in E. Kienle (ed.), *Contemporary Syria: Liberalization between Cold War and Cold Peace* (London: British Academic Press, 1994), p. 108.

154 V. Perthes, "The Private Sector, Economic Liberalization, and the Prospects of Democratization: The Case of Syria and Some Other Arab Countries" in G. Salame (ed.), *Democracy without Democrats? The Renewal of Politics in the Muslim World* (London: I.B. Tauris, 1994), p. 218.

155 Interview with Patrick Seale, Durham, November 1994.

156 *Syria – Country Profile* (London: Economist Intelligence Unit, August 1979), no. 3, p. 5.

157 Ibid.

158 *Syria – Country Profile* (London: The Economist Intelligence Unit, December 1981), no. 4, p. 7.

159 Ibid., p. 6.

160 A. Drysdale, "The Asad Regime and Its Troubles", *Middle East Report* (*MERIP*), no. 110 (November/December 1982), pp. 3–11, and R. Fisk, *Pity the Nation: Lebanon at War* (Oxford: Oxford University Press, 1991), pp. 181–7.

161 A peaceful Islamic movement focused on pious personal behaviour is starting to spread again, and so long as it does not challenge the regime, this safety-valve will be tolerated. The regime knows that under political liberalisation the Islamists, the main beneficiaries of the ideological vacuum, would widen their base. It is unlikely to allow them to operate politically unless they support the regime. Moderate conservative Islamic leaders who have cooperated with the government, such as Muhammad Said Rahman al-Buti, professor of shariah, and the mufti, Ahmad al-Kaftaro, have some followings in Sufi brotherhoods and old quarters like al-Midan.

162 *Syria – Country Profile* (London: The Economist Intelligence Unit, March 1984), no. 1, p. 9.

163 P. Seale, *Asad of Syria: The Struggle for the Middle East* (London: I.B. Tauris, 1988), p. 424.

164 Ibid.

165 Ibid.

166 Notes from Hinnebusch's interview with Seale, London, May 1994.

167 V. Perthes, *The Political Economy of Syria under Asad* (London: I.B. Tauris, 1995), p. 138.

168 R. Hinnebusch, "Liberalization in Syria: The Struggle of Economic and Political Rationality" in E. Kienle (ed.), *Contemporary Syria: Liberalization between Cold War and Cold Peace* (London: British Academic Press, 1994), p. 107.

169 R. Hinnebusch, "Asad's Syria and the New World Order: The Struggle for Regime Survival", *Middle East Policy*, vol. ii, no. 1 (May/June 1993), pp. 11–12.

170 V. Perthes, "Stages of Economic and Political Liberalization" in E. Kienle (ed.), *Contemporary Syria: Liberalization between Cold War and Cold Peace* (London: British Academic Press, 1994), p. 66.

171 Ibid.

172 R. Hinnebusch, "Liberalization in Syria: The Struggle of Economic and Political Rationality" in E. Kienle (ed.), *Contemporary Syria: Liberalization between Cold War and Cold Peace* (London: British Academic Press, 1994), p. 108.

173 *BBC Summary of World Broadcasts*, ME/1131, A/3, 23 July 1991.

4

The Regional Balance
of Power

___

Introduction

Syria's foreign policy has been consistent for the past twenty-five years. Comprehensive peace with Israel has been an obtainable and desired goal of the Syrian regime since the early 1970s, but the structural determinants within the region pushed the Syrian state to pursue a balance of power before taking a place at the negotiating table.

The consolidation of the state, forged through the policies of Asad, has afforded it the opportunity to pursue a rational foreign policy. Syria's foreign policy can be mainly accounted for by the realist paradigm of international relations. It is based upon: preserving the security of the state; following the national interest; maximising the available amount of power.

Syrian foreign policy has been guided by this set of principles; despite its tactical flexibility, Syria has remained committed to securing the state and maintaining its sphere of influence in the Levant.

Commentators such as Pipes[1] and Lawson[2] cast doubt over Syria's consistency in the execution of foreign policy. Their analyses, which belong to the domestic politics model, attribute Syrian foreign policy to the goal of satisfying the demands of its various domestic constituencies. Thus, an irrational pattern of behaviour emerges. As in the case of other Third World states, domestic constraints impinge upon the Syrian state's room for manoeuvre. Foreign policy is open to the centrifugal forces inherited from the period of colonialism; the state is not unitary, nor is it the principal actor because of the fractious and permeable nature of society.

In the following section, I shall present the arguments of the domestic politics and rational actor models of foreign policy analysis. It is my contention that the rational actor model, put forward by the realist paradigm, is the most appropriate explanatory model for the Syrian case.

Domestic politics model

The domestic politics model places emphasis on domestic interests in the formulation of foreign policy. It stresses the role of classes or interest groups and their access to the decision-making process. In this interpretation, the state is subjected to a loss of autonomy. Proponents of this model refute the primacy of the international political system as the major determinant for the actions of a state. Conversely, they focus upon the domestic configurations of power.

Domestic politics models are the dominant form for analysing the foreign policies of Third World states. The emphasis of the domestic politics models is on the instability that characterises Third World states,[3] whose foreign policy is portrayed as irrational by this school of thought.[4] Third World states are considered to lack legitimacy and autonomy from their societies; the regimes are notoriously authoritarian and depend upon foreign policy to cohere otherwise divisive social and political communities. The utility of an external threat provides a locus of attention for the population of a state. According to Goode, foreign policy is domestic politics pursued by other means.[5] In other words, Goode suggests that the continuous presence of an external threat to security is a useful device for generating allegiance to unconsolidated states. Regimes exaggerate the significance of security threats in order to divert attention away from domestic problems.

Calvert adds another dimension to this analysis when he highlights the intra-elite struggles that also characterise poorly consolidated states. He asserts that where this is a prominent feature of Third World states foreign policy loses all sense of coherence as it becomes an instrument in the hands of warring factions. The result is a belligerent and largely irrational foreign policy often grounded in anti-imperial rhetoric.[6]

Pipes and Lawson apply the domestic politics model in their analysis of Syrian foreign policy. Pipes emphasises the sectarian nature of the Syrian regime ('Alawi), and contrasts it with the majority (Sunni) interest of the population. He portrays Syrian foreign policy as irrational and founded upon two principles that support the 'Alawi-dominated regime: the perpetuation of the state of war with Israel and the irredentist ambition of recreating Greater Syria.[7] According to them, Syrian foreign policy serves the minority interests of the 'Alawis because the state of war with Israel provides a pretext for maintaining a strong domestic military presence in the cities. Basically, foreign policy acts as a tool for legitimising an unpopular regime. Furthermore, the promotion of Greater Syria envelops and hides the sectarian character of the 'Alawi regime.[8]

The domestic politics model accounts for a foreign policy that is grounded in praetorian politics (mosaic model) or economics (Marxist analysis). The use of the mosaic model to explain Syria's foreign policy is valuable as it enables us to correlate the execution of foreign policy decisions with domestic policy.[9] It is, however, limited in its applicability as it is too unidimensional. To say that the Syrian regime is sectarian is tautological. The sectarian composition of the regime is self-evident; the mosaic approach cannot account for the complex operations of the state. The 'Alawis hold the key positions in the security apparatus of the state, but the business community and the Ba'th constituency are functional in the decision-making process.

Lawson works with a model where foreign policy is instrumental in managing class cleavages.[10] The perpetual threat of war creates an environment which allows the state to enjoy a degree of autonomy from domestic social forces. Lawson suggests that Syria goes to war when the dominant ruling coalition is faced with a serious domestic threat that pre-eminently comes about through economic crisis.[11] War provides the solution for bridging the deep social divisions within Syrian society and healing the fractures within the dominant ruling coalition. This approach refutes the ability and ambitions of the regime to reach a peace agreement with Israel.

There is an economic variant of the domestic politics model which has been applied to the Syrian case.[12] According to this variant, economic crisis is believed to force the regime to sell foreign policy decisions for financial aid needed to service patronage networks on which its survival depends.[13] This is a familiar explanation of Syria's entry into the Gulf War coalition and its engagement in the Madrid peace process. In Chapters 6 and 7, I will give another explanation, showing that Syria's participation in both events was determined more by politico-strategic considerations.[14]

Although domestic politics models may apply to many Third World states, their suitability to the Syrian case is limited. The three most salient features of the Syrian case, namely, the durability of the Asad regime, the intensity of the Syrian–Israeli conflict, and its consistency in foreign policy, refute the basic assumptions of the domestic politics models. The Syrian regime has indubitably used external threats and foreign policy performance to legitimise its rule. It is difficult, however, to discount the threat posed by Israel. Israel's invasion of Lebanon, in 1978 and 1982, presented a direct challenge to Syria and its role in the Levant.[15] Syria's pursuit of a balance of power with Israel is a testament to the real threat it perceives from its southern neighbour.

Internal politics cannot be unlinked from foreign policy, but their explanatory power in the Syrian case is far more limited and indirect than domestic politics models suggest. The one quantitative study of linkage politics, which was conducted by Burrows and Spector, found that there was no direct link between the domestic and foreign policy behaviour of Syria.[16] Evron intimates that realist (deterrence) analysis is most useful for explaining Syria's quest for strategic parity with Israel.[17]

The rational actor model

According to the rational actor model, which belongs to the realist and neo-realist paradigms, foreign policy is determined primarily by security concerns.[18] Survival in an anarchic arena requires all states, in the long term at least, to adopt certain rational behaviour, such as power maximisation and balancing strategies. In the realist paradigm, foreign policy is substantially dictated by the international system, regardless of ideology and internal politics.[19]

The rational actor model explains the behaviour of states according to international events and by recounting the aims and calculations of states.[20] The value of this method, according to Morgenthau, is that:

> it provides for rational discipline in action and creates astounding continuity in foreign policy . . . [which] appears as an intelligible, rational continuum . . . regardless of the different motives, preferences, and intellectual and moral qualities of successive statesmen.[21]

Cross-national studies have tended to support the realist case, intimating that inter-state conflict is more closely associated with variations in international circumstances than domestic affairs. No strong consistent association was found between foreign policy and internal factors, such as authoritarian regimes and ethnic heterogeneity.[22] Where external threats are high, as in the Middle East, the realist paradigm is deemed particularly apposite.[23]

One proposition of the realist model is that adaptation to the external arena is best achieved in a strong state where the foreign policy machine is a unified autonomous rational actor. In this case, the foreign policy machine is able to harness policy in the service of an historically or geopolitically shaped national interest. The state is sufficiently autonomous to pursue foreign policy goals based on rational criteria. The state is also unitary and able to execute a coherent policy without accounting for the intra-state interests of dominant social actors or groups. Seale and Hinnebusch apply this analysis to Syria.[24]

The realist paradigm, with its focus on systemic variables, takes a leader's ability to mobilise domestic resources for external objectives as non-problematic. This is where the realist paradigm is weak in its analysis. Without an analysis of state–society relations, the realist paradigm invites criticism, especially when applied to the Third World. Protagonists of the domestic politics models are dismissive of realism; they discount the possibility that Third World states can act according to a set of rational considerations because they often lack legitimacy, strong state institutions and a national agenda.[25]

I contend that Syria's foreign policy has been tempered by the international political system and the peculiarities of the regional state sub-system of the Middle East. The Syrian state, as explained in Chapter 3, is particularly vulnerable because of its recent history, demography, and geopolitical position. Located on one of the major trading routes between the Occident and the Orient, Syria has been subject to the political machinations of the region.

Syria's foreign relations have traditionally been dependent upon external factors. Consequently, Syria has been a pawn among the regional hegemons, often constituting a sphere of influence for regional actors, such as Iraq and Egypt.[26] The struggle for Syria intensified after independence: it became a prize in the regional contest between the two tributary states, Egypt and Iraq, which competed for influence in the fractious state of Syria.

Belonging to the Arab nation, and dissected from its regional base, Syria had an unclear political identity. The pan-Arab appeal of Arab nationalism, and the pan-Islamic call of Islam contradicted the notion of Syrian statehood. Cross-state loyalties undermined the sovereign base of the new Syrian state, and allowed its centrifugal forces to disrupt a cohesive central polity. The state was porous to the covert interventions of the region's main power centres. Egypt, Saudi Arabia, and Iraq all played instrumental roles in subverting the independence of Syria, whilst promoting their own political agendas.[27]

On the international level, Syria became a cornerstone in the zero-sum game between the Soviet Union and the US.[28] The US Central Intelligence Agency (CIA) was also reputed to have undertaken covert operations in order to dissuade local actors from cultivating ties with the Soviet Union.[29] As a small, ethnically divided and vulnerable state, Syria could not emerge from its passivity without significant internal changes. The new state of Syria, struggling to construct its own identity, was beset by regional and international actors intervening to assert their hegemony.[30]

The creation of Israel has been considered, by Syrian regimes, to be an extension of imperial rule.[31] In other words, Israel represented a combined regional and international threat to the indigenous peoples of the region. Israel's occupation of Palestinian land, orchestrated through the channels of the Great Powers, engendered a permanent agenda for war. The struggle between Syria and Israel set a precedent that determined the orientation of Syrian foreign policy, which has been based on security, national interest, and power maximisation since 1970. The security of the state has been a preoccupation of the political elite and the occupation of the Golan Heights has served as a constant reminder of the threat posed by Israel.[32]

Asad's rise to power in 1970 marked a distinctive change in Syria's role in the region. The centralisation of the decision-making process, the institutionalisation of the political process, and the suppression of inter-state activists enabled the regime to consolidate its domestic position. Through this process of state-building, Asad, understanding the significance of power in shaping relations, started to translate Syria's inherent vulnerability into a source of power. This was achieved through a policy of alliance-building and -breaking, with the region's hegemonic powers.[33]

Instead of remaining the pawn, Syria began to exploit both the presence of Israel in the region and the presence of other revolutionary forces within the Arab world in order to extract political, military, and economic assistance from Egypt, the Gulf Arab states, and the Soviet Union. Syria has since then attempted to free itself from the constraints imposed by the superpowers, or other regional actors, in order to pursue an independent foreign policy.

Syria's foreign policy

Syria's foreign policy has been driven by its recent historical experience. The amputation of Lebanon, Palestine, and Jordan from historical Syria left the Syrian regimes of the post-independence period with an irredentist vision of recreating Greater Syria as a constituent of the wider Arab nation. Thus, Syria's foreign policy has been moulded and justified by Arab nationalism since independence.

Pan-Arabism, as a concept, has ceased to be the foremost determinant of Syria's foreign policy. This is now shaped primarily by assessments of how best to defend and enhance the power and prestige of Syria within the regional state system.[34] Seale labelled Syria's foreign policy as the "Levant Security Doctrine", which incorporated the following concepts:

(a) The security of the Arab East is indivisible, and any defection from the Arab front against Israel would undermine the chance for peace.

(b) Peace in the region is only possible through unity. Separate agreements between Arab states and Israel would weaken the common front and result in settlements that hurt the Arab side.

(c) Syria and Israel are engaged in an ongoing competition for hegemony over the western buffer zones.

(d) Syria must fight any policy that, intentionally or not, impinges upon its front-line defences.[35]

Seale's analysis is based on Syria's desire to provide the state with security from external threats. Because of Syria's geopolitical location the threats to its security are numerous and can be found on Syria's northern, southern, eastern, and western flanks. Israel represents the most significant and dynamic threat and has therefore been the focus of Syrian foreign policy since 1948. Israel's separate peace deals with Egypt, the PLO, and Jordan have increased the extent of Syria's insecurity.[36] Iraq's contention for the leadership of the Arab world has posed a dynamic threat to Syria's security, and ensured that inter-Arab rivalry has focused upon the Syrian–Iraqi relationship.[37]

In order to balance the threats imposed by Iraq and Israel, the Levant Security Doctrine set out to incorporate the potential of the Lebanese, the Jordanians, and the Palestinians. In an effort to extract Syria from the struggle among the regional powers, Asad sought to develop a base from which to challenge the hegemonic pretensions of its neighbours. This would enable Syria to maximise its power projection.

The drawing together of the Levant states' foreign policies into a unified policy could have provided a counterbalance to the power projections of Iraq and Israel. Asad's objective, however, was not the territorial annexation of Syria's neighbours, but their incorporation into its sphere of influence.[38] The tangible objectives of Syria's foreign policy can be translated into:

(a) Recovering the territories lost in the 1967 war, which included Gaza, the West Bank, the Golan Heights, and Sinai;
(b) The restoration of Palestinian rights.

The signing of the Camp David Accords between Israel and Egypt, and of the Oslo Accords between Israel and the PLO, curtailed Syria's ambitions. Syria's goals were contained in UN Resolution 242, which had constituted a basis for comprehensive peace talks prior to the Oslo Accords of 1993.[39] Dispensing with the rhetoric of his predecessors, Asad implicitly accepted UN Resolution 242 when he agreed to Resolution 338, on 15 October 1973, which called for a cease-fire between Syria and Israel and the implementation of Resolution 242.[40]

Seale and Hinnebusch assert that Syria's foreign policy has been consistent since 1972, and has been founded upon a set of rational principles. Asad relegated the role of ideology in the decision-making process, and formulated foreign policy according to Syria's power potential. Since coming to power, Asad has employed various strategies, and has effected numerous culpable tactical moves that have alienated large sections of the Syrian population. Syria's foreign policy has, however, remained anchored to the Levant Doctrine, but the transmuting international and regional configurations of power have pushed Syria towards unpopular tactics and new strategies.[41]

The balance of power has determined the strategies employed by the Syrian state in its competition with Israel. These strategies have taken three distinct forms since 1970:

(a) The Egyptian axis: 1970–8;
(b) Strategic parity: 1979–88;
(c) Strategic deterrence: 1989–96.

The following section will explore the content of Syria's strategies, and its pursuit of foreign policy goals.

The Egyptian axis: 1970–8

As soon as Asad seized power in Damascus, he started to court the financial and political support of the conservative Gulf monarchies whilst reinforcing the symbiotic military relationship with the Soviet Union.[42] Although Asad was not an ideologue, he understood the support that the Soviet Union could lend the Arabs in terms of military aid and strategic depth.[43]

The outcome of the 1967 war appeared to signify that the Arab effort to eradicate Israel had retreated into the annals of history. A new sense of realism emerged among the front-line Arab states. Between 1970 and 1978, Syria's military doctrine was cast within the rubric of Arab military and economic coordination.

The Middle Eastern equation, according to Asad and Sadat, required Syria and Egypt to coordinate their military manoeuvres, under the auspices of the Soviet Union, in order to balance the power of the Israeli military. Achieving a balance of power determined Syria's and Egypt's potential to strike Israel, reclaim the territories lost in 1967 and recover diplomatic prestige.[44] The Syrian–Egyptian axis, operating with the support of the Soviet Union, appeared to offer a realist strategy to recover the lands lost in the 1967 war, and deliver a political advantage. The two-front strategy received economic support from the Gulf Arab states. This represented a new era in the Middle East based on the balance of power.

Developing the two-front strategy entailed a commitment from the Soviet Union to rearm and train the Syrian and Egyptian military. By June 1973, according to Ramet's source, Syria had acquired 300 fighter aircraft, which meant an additional 200 to the stockpile of the 1967 war. Syrian military expenditure per capita increased quite substantially, from $115 in 1972 to $148 in 1973 and $151 in 1974.[45] The armed forces also started to grow in strength throughout this period. The strength of the armed forces increased from 17.2 per 1,000 people in 1972 to 18.1 per 1,000 in 1974.[46]

The consolidation of Soviet–Syrian ties, and the improvement in the quality and quantity of the military hardware transferred, were not sufficient, however, to sustain a prolonged offensive against Israel. Although the Soviets re-supplied the Syrians and the Egyptians during the October War, the disjointed approach to the war caused Syria and Egypt to cede their early military and territorial advantages.[47] After 72 hours, Israel was able to mobilise its reserves and concentrate upon its northern border. The initial gains were lost as Israel pushed Syria back towards Damascus, and the war was effectively lost.[48]

The different objectives of Asad and Sadat were considered to be largely responsible for the failings of the Syrian–Egyptian axis. Seale suggests:

> Asad went to war because he believed there could be no satisfactory negotiation with Israel until the Arabs had snatched back some of their lost land. Peace-making, he believed, could be a product of war, but not a substitute for it. Sadat went to war because the peace diplomacy he was already conducting, covertly as well as overtly, had faltered. He thought a shock would revive it.[49]

Egypt's limited military strategy, dubbed "High Minarets", was ultimately tied to Sadat's political ambitions. The tactical delay employed after seizing control of the Suez Canal, during the first phases of the war, allowed Israel sufficient space and time to redirect its aggression towards the more threatening Syrian advances.[50] The initial gains of the October War were lost as Egypt pursued a cease-fire with Israel through the secret diplomatic offices of US Secretary of State Henry Kissinger.[51] Apparently, Sadat was more willing and ready to accept the imposition of a cease-fire than Asad, but the military failure of the two-pronged attack led to the US-brokered Disengagement Agreements of 1974.[52]

The climax of the division of Syrian and Egyptian objectives was President Sadat's visit to Jerusalem in 1977, and the signing of the Camp David Accords in 1979. This signified the end of the Syrian–Egyptian alliance. Egypt was effectively removed from the Arab–Israeli conflict through its peace treaty with Israel, thus forcing Syria to adopt a new strategy.[53]

Strategic parity: 1979–89
The regional environment of the Middle East during 1979, which witnessed the signing of the Camp David Accords, the Iranian revolution, and the Soviet invasion of Afghanistan, impinged upon Syria's scope for strategic planning and tactical manoeuvring.

The absence of Egypt from the theatre of war forced Syria to seek alliances elsewhere. The temporary *rapprochement* between Syria and Iraq, through the formation of the Steadfastness Front, provided Syria with strategic depth. Nevertheless, its effectiveness was limited. The traditional competition for regional hegemony between these tributary states, expressed in the balance of power, determined the transitory nature of their alliance.[54] Syria's support of Iran in the Iran–Iraq War of 1980 demonstrated the intense rivalry between Syria and Iraq, which emanated from two sources:

(a) The balance of power;
(b) Syria's quest for regional leadership.

Syria's support of Iran during the Iran–Iraq War offered a classic example of the balance of power in operation. Syria's interests were enhanced through its alliance with Iran.[55] The perpetuation of the conflict enabled Syria to pursue its goal of regional leadership through its offices in Lebanon, and of control of Palestinian activities through Sa'iqa (meaning 'thunderbolt' – a Syrian-sponsored Palestinian unit which falls under the aegis of the Syrian army) and the Popular Front for the Liberation of Palestine–General Command (PFLP–GC).[56] There were a number of other factors that reinforced Syria's decision to oppose Iraq in its conflict with Iran, such as the Syrian and Iraqi claims to Ba'th party authenticity, and the personal animosity between President Asad and President Saddam Hussein.[57]

Syria's policy towards Iraq, its endorsement of the Soviet invasion of Afghanistan, and its continuing intervention in Lebanon, led to a period of regional isolation.[58] This set of conditions produced an environment which led to the development of the Syrian doctrine of strategic parity.[59]

Syria's search for strategic parity was initiated by the conclusion of the Camp David Accords and the deflection of regional attention towards the Iran-Iraq war, which implied that the balance of power between the Arabs and Israel worked in favour of Israel. Strategic parity was a doctrine that implied that Syria would reduce the military, societal, and political imbalance between Israel and itself. In other words, strategic parity signalled an expansion of Syrian power.[60]

The doctrine of strategic parity was designed to provide Syria with the capability of building a credible deterrent to Israel founded on two interrelated notions:

(a) Syria could not enter into a full-scale war with Israel, but by expanding its missile systems (SS-21s), and equipping them to carry chemical warheads, Syria could inflict devastating damage on an Israeli society that is acutely sensitive to civilian casualties.[61]

(b) In order to participate in an international peace conference, and to negotiate from a position of strength, Syria was required to compensate for the loss of its regional allies by developing its armed forces.[62]

Only by developing its military capabilities could Syria enter the peace process in pursuit of a durable and honourable peace. The achievement of a balance of power alone, Hinnebusch suggests, would not be sufficient reason to initiate an offensive: "Decisions to go to war are rarely based only on a calculus of the balance of power, but are also shaped by frustrations."[63]

Strategic parity represented a radical departure from previous functional military cooperation structures, as it implied that Syria would seek to achieve a balance of power with Israel.[64] The concept itself was far-reaching as it aimed at equating Syria with Israel in military and diplomatic terms.[65]

Syria's military expansion

The doctrine of strategic parity prescribed that the Syrian forces should be upgraded in both qualitative and quantitative terms. The central tenet of the doctrine focused on the inadequacy of the Syrian military.[66] Syria's military technology was relatively old so in order to move closer to the cutting edge (enjoyed by Israel), it needed to formalise its relations with the Soviet Union.[67] Mutual Soviet and Syrian vulnerability propelled the two states towards a more intense patron–client relationship which resulted in the Treaty of Friendship and Cooperation in 1980.[68] The Soviet Union's loss of Egypt as its major client in the region served to elevate Syria's importance and this resulted in a new Soviet arms supply policy aimed at securing Syria's allegiance.[69] Soviet–Syrian relations, from the Syrian perspective, played a vital role in the quest for strategic parity. Syria needed to equip itself in order to compensate for the absence of Egypt, and to balance the military power of Israel.

Syria's military experienced a period of intense and rapid expansion between 1982 and 1989. This included:

(a) An 80 per cent increase in the regular armed forces personnel from 240,000 to 400,000;

(b) A 50 per cent increase in the number of armoured and mechanised divisions (from 6 to 9);

(c) A 35 per cent increase in the number of Main Battle Tanks (MBTs) from 3,200 to 4,200;

(d) A 200 per cent increase in the number of tactical ballistic missile launchers (from 33 to 100);

(e) A 50 per cent increase in the number of surface-to-air batteries (from 100 to 150);

(f) A 45 per cent increase in the number of fighter planes (from 440 to 650);

(g) A 150 per cent increase in the number of attack helicopters (from 40 to 100);

(h) A 40 per cent increase in the number of missile attack aircraft (from 20 to 28);

(i) An absolute increase in the number of submarines (from 0 to 3).[70]

Syria's military power also increased from a qualitative perspective between 1982 and 1989. The Soviet commitment to Syrian ambitions, linked to Soviet vulnerability in the region, ensured that higher quality hardware was provided on soft terms.[71] The following weapons systems entered the Syrian inventory after 1982:

(a) SS-21 tactical ballistic missiles;

(b) SAM-5, SAM-11, SAM-13, and SAM-14 surface-to-air missiles;

(c) T-80, T-72M, T-74 Main Battle Tanks;

(d) BM-27 220-mm multiple rocket launchers;

(e) MiG-29 strike fighters and MiG-23MF/Flogger-G;

(f) AA-7 "Acrid" and AA-8 "Aphid" air-to-air missiles;

(g) New tactical C3I and electronic warfare systems, including DR-30 and UR-1, remotely piloted drones (RPVs), and Mil Mi-17 "Elint" helicopters;

(h) Chemical warfare delivery systems.[72]

The armed forces expanded rapidly from 250,000 in 1982 to 404,000 in 1989.[73] The change in the ratio of reserves to regular forces in Syria's favour indicated a more responsive action force. It was estimated that Israeli mobilisation would take at least 24–72 hours,[74] thus offering Syria the opportunity to seize the Golan Heights without conceding defeat.[75]

Syria started to close the quantitative gap with Israel in number of combat aircraft between 1982 and 1989. Nevertheless, Syrian air power remained weaker than Israeli air power as the pace of technological advancement accentuated Israel's superiority. During the period in question, Syria had 65 high-quality combat aircraft from its total of 650 aircraft whilst Israel had 200.[76] Israel's alliance with the US guaranteed its superiority in air-to-air and air-to-ground operations, modern command, control, communication systems, and combat aircraft.[77]

Syria did manage to improve its air defences through an increase in the number of SAM batteries, radar and electronic jammers, and acquisition of an advanced command and control system, thereby creating an air-defence system deployed by the Soviets.[78] Israeli and US technology rapidly outmanoeuvred these initiatives with the development of the "Arrow" missile and the tested "Patriot" anti-missile system.[79]

The technological gap between Syria and Israel ensured that Israel continued to enjoy the military advantage. Whenever the gap in technology seemed to recede, the next cycle extended Israel's disproportionate advantage. For example, the delivery of MiG-29s to Syria was met with the arrival of the "Agile Falcon", the advanced tactical fighter (ATF), in Israel.[80]

Evidently, Syria's dependence on the Soviet Union was crucial to maintaining a semblance of strategic parity. Syria could not have acquired its sizeable arsenal without the assistance of the Soviet Union. Although Syria sought to diversify its military suppliers, it was severely hampered in this attempt by the European and US ban on military exports to Syria.[81] Syria's principal suppliers remained the Soviet Union (which accounted for 90 per cent of total supplies), Eastern Europe, China, and North Korea.[82]

Patron–client relations

Israel's advantage over Syria was not confined to technology; there was a discernible difference between the status of the US–Israeli alliance and that of the Soviet–Syrian relationship. The US–Israeli and the Soviet–Syrian patron-client relationships were formulated according to two distinct sets of principles.

THE UNITED STATES AND ISRAEL

The US–Israeli alliance has been built on more sustainable foundations than the Soviet–Syrian relationship and has been cemented through the relationship between the Jewish lobby in the US and the US administrative system. Although it seems a rather crude analysis, there is sufficient evidence to suggest that the US–Israeli relationship is guided by the aspirations of the multifarious Jewish associations in the US.[83] The influence of the Jewish lobby in both domestic policy and foreign policy articulation is well documented.[84] This instrumental presence of Israel supporters in the US operates in complete contrast to the avenues open to the Syrians in the Soviet Union.

The durability of the US–Israeli alliance is shown by the fact that it has outlived changes of US administrations and of ruling coalitions in Israel. At each juncture, the alliance has remained unchallenged as the fundamentals of the relationship are constant. There may be teething troubles as each new team settles into position, but the core of the allegiance is protected. For instance, US President Bush's resistance to providing the $10,000 million in loan guarantees in 1991, because of his objection to the expansion of Israeli settlements in the West Bank, marked a period of troubled relations between the US and Israel. Bush's reluctance, however, failed to prevent the expansion of settlements after Israel had obtained the loan guarantees.[85]

THE SOVIET UNION AND SYRIA

In the zero-sum game of the Cold War, the Soviet Union became increasingly marginalised in the Middle East. The conservative and monarchical states of the region resisted the ideological orientations of Soviet Communism, which were deemed more pernicious than the liberal ideologies of the West. Realising this, the US adopted a policy that successfully incorporated the inimical interests of the conservative oil-rich Arab states, Israel, Turkey, Iran (before 1979), and Egypt (after 1973).[86]

The loss of Egypt as a client state to the US in 1972, and the Soviet invasion of Afghanistan, resulted in a further diminution of Soviet influence and a concomitant increase in US prestige in the Middle East. Although the Iranian Revolution in 1979 disengaged Iran from the US sphere of influence, the Soviet Union did not become a beneficiary in the zero-sum game. Iran's post-revolutionary foreign policy was governed by Iran's neither-East-nor-West policy.

Soviet access to the states of the Middle Eastern region was limited; Syria and Iraq were the two radical/revolutionary states of the Mashreq that turned to the Soviet Union, but they extracted a high price for their allegiance. The limited Soviet penetration in the Middle East state-system provided Syria and Iraq with some autonomy to pursue their regional goals, even to the detriment of Soviet interests.[87] Bercovitch has labelled this style of patron–client relationship as *interdependent*.[88]

In the zero-sum game, Syria formed part of the Soviet Union's chessboard strategy. The Soviets lent the Syrians military, political, and diplomatic support for their regional designs. As part of the reciprocal bargain, Syria allowed the Soviet Union to use its ports at Latakia and Tartous, giving the Soviet navy access to the Mediterranean. The interdependent relationship was confined to serving the mutual interests of both superpower and regional state. This leads one to conclude that the Soviet–Syrian relationship was functional and based on strategic value rather than on cultural, religious, or ideological foundations.[89]

The Soviet–Syrian alliance was not sustainable beyond the strategic value that each state lent to the other. This became evident when "new thinking" was introduced into Soviet foreign policy, which challenged the very foundations of the relationship, for it disengaged their mutual interests. "New thinking" dictated a change in the strategic dimension of Soviet international relations, and a focus upon the ailing Soviet economy.[90]

NEW THINKING

The Soviet Union, through the Treaty of Friendship and Cooperation in 1980, pledged its support for Syria's pursuit of strategic parity. Syria's relationship with the Soviet Union enabled it to adopt its rejectionist stance throughout the 1980s. During the years of its association with the Soviet Union, Syria successfully avoided becoming a Soviet satellite, however; in particular, this strategic alliance gave Syria a considerable degree of autonomy of action whilst providing it with a cushion of strategic depth.[91] The arrival of Mikhail Gorbachev in 1985 was to alter radically the autonomy enjoyed by Syria.

The substance of Soviet–Syrian relations started to disintegrate when Gorbachev came to power. The Soviet foreign minister, Eduard Shevardnadze, spelt out the new concerns of Soviet foreign policy: "The *new thinking* logically led us to reject antagonism as the basis for foreign policy, to discard ideological clichés, and to de-ideologise international relations."[92]

Gorbachev's introduction of "new thinking" in Soviet foreign policy changed the nature of international politics. Global issues, such as nuclear arms reduction, the eradication of famine, and the inevitable destruction of the global environment, started to take precedence over the bipolar competition between the Soviet Union and the US.[93] With the shift of emphasis upon global cooperation, the radical states of the Middle East had to acclimatise to a new international environment. The Arab–Israeli conflict required reappraising according to the new tenets of Soviet foreign policy. In an after-dinner speech, Shevardnadze reflected: "The climate, both worldwide and in the Middle East, has changed significantly. The antagonism between the Soviet Union and the US in that region has ended. This alone is a factor that affects all of the elements of the Middle East equation."[94]

The immediate impact of "new thinking" upon Syrian foreign policy was severe. Until the advent of "new thinking", the relationship between the Soviet Union and Syria had existed on the basis of mutual dependence and insecurity. Nevertheless, the fabric of the relationship had been sustained because of their mutual isolation. "New thinking" undermined the flexibility of the partnership and removed Syria's margin of manoeuvre. Although the Soviets pledged their continued support of Syrian interests, Gorbachev seized the political opportunity and initiated a process of redefinition of relations. The first outcome was the rejection of strategic parity. This signified the end of their intimate military relationship and made it necessary for Syria to reassess its regional strategy.

During the bipolar period of modern history, Syria had been successful in extracting military advantages from the Soviet Union, based on the Soviet desire to gain a stronghold in the region. "New thinking" liberated the Soviet Union from this necessity, and granted it more freedom to redefine its role in the Middle East.

Gorbachev's address in Syria during 1987 revealed the fragility of the Soviet–Syrian bond. He commented on the Soviet–Israeli situation: "The absence of diplomatic relations between the Soviet Union and Israel cannot be considered normal."[95] During the meeting of Asad and Gorbachev, in April 1987, the Soviet leader stressed the inappropriateness of the military option and placed emphasis upon a political solution.[96] Asad remained resolute and mocked Gorbachev's naivety.

> Force in today's world, just as in the past, is what determines rights. Everyone speaks about rights and international norms, charters, and resolutions. However, you find that every international event is eventually settled by force.[97]

As part of the "new thinking", Gorbachev rejected the military solution in resolving international conflicts and paid particular attention to the Arab–Israeli conflict and the role of the peace process. The option of strategic parity, a policy that had gained momentum after the Camp David Accords, was abruptly abandoned by the Soviets.

The Soviet economic crisis forced Syria to abandon the policy of strategic parity, a change which was reflected in the pattern of Syrian arms purchases; as Rathmell says: "This drive for strategic parity was undermined by the sclerotic performance of the Syrian economy and the changes in the Soviet Union which ended Moscow's willingness to supply hardware on easy payment terms."[98] The Soviet demand for payment in hard currency altered the flexibility within the relationship.

The bipolar era was passing, a New World Order was forming and Asad had to seek a new strategy or co-sponsor to achieve his regional ambitions. The disjuncture between theory and application in Soviet foreign policy granted Asad a period of grace. The impact of "new thinking" was incremental during its early stages, and the Syrians continued to benefit from the contradiction in theory and application.[99]

After 1985, Soviet arms transfers to Syria declined; the deterioration in military relations between Syria and the Soviet Union should not be exaggerated, however. Although the Soviet Union was embarking upon its new philosophy, residues of former attitudes still prevailed. The geographic and strategic dimensions of the Soviet–Syrian relationship could not be unconditionally discounted for the Soviet Union continued to share its southern borders with the Middle East, and still required strategic allies. There were occasions when "new thinking" was subordinated to the immediate interests of Soviet security.[100]

The Soviet rejection of the military option, and its recognition of the state of Israel, signified the end of Syria's pursuit of strategic parity.[101] This became manifest when Asad restored diplomatic relations with Egypt in December 1989.[102] The functional capacity of the Soviet–Syrian relationship came to its conclusion with the breakup of the Soviet Union in August 1991.[103] The structural changes in the relationship were responsible for engendering Syria's search for a new strategy.[104]

Strategic deterrence: 1989–96

The transition in superpower relations, following the withdrawal of Soviet support, and the fluidity in the regional configurations of power after 1988, encouraged Syria to pursue a more inclusive regional strategy. This included:

(a) Engaging in a more constructive dialogue with the US, carried out through Syrian–US complicity in Lebanon;[105]
(b) Getting involved in a more rigorous realignment with the Gulf Arab states and Egypt.[106]

Iraq's respite from the Iran–Iraq War in 1988 allowed Saddam Hussein to reclaim the central role in the Arab–Israeli conflict, a move which deliberately challenged Syria's regional and Levantine role. Asad needed an opportunity to maintain Syria's hegemony in Lebanon, and its claim to Arab nationalism.

The Iraqi invasion of Kuwait, on 2 August 1990, was fortuitous for Asad for it provided Syria with the opportunity to secure its regional position in the post-Cold War era. Although Asad's decision to join the US-led coalition appeared to contradict Syria's Arab nationalist credentials, the reward for its support was substantial: it elevated Syria's role in the postwar Arab and global orders, and it allowed Syria to obtain $700 million in credits from the Europeans and the Japanese, and over $2,000 million in pledges from Saudi Arabia and the Gulf states.[107]

These funds allowed Syria to diversify its military suppliers and to purchase more sophisticated weaponry. The build-up of Syria's military hardware was financed with the hard currency earned from the liberation of Kuwait. With the financial rewards, Syria was able to conclude deals with Russia, Bulgaria, and Czechoslovakia. In 1991–2, Syria procured 400 T-72M main battle tanks and 300 self-propelled artillery pieces from these deals.[108] In 1993, it was believed that Syria had placed an order with Russia for 68 MiG-29 strike fighters, 24 Su-24 attack aircraft and SA-11 "Gadfly" missile batteries. Syria managed to diversify its military supplies and obtained the North Korean Scud-C and the Chinese solid-fuel M-9 missile.[109] Ironically, it led some commentators, namely Shahak and Lucas, to admit that "the Syrian army is much better equipped than it was when Syria depended on Soviet supplies".[110]

Sadowski, however, disputed some of the above claims when he wrote:

> By late 1992, however, the expected rearmament of Syria had not materialised. Moscow signed no new arms agreement. In 1992 the

Czechs announced that they would complete a standing contract for the delivery of T-72 tanks to Damascus but would not make any future sales. The North Korean ship suspected of carrying missiles returned to port without docking in Syria, and in February 1992 a second freighter supposedly carrying Scuds for Damascus failed to reach the Mediterranean, although it did make port in Iran.[111]

Sadowski assigned Syria's failure to purchase these items to US pressure on China and North Korea. Syria's failure to conclude a deal to buy military hardware from South Africa in January 1997 illustrates the extensive influence of the US and the limitations Syria faces.[112]

Although it was a casualty of the change in the global and the regional balance of power, Syria managed to pursue an alternative path to achieving a balance with Israel. The new strategy for Syria, engaging the US, Egypt, Saudi Arabia, and the other Gulf Arab states in a new balance-of-power formula, enabled it to develop a military doctrine based on a strategic deterrent. Syria's new military doctrine can be identified as "the capability to deter [a regional enemy] through power projection and through suitable alliances with one or more regional players".[113]

Syria's goal of providing a strategic deterrent, whilst participating in the peace process, has been achieved through the possession of ballistic missiles, together with chemical and biological warheads. But as Sayigh says: "not only does Israel possess chemical weapons, but it is also the only Middle Eastern country to have developed nuclear warheads for its Jericho missiles."[114] Therefore, the power projection of Syria can only be conceived of in defensive terms.

Syria's intervention in Lebanon

Syria's foreign policy has been determined by the regional balance of power. Its pursuit of strategic parity in the 1980s was a quest to achieve such a balance with Israel. The conclusion of the Camp David Accords reduced Syria's regional importance and circumvented its centrality to the peace process. The signing of a separate peace deal threatened the very notion of Arab unity, or at the very least Arab cooperation, and, therefore, Syrian security. Egypt's departure, motivated by national interest, risked establishing a precedent among the Arab states. In the aftermath, Syria tried to mould the policies of the Arab states to accommodate the Levant Security Doctrine.

The rational actor model helps to explain the strategy of Syria during its tumultuous engagement in the Lebanese civil war. Preservation of Syria's security and the maximisation of its power by extending its hegemony accords with the realist paradigm and most accurately accounts for Syria's actions in Lebanon. Syria entered Lebanon and broke numerous alliances, often trading its traditional allies for less ideologically disposed clients, but each instance can be attributed to the broader goal of Syrian security, and Asad's determination to prevent separate Israeli peace deals from disrupting the prospect for comprehensive peace. In the very early stages of the war, Syria was still smarting from Egypt's defection, and tried to construct an Eastern bloc comprising Jordan, Lebanon, and the PLO. It was designed to counter the effect of the Camp David Accords by ruling out the possibility of another separate peace agreement. Syria's attempt to create a cohesive bloc also served its security interests, which had become paramount to Syrian foreign policy. At the focal point of the Eastern bloc's and Syria's security concerns was Lebanon.

Lebanon has been central to Syria's foreign policy since the outbreak of the Lebanese civil war in 1975, and has remained a cornerstone of Syria's Levant Doctrine. During the civil war, Lebanon became an intense battleground for the region's interests; it resembled a microcosm of the Middle East's numerous political contests. The Arab–Israeli conflict, the inter-Arab competition, the export of the Iranian Revolution, and the superpower zero-sum game all found an expression in Lebanon. Syria has played a pivotal role in each of these conflicts, illustrating its centrality to the political machinations of the Levant.

Syria's interests have been irrevocably intertwined with the fortunes of Lebanon and have manifested themselves in a variety of forms. Syria's historical claim to be the parent state of the Levant, its role in the Arab–Israeli conflict, and its contentious relationship with Iran, have all served to embroil Syria in the struggle for Lebanon.[115] Syria's role in Lebanese affairs can be accounted for by the two factors of history and security.

History

As the cornerstone of the Levant, Syria has historically played a role in the political organisation and administration of the region. Under the rule of the Ottomans, Aleppo and Jerusalem were local administrative centres that deferred to Damascus. Syria was the dominant Arab actor in Bilad al-Sham, and drew its allegiance from the indigenous Arab population. The assault of the Arab armies on Damascus in 1918, and their effort to liberate it from Turkey, remains a testament to the parental status of Damascus.[116]

The secret Sykes–Picot agreement of 1916 and the postwar San Remo Conference of 1920, however, undermined Syria as a regional centre of power. The dismemberment of Bilad al-Sham, referred to in Chapter 3, has left an indelible imprint on the domestic and foreign policies of Syria. The creation of the modern states of Lebanon, Syria (under French mandate), Palestine, Iraq and Transjordan (under British mandate) after World War I, led to the diminution of Syria's power at the centre of the region.

This period in history, from 1920 to the present, fostered a revisionist agenda for the restoration of Bilad al-Sham by the more radical nationalists belonging to the Ba'th party and the Syrian Socialist National Party (SSNP).[117] The ideology and the ambitions of the Ba'th party and the SSNP, however, were incompatible. Whereas the Ba'thists believed that the recreation of Bilad al-Sham was a staging post to achieving comprehensive Arab unity, the SSNP was less ambitious with its intention of rebuilding Greater Syria.[118]

Modern Lebanon was carved from Syria and the two states share a cultural, linguistic, and political heritage. The extraction of Lebanon from Syria has left a psychological scar on the Syrian political landscape. Lebanon was part of the jigsaw puzzle, and according to Arab nationalists, its adherence to Bilad al-Sham would have guaranteed Lebanon's Arab character and restored Syria's regional prominence. Hence, Syrian politicians have viewed Lebanon with a covetous eye over the years.

With this common history, it might present itself as an attractive option to reunite these two independent states under the dominant supervision of Syria; indeed, it has been suggested that Syria's ambitions, under 'Alawi rule, have included the annexation of Lebanon.[119] The complex realities of the Lebanese political system, in which seventeen confessions compete, however, make the prospect of unity or annexation unlikely. In addition, the global and regional powers would prevent such a move. One only has to observe Syria's dependence upon receiving the *green light* from the US before intervening in Lebanon during the civil war to realise the limitations placed on Syria by these powers.[120]

Asad's foreign policy has been partially motivated by the historical connection between Syria and Lebanon. He has frequently stressed the historic indivisibility of the two countries. He once commented: "the Syrians and Lebanese are one people. What binds us is stronger than any treaty. Syria is concerned with defending Lebanon and Lebanon is concerned with defending Syria, whether this is written on paper or not."[121] The notion of defence appears to have taken priority in the definition of their relationship.

Security
The issue of security has been the most dynamic aspect of the relationship between Syria and Lebanon. As implied earlier, security has been a priority of Syrian foreign policy since 1970 and has dominated the formulation and implementation of that policy. Immersed in a regional contest with Israel, that has its roots in the imperial policy of the British, Syria's main preoccupation has been securing its borders.

The rise of Asad to power in 1970 and the advent of the Lebanese civil war in 1975 have joined the two states in a complex symbiotic relationship. The introduction of realism into Syrian foreign policy in 1970 has placed the Syrian–Lebanese relationship in a context of power politics, where Lebanon has been used to serve the security interests of Syria.[122] As part of the equation, Syria has provided stability, through the use of force, for the weak state. One should not be under the impression that this status quo has been arrived at by mutual consent, however.

Moreover, the political, confessional, cultural, and demographic contortions of the Lebanese civil war challenged the fabric of the Syrian–Lebanese relationship.[123] Asad colluded with all of the main Lebanese actors of the war, and subsequently dissolved his alliance with each. The Syrian president has been consistent in trying to forge a durable alliance to protect Syria's security, but the efficacy of each client has waxed and waned according to local conditions and the intervention of the US and other regional actors.

The weak state within Lebanon, together with the volatile nature of its multifarious confessional composition, was acutely sensitive to any demographic change. The political balance of the confessions was institutionalised in the National Charter of 1943 but this form of co-associational democracy was not designed to accommodate the demographic change that was taking place in Lebanon. The political structure was particularly susceptible to the influx of members of the Palestinian resistance movement after Black September in 1970.[124]

Amidst these fluctuations in the composition of the population, Syria sought to balance the interests of each party in order to extend its hegemony over Lebanon, whose stability was of paramount importance to Syrian security. To provide security, Syria found it necessary to ensure that:

(a) The confessional balance that governed the state was maintained;
(b) The Palestinians did not radicalise Lebanon and invite an Israeli invasion;
(c) The Christian community did not create an alliance with the Israelis;
(d) Lebanon did not disintegrate into numerous statelets, inviting Israel and Iraq to foster client states adjacent to Syria's borders.[125]

The history and the structure of the political system in Lebanon made it a tinder-box that was waiting to be lit. The influx of the Palestinians after 1970 became the match that ignited the Lebanese civil war, and enflamed the hostilities between the different communities. The Palestinians tipped the balance of forces between the Christians and Muslims, fuelling the emergent animosity. Syria was unable to preserve the status quo, and chose to adopt an interventionist policy. Far preferable for Syria to a radicalised Lebanon was a situation in which it could play the role of balancer between two rival alliances, Christian rightist forces, and the Palestinian and Muslim leftist forces. Hence, Syria would be able to exercise hegemony in Lebanon.[126]

With its weak state structure, amorphous demography, and contiguous borders with Syria and Israel, Lebanon became the foremost of Syria's security concerns. In their perennial conflict with Israel, Syrian decision-makers have tended to consider the mountains of southern Lebanon as natural defensive frontiers that could be utilised to stop, or at least crucially delay, an Israeli middle thrust should a war suddenly occur.[127] Israel's military advance into Syria could take two possible routes: through the Golan Heights, and/or through Lebanon's Beqa' valley. The pincer movement would encircle the Syrian capital, thus threatening the very heart of the Syrian state. The security threat has been unquestionably the dominant ingredient in Syria's foreign policy calculations.[128] Consequently, Lebanon's security became concomitant with Syria's security.

For Syria, the Lebanese civil war offered a mixture of opportunities and risks.[129] The opportunity for Syria was the chance to extend its hegemony over Lebanon, and to secure its eastern borders. Lebanon would fall under Syria's sphere of influence enhancing its power in the regional contest with Israel. Lebanon, as the microcosm of the region, also offered Syria the opportunity to contain the PLO, the Leftist National Movement (LNM), the growing disaffected Shi'a population in the south, and the Lebanese Forces (LF).[130] The risks, however, far outweighed the advantages to be gained. The schizophrenic nature of Lebanon's foreign policy, and its split allegiance between the West and the Arab world, polarised the Lebanese arena. Successfully balancing of the forces among Lebanon's confessions was destined to be a tempestuous affair, as the Muslims looked towards the Arab fold for support, and the Christians looked favourably towards the Israelis.[131]

The civil war

At the outset of the civil war, Israel issued the Syrians a warning not to intervene beyond the agreed red-line. Asad remained committed to this agreement, as it would have been untimely to enter a conflict with Israel as the balance of power was firmly in favour of the Israelis.[132]

During the course of the Lebanese civil war, Syria was at times pitted against the Palestinian–Leftist alliance and at times against the Christian–Rightist forces. It was engaged in an indirect conflict with Israel and the US at different stages of the war. It entered a quagmire, which left it regionally isolated and increasingly dependent upon the support of its patron, the Soviet Union.

Syria entrenched its position in Lebanon as a matter of necessity to secure the Beqa' valley against Israeli incursion, and preserve its regional and international prestige. There is no space here to give details of the Lebanese civil war.[133] The most significant point for this study is the motivation behind Syria's intervention policy in Lebanon, and the flexibility with which it was pursued. Syria's intervention was fraught and tortuous; it appeared, on first inspection, to be governed by irrational impulses. Its first military engagement was conducted in accordance with the red-line agreement brokered by the US, satisfying both Israeli and US interests.[134] Syria unleashed its forces against the Palestinian–Leftist alliance, on 31 May 1976, in order to break its emerging dominance in the politico-military balance with the Christian alliance.[135]

This action was difficult to justify to its domestic constituency, particularly as Arab nationalism was the state's main source of legitimacy, and the Palestinians remained symbolic of the Arab cause. Syria's pro-Christian tendency in Lebanon also enflamed the Sunni population in Syria, and the regime was accused of pursuing a sectarian policy; the prospect of an 'Alawi–Christian alliance tainted the regime's Arab credentials.[136]

The intervention in Lebanon produced a number of political dividends in the early stages of the civil war. During the Riyadh Conference of October 1976, Syria again received the green light to continue its policy in Lebanon; furthermore, it received a financial endorsement from the Arab League to pursue its balanced policy. The 30,000-strong Arab peace-keeping force was predominantly composed of Syrian soldiers, and financed by the Gulf Arab sheikhdoms.[137]

A change in the political orientation of the regime took place after the Israeli invasion of Lebanon in 1978. The switch in policy was activated by Syria's growing impatience with the delaying tactics of the Christian Maronite rightists and their attempts to thwart any political solutions offered or imposed by Syria. Syrian bombardments of East Beirut in July 1978, in which 350 civilians were killed, was an indication of a more aggressive and intrusive policy in Lebanon.[138]

The number of troops in Lebanon rose from the regular level of 28,000, approved by the Arab League, to 40,000–50,000, indicating Syria's broader strategy for containing the conflict.[139] Naturally, US and Israeli interests were at stake through Syria's pervasive intervention in Lebanon. As Syria began to lose international support for its Lebanon policy, Israel colluded with the Lebanese rightists to cement their interests in Lebanon.[140]

Although the Maronites could not hope to re-establish their supremacy in the whole of Lebanon, some of them seemed determined to fall back on the notion of a smaller Christian Lebanon.[141] Thus, the Maronites overtly aligned with Israel, thereby forming a stubborn obstacle to the reconstruction of a united Lebanon whilst posing a serious threat to Syrian security. By this stage, Israel, assuming the role of protector of the Christians, had, as much as Syria, become the arbiter of Lebanon.[142] Syria's nightmare looked like tipping the balance of power in Lebanon back in Israel's favour. Consequently, Syria was compelled to return to its traditional allies, and to offer them limited protection against the imperial policies of Israel.

Syria's intervention in Lebanon enabled the Syrian regime to exercise some control over the Palestinian resistance movement. The Palestinians became a useful pawn in the game of international diplomacy; the Syrians, through their increasing military role in Lebanon, could enhance or constrain the activities of the Palestinians. The imposition of a cease-fire on 22 January 1976 acted as a restraining order on the Palestinian resistance fighters, and Asad encouraged the Palestinians to conform with an iron fist.[143]

The Palestinians

The Palestinians were problematic for the Syrians. Their cause was the main source of legitimacy for the Syrian regime and they were strategic allies in the struggle with Israel, but they were also a formidable force that threatened the security of Syria through their presence and opportunistic operations in Lebanon. To serve the Syrian interests, and what Asad considered to be the broader Arab interest, the Palestinians needed to be ordered and disciplined according to Syria's criteria.

Asad's strategy to forge a common Arab position was not shared by Yasser Arafat and his followers. Their different visions of how to liberate Palestine, and their conflictual *national* interests, prevented the pro-Fatah groups of the PLO and the Syrians from maintaining a consistent unified policy. Asad wished to discipline the resistance fighters of the PLO, and incorporate them into a projected balance-of-power formula. Such a formula would enhance Syria's security by restraining the Palestinians' impetuous modes of resistance. Asad's Levant Security Doctrine incorporated the Palestinian movement as an integral element of Syria's regional strategy. For Arafat, the solution to the Palestinian question belonged exclusively to the Palestinians.[144]

After the Palestinian resistance movement had been expelled from Jordan in 1970, it reassembled in Lebanon. Its activities were initially governed by the terms of the Cairo Accords of 1969, in an attempt to avoid alienating its host country.[145] The activities of the PLO under the leadership of Arafat were not constrained by the Cairo Accords for long, however. The fomentation of a state within a state was starting to take place as the PLO infrastructure was transferred from Jordan to Lebanon.

Not only did the PLO's military operations invite Israeli retaliation, but its presence also created a distinct imbalance in the composition of Lebanon's confessional mixture.[146]

In Lebanon, the PLO, as an umbrella organisation, was unable to conceal the tensions among its factions. All were united in their aim to liberate Palestine or the occupied territories, but there was a significant disagreement on how to liberate their homeland. The main contenders of the time were:

Fatah, led by Arafat;

The Popular Front for the Liberation of Palestine (PFLP), led by George Habash;

The Popular Democratic Front for the Liberation of Palestine (PDFLP), led by Nayif Hawatmeh;

The Popular Front for the Liberation of Palestine – General Command (PFLP-GC), led by Ahmed Jibril;

Sa'iqa and the Palestine Liberation Army (PLA) which owed their loyalty to the Syrian Ba'th party.

Arafat's Fatah was the most dominant faction in the PLO, and was often able to persuade its partners, the PFLP and PDFLP, to support its motions in the Palestine National Council (PNC). Fatah was the faction least ideologically opposed to the existence of the state of Israel. It was more willing to negotiate a final agreement with the Israelis based on a two-state solution.[147] The motivations of Saiqa and the PLA were less obvious than those of Fatah as they were guided by Syrian national interests.[148]

One can perceive from the factional structure of the PLO that it has been accessible to external forces. This has helped to produce a disparate organisation which has often lacked a coordinated policy. Consequently, the lack of consensus has invoked a series of internecine struggles among its factions occasionally fuelled by external powers. This was the case in Lebanon when the PLO temporarily disintegrated into its constituent parts.[149]

In May 1983, because of Arafat's decision to explore the possibilities of the Reagan Plan, a deep division within the ranks of Fatah occurred. The Abu Musa group, a rejectionist component within Fatah, rejected the adoption of the provisional political programme of 1974, where reconciliation, recognition, and negotiation were welcomed. Arafat's autocratic rule also caused consternation among his followers. The decision to engage in the Reagan Plan, despite the PLO Central Committee's rejection of the Plan, exemplified the multidirectional forces within the PLO.[150]

Asad lent military support to the anti-Arafat groups and helped to oust the Arafat loyalists from the Beqa' valley towards Tripoli.[151] In November 1983, the Syrian-backed insurrection against Arafat began. Numerous battles took place in the refugee camps of Nahr al-Bared and Badawi, where Abu Jihad took command of the loyalist soldiers. Open rebellion against Arafat was backed by the PFLP and the PDFLP, as well as by its main protagonists, Abu Musa, PFLP-GC and Sa'iqa.[152] The internecine struggle among the Palestinians added another surreal dimension to the Lebanese civil war; Asad waited to reorder the emasculated Palestinian resistance movement under the auspices of the Damascus regime.

> The PLO, Asad declared, no longer spoke for the Palestinian cause; henceforth, Syria would lead the struggle. Nevertheless, Asad was not prepared to support the resumption of armed struggle by Palestinian radicals, which might have made their strategy a credible alternative to Arafat's diplomacy.[153]

Asad's policies, however, proved to be short-sighted as his intervention in the fratricidal fight raised Palestinian consciousness, and provided a reinvigorated mandate for Arafat and his loyalists. The PDFLP and PFLP returned to the moderate PLO fold and turned against Syria. Two days after leaving Tripoli, Arafat scored a diplomatic victory against his Syrian adversary by meeting President Hosni Mubarak of Egypt. It was the first meeting between the Palestinian leader and an Egyptian president since the signing of the Camp David Accords and was designed to circumvent Syria's role in the Middle East peace process.[154]

Syria claimed a kind of protectorate over the PLO; but in 1982 it failed to fulfil the responsibilities incumbent on this self-assumed role, as the Palestinian resistance movement was expelled from Lebanon.[155] Whilst the immediate object of Israel's invasion of Lebanon was to uproot the PLO from the Lebanese arena, its grander objective was to humble Syria militarily, and dislodge Lebanon from Syria's sphere of influence.[156] The Lebanon–Israel agreement made some headway in diminishing Syria's influence in Lebanon.

The Lebanese–Israeli agreement

Israel's invasion of Lebanon in 1982 was comprehensive as it consumed the small Levantine state and its capital within days. The Syrians suffered a humiliating defeat as their air force was no match for the Israeli air force, and the Israelis destroyed Syria's air-defence systems. Iran's offer of active support contrasted sharply with the virtual immobility of the rest of the Arab world and the Soviet Union.[157]

Because of the imbalance of power between Syria and Israel, Syria was unable to confront the Israelis directly, and so began a game of spoils. As Syrian influence waned, Syria's forces entrenched themselves in and around the Beqaʻ valley. Syria and Iran fuelled the activities of their proxies, Amal and the new resilient force that became Hizbollah; they began a campaign of liberation based upon martyrdom and hostage-taking.[158]

In the wake of the 1982 Israeli invasion of Lebanon, Israel installed a regime friendly to its cause. Bashir Gemayel, the leader of the Phalange, was the ideal candidate for the presidency, but his assassination forced the Israelis to deal with his brother, Amin Gemayel.[159] The Lebanese–Israeli agreement, which constituted a separate peace treaty, was signed by Amin Gemayel. The terms of the treaty opened Lebanon to an exchange of diplomats, military influence, and goods with Israel which maintained the right to extend and legitimise the role of Haddad's army in the south. The Arab character of Lebanon was to be effaced with Israel providing the initiative for foreign policy, which stipulated the withdrawal of all Arab forces from Lebanese soil. As part of the agreement, Israel's withdrawal from Lebanese territory was made contingent upon the evacuation of Syrian forces.[160]

Syria was confronted by a triumphant Israel. Egypt had signed the Camp David Accords; an Israel-friendly regime had been installed in Lebanon; Jordan and Saudi Arabia were accommodating to the Reagan Plan; and Iraq was engaged in a war deflecting its attention away from the Arab–Israeli conflict. Syria's regional position was weakened and capitulation appeared to be a prospect.

Syria naturally rejected the Lebanese–Israeli agreement and strove to disrupt it. To counter the terms of the treaty, Asad set about constructing a rejectionist front from the alienated parties within Lebanon. A coalition of forces was established around the resentments caused by the exclusive deal between the Maronites and Israel. The National Salvation Front (NSF) was formed after the promulgation of the treaty on 17 May 1983.

A coalition of Lebanese Shiʻa, Druze, and Palestinian forces joined under the leadership of Syria with the intention of destroying the imposition of the Lebanese–Israeli agreement.[161]

An intense period of resistance commenced with the US and the Israeli military experiencing high fatalities from suicide bombers. US support of the Lebanese–Israeli agreement was punished, on 23 October 1983, when 236 US marines died in a suicide bombing mission. Although Syria was not directly implicated in the attack, its alliance with the pro-Iranian Shiʻa group Amal did not go unnoticed. The Syrian–Iranian connection, perpetuated through the role of Hizbollah and Amal, fomented an alternative bargaining chip for Syria.[162]

The US did not leave Lebanon without a show of force off the Lebanese coast. This consisted of three aircraft-carriers, 40 ships, 300 aircraft, and 2,000 marines.[163] The subsequent withdrawal of the US marines, and the partial withdrawal of the Israeli forces, created a vacuum which the Druze and Muslim militias filled. They defeated the isolated Phalangists in the Shouf mountains and West Beirut.[164] The strained Gemayel government could no longer withstand the unified resistance to the Lebanese-Israeli agreement, and so annulled it in February 1984.[165] Through a policy of coalition-building, military entrenchment, and an extension of Soviet–Syrian ties, Asad successfully unravelled the agreement brokered by the US between Israel and Lebanon.[166]

The Taʾif Agreement

Syria thus prevented another Arab state from concluding a durable peace treaty with Israel. From this perspective, the Levant Security Doctrine was successful. Throughout the late 1980s, Syria was able to extend its military presence in Lebanon, as the casualties sustained by the Israelis, inflicted by the martyrs of Hizbollah, forced the Israeli Defense Forces (IDF) to retreat to their self-imposed security in south Lebanon. Syria's hegemony in Lebanon was organized in the terms of the Taʾif Agreement, which eventually delivered Lebanon from the civil war in September 1989.

According to the Taʾif Agreement, an agreement underwritten by Saudi Arabia, Algeria, and Morocco, the special nature of the Lebanese–Syrian relationship recognised that future coordination and cooperation between the two states would be determined by bilateral agreements in all domains. These domains were to include foreign policy, security and military affairs, economic relations, educational affairs and information.[167] Indeed, Syrian–Lebanese security coordination was formalised in a mutual Defence Pact in 1991. This pact made provision for the continued deployment of Syrian troops in Lebanon. They were held accountable to the Syrian state and enjoyed a large degree of autonomy from the Lebanese authorities.[168]

Although the Israelis have maintained their military presence in southern Lebanon, and still influence the policies of their Christian proxy, the South Lebanese Army, Syria has managed to extend its sphere of influence throughout the remainder of Lebanon. Its hegemony is enshrined in the Ta'if Agreement despite the commitment to troop redeployment contained in chapter 4 of the agreement. With some irony, Syria's domination over Lebanese affairs was facilitated by Iraq's invasion of Kuwait. Syria received yet another green light from the US to crush the 'Aoun rebellion in reward for its participation in the Gulf War coalition.[169]

Conclusion

In Chapter 4, I have attempted to illustrate that the international political system has been the ascendant variable in determining Syria's foreign policy. Its foreign policy has been consistent since Asad came to power in 1970 and injected a dose of realism into the decision-making process. If one examines this process, one can identify a consistency of objectives which derive from national security and the national interest. A tribute to its consistency can be found in the three strategies that have been utilised by the state since 1970, which engaged Israel in the regional contest for hegemony.

Prior to 1979, Syria participated in the two-front strategy with Egypt. This was designed to strengthen the diplomatic position of the Arab states in their postwar negotiations with the Israelis. The strategy was based on achieving the balance of power between Egypt and Syria, on the one hand, and Israel on the other. But the conclusion of the Camp David Accords in 1979 pushed Syria towards a new strategy.

The doctrine of strategic parity encouraged Syria to pursue a bilateral balance of power with Israel.[170] The source of Syria's power, however, was not indigenous as it was dependent upon the strategic support of the Soviet Union. The transformation of Soviet foreign policy from 1985 onwards, and the dissolution of the Soviet Union in 1991, left Syria without a patron.

The transition in global affairs at the end of the 1980s rendered Syria's search for strategic parity redundant, and increased its regional and international vulnerability. Nevertheless, Syria remained constant in its objectives, and endeavoured to find a new strategy. In order to understand the determinants of Syria's foreign policy, I have referred to two explanatory models of analysis.

The rational actor and the domestic politics models offer us two possible alternatives for explaining state behaviour. The rational actor model, noted by Allison, is a useful model for examining the decision-making process within states. It enables us to examine the structural determinants that affect a state's decision-making process, but it is unable to account for the behaviour of Third World states. Belonging to the paradigm of realism, the rational actor model bases its assumptions upon the unitary character of states. Many states of the Third World, however, have yet to consolidate their status, and are open to the protracted domestic struggle for power.

The domestic politics model may be more suitable for analysing the behaviour of Third World states. Instead of attributing state behaviour to the international political system, it ascribes the formulation of foreign policy to the interplay of domestic forces. In this case, foreign policy becomes an outward expression of domestic politics. The inability of many Third World states to achieve a unitary status, and to resist the continual intervention of the military, gives this model of inquiry credence. However, this particular model is not apposite to the Syrian case, where the state has managed to elevate itself above the dominant social forces in society. Omnibalancing, with its emphasis on the link between the international political system and domestic politics, appears to be the most applicable explanation for Syrian foreign policy.

The international political system has been the primary determinant in the formulation of Syrian foreign policy. The anarchy of the international political system has compelled the Syrian state to protect its national security, especially in the hostile environment of the Middle Eastern state-system. Syria's foreign policy, motivated by the national interest and national security, has manifested itself in the struggle for regional hegemony with Israel.

One arena of Syrian–Israeli contest has been Lebanon. Both states have competed to incorporate Lebanon into their spheres of influence.[171] For Syria, Lebanon's strategic value is paramount, and their shared history symbolises the destiny of both states. Syria's tenacity in Lebanon, notwithstanding Israel's invasions and US intervention, demonstrated its value to Syria. In the regional balance of power, Lebanon constituted a critical piece in Syria's game plan.

The balance of power has determined Syria's pursuit of regional hegemony. Syria has tried to achieve this balance by employing the different strategies described above. The end of the bipolar era dictated a search for a new strategy. In the ensuing reconfiguration of global power, Syria tried to anchor a new strategy to the epicentre of the New World Order. In other words, Syria's adjustment to the New World Order presaged a propitious move towards the US.

NOTES

1 D. Pipes, *Greater Syria: The History of an Ambition* (Oxford: Oxford University Press, 1990).
2 F. Lawson, *Why Syria Goes to War? Thirty Years of Confrontation* (London: Cornell University Press, 1996).
3 C. Clapham, *Third World Politics: An Introduction* (London: Croom Helm, 1985), pp. 40–1.
4 P. Calvert, *The Foreign Policy of New States* (Sussex: Wheatsheaf, 1986).
5 R. Goode, "State Building as a Determinant of Foreign Policy in the New States" in L. Martin (ed.), *Neutralism and Non-Alignment* (New York: Praeger, 1962).
6 P. Calvert, *The Foreign Policy of New States* (Sussex: Wheatsheaf, 1986).
7 D. Pipes, *Greater Syria: The History of an Ambition* (Oxford: Oxford University Press, 1990), p. 175.
8 Ibid., pp. 184–5.
9 J. Bill and R. Springborg, *Politics in the Middle East* (New York: HarperCollins, 1994), pp. 98–105.
10 F. Lawson, *Why Syria Goes to War? Thirty Years of Confrontation* (London: Cornell University Press, 1996).
11 Ibid., pp. 179–81.
12 L. Brand, "Economics and Shifting Alliances: Jordan's Relations with Syria and Iraq, 1975–81", *International Journal of Middle East Studies*, vol. 26 (1994), pp. 393–413.
13 See M. Sarkees and S. Zunes, "Disenchantment with the 'New World Order': Syria's Relations with the United States", *International Journal of Middle Eastern Studies*, vol. XLIX, no. 2 (April 1994), p. 361.

14 Ibid.
15 D. Hopwood, *Syria 1945–1986: Politics and Society* (London: Unwin Hyman, 1988), pp. 60–72.
16 R. Burrows and B. Spector, "The Strength and Direction of Relationships between Domestic and External Conflict and Cooperation" in J. Wilkenfield (ed.), *Conflict Behaviour and Linkage Politics* (New York: David McKay, 1973), pp. 294–321.
17 Y. Evron, *War and Intervention in Lebanon: The Syrian–Israeli Deterrence Dialogue* (Baltimore: Johns Hopkins University, 1987).
18 G. Allison, *Essence of Decision: Explaining the Cuban Missile Crisis* (Boston: Little, Brown, 1971), pp. 4–5.
19 K. Waltz, *Theory of International Relations* (Reading, Mass.: Addison-Wesley, 1979).
20 G. Allison, *Essence of Decision: Explaining the Cuban Missile Crisis* (Boston: Little, Brown, 1971), p. 10.
21 H. Morgenthau, *Politics Among Nations: The Struggle for Power and Peace* (New York: Knopf, 1968), p. 5.
22 P. McGowan and H. Shapiro, *The Comparative Study of Foreign Policy: A Survey of Scientific Findings* (London: Sage, 1973), pp. 75–124.
23 A. Yaniv, "Alliance Politics in the Middle East" in A. Braun (ed.), *The Middle East in Global Strategy* (London: Westview Press, 1987), pp. 133–52.
24 See R. Hinnebusch, "Does Syria Want Peace? Syrian Policy in the Syrian–Israeli Peace Negotiations", *Journal of Palestine Studies*, vol. XXVI, no. 1 (Autumn, 1996), pp. 44–6.
25 S. David, "Explaining Third World Alignment", *World Politics*, vol. 43, no. 2 (January 1991), pp. 235–7.
26 P. Seale, *The Struggle for Syria: A Study of Post-War Arab Politics, 1945–1958* (London: Oxford University Press, 1965), p. 46.
27 For more details of this protracted struggle see P. Seale, *The Struggle for Syria: A Study of Post-War Arab Politics, 1945-1958* (London: Oxford University Press, 1965).
28 B. Saunders, *The United States and Arab Nationalism: The Syrian Case, 1953–1960* (London: Praeger, 1996), p. 15.
29 A. Rathmell, *Secret War in the Middle East: The Covert Struggle for Syria, 1949–1961* (London: I.B. Tauris, 1995), pp. 36–7.
30 Ibid. Chapters 3, 4 and 5.
31 A. Drysdale and R. Hinnebusch, *Syria and the Middle East Peace Process* (New York: Council on Foreign Relations, 1991), p. 54.
32 M. Ma'oz, *Syria and Israel: From War to Peace-making* (Oxford: Clarendon Press, 1995), p. 104.
33 Syria's *détente* with Iraq, after Egypt's defection, was short-lived because of the rivalry between the two states. Motivated by geopolitics and the need to balance Iraq's power, Syria entered into an alliance with Iran.
34 A. Drysdale and R. Hinnebusch, *Syria and the Middle East Peace Process* (New York: Council on Foreign Relations, 1991), p. 57.
35 L. Brand, "Asad's Syria and the PLO: Coincidence or Conflict of Interests?", *Journal of South Asian and Middle Eastern Studies*, vol. XIV, no. 2 (Winter 1990), pp. 23–4.

36 M. Ma'oz, *Syria and Israel: From War to Peace-making* (Oxford: Clarendon Press, 1995), p. 273.

37 For a detailed account of the rivalry between Syria and Iraq see: E. Kienle, *Ba'th v. Ba'th: The Conflict between Syria and Iraq 1968–1989* (London: I.B. Tauris, 1990).

38 A. Drysdale and R. Hinnebusch, *Syria and the Middle East Peace Process* (New York: Council on Foreign Relations, 1991), p. 60.

39 For more details and discussion of UN Resolution 242, the Madrid Peace Conference, and the Oslo Accords see Chapter 7.

40 J. Lorenz, *Egypt and the Arabs: Foreign Policy and the Search for National Identity* (Boulder: Westview Press, 1990), p. 49.

41 M. Ma'oz, *Syria and Israel: From War to Peace-making* (Oxford: Clarendon Press, 1995), p. 187.

42 R. Hinnebusch, *Peasant and Bureaucracy in Ba'thist Syria: The Political Economy of Rural Development* (London: Westview Press, 1989), p. 24.

43 E. Karsh, *The Soviet Union and Syria: The Asad Years* (London: Routledge, 1988), pp. 5–8.

44 J. Lorenz, *Egypt and the Arabs: Foreign Policy and the Search for National Identity* (Boulder: Westview Press, 1990), p. 46.

45 These figures are calculated at constant 1981 dollars.

46 P. Ramet, *The Soviet–Syrian Relationship Since 1955: A Troubled Alliance* (Boulder: Westview Press, 1990), pp. 95–6.

47 E. Karsh, *The Soviet Union and Syria: The Asad Years* (London: Routledge, 1988), pp. 12–13, and A. Khalidi and H. Agha, "The Syrian Doctrine of Strategic Parity" in J. Kipper and H. Saunders (eds.), *The Middle East in Global Perspective* (Boulder: Westview Press, 1991), p. 196.

48 "The October War and its Aftermath", *Middle East Economic Digest Annual Review 1973*, vol. 17, no. 52, 28 December 1973, p. 1498.

49 P. Seale, *Asad of Syria: The Struggle for the Middle East* (London: I.B. Tauris, 1988), p. 195.

50 Ibid., p. 198.

51 Ibid., p. 208.

52 V. Israelyan, "The October 1973 War: Kissinger in Moscow", *Middle East Journal*, vol. 49, no. 2 (Spring 1995), p. 262.

53 H. Agha and A. Khalidi, *Syria and Iran: Rivalry and Cooperation* (London: Pinter, 1995), p. 45.

54 E. Kienle, *Ba'th v. Ba'th: The Conflict between Syria and Iraq, 1968–1989* (London: I.B. Tauris, 1990), pp. 149–51.

55 J. Goodarzi, "The Syrian–Iranian Axis: An Enduring Entente?", *Middle East International*, no. 522, 29 November 1996, p. 19, and A. Ehteshami and R. Hinnebusch, *Syria and Iran: Middle Powers in a Penetrated Regional System* (London: Routledge, 1997), pp. 112–15.

56 Interview with press secretary of the DFLP, Maher Hamdi, 10 October 1995.

57 Saddam Hussein's accusation that the High Command of Syria had played an instrumental role in an attempted *coup* against him exacerbated the personal rivalry between the two leaders.

58 I. Rabinovich, "The Foreign Policy of Syria: Goals, Capabilities, Constraints and Options" in C. Tripp (ed.), *Regional Security in the Middle East* (New York, St Martin's Press, 1984), pp. 40–1.

59 A. Khalidi and H. Agha, "The Syrian Doctrine of Strategic Parity" in J. Kipper and H. Saunders (eds.), *The Middle East in Global Perspective* (Boulder: Westview Press, 1991), p. 186.

60 R. Freedman, "The Soviet Union and Syria: A Case Study of Soviet Policy" in M. Efrat and J. Bercovitch (eds.), *Superpowers and Client States in the Middle East: The Imbalance of Influence* (London: Routledge, 1991), p. 171.

61 Y. Sayigh, "The Middle East Strategic Balance: Capabilities for Waging War", *Middle East International*, no. 378, 22 June 1990, pp. 15–16.

62 A. Khalidi and H. Agha, "The Syrian Doctrine of Strategic Parity" in J. Kipper and H. Saunders (eds.), *The Middle East in Global Perspective* (Boulder: Westview Press, 1991), p. 189.

63 A. Drysdale and R. Hinnebusch, *Syria and the Middle East Peace Process* (New York: Council on Foreign Relations, 1991), p. 141.

64 Ibid., p. 135.

65 Ibid., p. 141.

66 A. Ehteshami, "Defence and Security Policies of Syria in a Changing Regional Environment", *International Relations*, vol. XIII, no. 1 (April 1996), pp. 53–4.

67 A. Drysdale and R. Hinnebusch, *Syria and the Middle East Peace Process* (New York: Council on Foreign Relations, 1991), pp. 135–6.

68 P. Ramet, *The Soviet–Syrian Relationship Since 1955: A Troubled Alliance* (Boulder: Westview Press, 1990), pp. 263–7.

69 E. Karsh, *The Soviet Union and Syria: The Asad Years* (London: Routledge, 1988), pp. 52–3.

70 A. Khalidi and H. Agha, "The Syrian Doctrine of Strategic Parity" in J. Kipper and H. Saunders (eds.), *The Middle East in Global Perspective* (Boulder: Westview Press, 1991), p. 192.

71 A. Cordesman, "United States Power-projection Capabilities in the Gulf and South-West Asia: Changing Forces for a Changing World" in C. Davies (ed.), *Global Interests in the Arab Gulf* (Exeter: University of Exeter Press, 1992), p. 249.

72 A. Khalidi and H. Agha, "The Syrian Doctrine of Strategic Parity" in J. Kipper and H. Saunders (eds.), *The Middle East in Global Perspective* (Boulder: Westview Press, 1991), p. 193.

73 A. Ehteshami, "Defence and Security Policies of Syria in a Changing Regional Environment", *International Relations*, vol. XIII, no. 1 (April 1996), p. 54.

74 A. Khalidi and H. Agha, "The Syrian Doctrine of Strategic Parity" in J. Kipper and H. Saunders (eds.), *The Middle East in Global Perspective* (Boulder: Westview Press, 1991), p. 193.

75 A. Drysdale and R. Hinnebusch, *Syria and the Middle East Peace Process* (New York: Council on Foreign Relations, 1991), p. 140.

76 A. Ehteshami, "Defence and Security Policies of Syria in a Changing Regional Environment", *International Relations*, vol. XIII, no. 1 (April 1996), p. 54.

77 A. Khalidi and H. Agha, "The Syrian Doctrine of Strategic Parity" in J. Kipper and H. Saunders (eds.), *The Middle East in Global Perspective* (Boulder: Westview Press, 1991), p. 195.

78 A. Drysdale and R. Hinnebusch, *Syria and the Middle East Peace Process* (New York: Council on Foreign Relations, 1991), p. 137.

79 A. Khalidi and H. Agha, "The Syrian Doctrine of Strategic Parity" in J. Kipper and H. Saunders (eds.), *The Middle East in Global Perspective* (Boulder: Westview Press, 1991), p. 197.

80 Ibid.

81 A. Ehteshami, "Defence and Security Policies of Syria in a Changing Regional Environment", *International Relations*, vol. XIII, no. 1 (April 1996), p. 54.

82 A. Khalidi and H. Agha, "The Syrian Doctrine of Strategic Parity" in J. Kipper and H. Saunders (eds.), *The Middle East in Global Perspective* (Boulder: Westview Press, 1991), p. 200.

83 N. Chomsky, *The Fateful Triangle: The United States, Israel & the Palestinians* (Boston: South End Press), pp. 13–17.

84 S. Dallal, "The Zionist Bureaucracy in the US Government", *Middle East International*, no. 381, 3 August 1990, pp. 16–17. Because of the limitation of space, it is not possible to develop this idea here, but the following readings are recommended: C. Rubenburg, *Israel and the American National Interest* (Urbana: University of Illinois Press, 1986); S. Tillman, *The United States in the Middle East* (Bloomington: Indiana University Press, 1982); M. Kerr, *America's Middle East Policy: Kissinger, Carter and the Future* (Beirut: Institute for Palestine Studies, 1980), and R. Curtiss *Stealth PACs: How the Israeli–American Lobby Took Control of US Middle East Policy*, (Washington: American Educational Trust, 1990).

85 D. Neff, "The Bruising Battle between Bush and Shamir", *Middle East International*, no. 404, 13 September 1991, pp. 3–4.

86 J. Bercovitch, "Superpowers and Client States: Analysing Relations and Patterns of Influence" in M. Efrat and J. Bercovitch (eds.), *Superpowers and Client States in the Middle East: The Imbalance of Influence* (London: Routledge, 1991), pp. 22–3.

87 Syria's intervention in Lebanon went against Soviet advice. For more details of this episode see G. Golan, *The Soviet Union and the Palestine Liberation Organisation: An Uneasy Alliance* (New York: Praeger, 1980), p. 187. Furthermore Syria's support of the Abu Musa rebellion against Arafat's Fatah group contravened Soviet interests as two of its clients were engaged in military confrontation in 1983. See H. Cobban, *The Superpowers and the Syrian–Israeli Conflict: Beyond Crisis Management?* (London: Praeger, 1991), p. 234.

88 J. Bercovitch, "Introduction" in M. Efrat and J. Bercovitch (eds.), *Superpowers and Client States in the Middle East: The Imbalance of Influence* (London: Routledge, 1991), p. 12.

89 V. Yorke, *Domestic Politics and Regional Security: Jordan, Syria and Israel. The End of an Era?* (Aldershot: Gower, 1988), pp. 142–3.

90 M. Gorbachev, *Perestroika: New Thinking for Our Country and the World* (London: Fontana Press, 1987).

91 E. Karsh, *The Soviet Union and Syria: The Asad Years* (London: Routledge, 1988), pp. 46–7.

92 E. Shevardnadze, *The Future Belongs to Freedom* (London: Sinclair-Stevenson, 1991), p. 102.

93 M. Gorbachev, *Perestroika: New Thinking for Our Country and the World* (London: Fontana Press, 1987), p. 102.

94 E. Shevardnadze, *The Future Belongs to Freedom* (London: Sinclair-Stevenson, 1991), p. 108.
95 J. Hannah, *At Arms Length: Soviet–Syrian Relations in the Gorbachev Era* (Washington: Washington Institute for Near East Policy, 1989), p. 21.
96 M. Gorbachev, *Perestroika: New Thinking for Our Country and the World* (London: Fontana Press, 1987), p. 106.
97 J. Hannah, *At Arms Length: Soviet–Syrian Relations in the Gorbachev Era* (Washington: Washington Institute for Near East Policy, 1989), p. 21.
98 A. Rathmell, "Syria's Search for an 'Honourable Peace'", *Middle East International*, no. 480, 22 July 1994, pp. 16–17.
99 J. Hannah, *At Arms Length: Soviet–Syrian Relations in the Gorbachev Era* (Washington: Washington Institute for Near East Policy, 1989), p. 52.
100 G. Golan, *Moscow and the Middle East: New Thinking on Regional Conflict* (London: Pinter, 1992), p. 32.
101 Y. Sadowski, *Scuds or Butter?: The Political Economy of Arms Control in the Middle East* (Washington: Brookings Institute, 1993), p. 35.
102 Ibid., p. 37.
103 T. Shad, S. Boucher and J. Gray-Reddish, "Syrian Foreign Policy in the Post-Soviet Era", *Arab Studies Quarterly*, vol. 17, no. 1&2 (Winter/Spring 1995), p. 77.
104 Y. Sadowski, *Scuds or Butter?: The Political Economy of Arms Control in the Middle East* (Washington: Brookings Institute, 1993), p. 37.
105 J. Muir, "Why Asad Turned to Cairo?", *Middle East International*, no. 366, 5 January 1990, p. 3.
106 Ibid.
107 Y. Sadowski, *Scuds or Butter?: The Political Economy of Arms Control in the Middle East* (Washington: Brookings Institute, 1993), p. 33.
108 A. Rathmell, "Syria's Search for an 'Honourable Peace'", *Middle East International*, no. 480, 22 July 1994, pp. 16–17.
109 M. Ziarati, "The Regional Balance of Power in the Air", *Middle East International*, no. 463, 19 November 1993, p. 21.
110 I. Shahak, "Israel and Syria: Peace through Strategic Parity?", *Middle East International*, no. 490, 16 December 1994, pp. 18–19.
111 Y. Sadowski, *Scuds or Butter?: The Political Economy of Arms Control in the Middle East* (Washington: Brookings Institute, 1993), p. 35.
112 G. Jansen, "South Africa Caves In on Arms", *Middle East International*, no. 543, 7 February 1997, p. 11.
113 A. Ehteshami, "Defence and Security Policies of Syria in a Changing Regional Environment", *International Relations*, vol. XIII, no. 1 (April 1996), p. 64.
114 Y. Sayigh, "The Middle East Strategic Balance: Capabilities for Waging War", *Middle East International*, no. 378, 22 June 1990, pp. 15–16.
115 R. Hinnebusch, "Syrian Policy in Lebanon and the Palestinians", *Arab Studies Quarterly*, vol. 8, no. 1 (Winter 1986), p. 3.
116 T. Lawrence, *Seven Pillars of Wisdom: A Triumph* (London: Cape, 1990), p. 515.
117 L. Yamak, *The Syrian Social National Party: An Ideological Analysis* (Cambridge: Harvard University Press, 1966), pp. 76–88.
118 D. Pipes, *Greater Syria: The History of an Ambition* (Oxford: Oxford University Press, 1990), chapter 2.

119 Ibid., chapter 3.
120 I. Rabinovich, "The Changing Prism: Syrian Policy in Lebanon as a Mirror, an Issue and an Instrument" in M. Ma'oz and A. Yaniv (eds.), *Syria Under Asad: Domestic Constraints and Regional Risks* (London: Croom Helm, 1986), p. 182.
121 A. Dawisha, *Syria and the Lebanese Crisis* (London: Macmillan, 1980), p. 72.
122 F. Nasrallah, "Syria after Ta'if: Lebanon and the Lebanese in Syrian Politics" in E. Kienle (ed.), *Contemporary Syria: Liberalization between Cold War and Cold Peace* (London: British Academic Press, 1994), p. 134.
123 Ibid., pp. 134–5.
124 M. Ma'oz, *Syria and Israel: From War to Peace-making* (Oxford: Clarendon Press, 1995), p. 162.
125 H. Agha and A. Khalidi, *Syria and Iran: Rivalry and Cooperation* (London: Pinter, 1995), p. 14.
126 R. Hinnebusch, "Syrian Policy in Lebanon and the Palestinians", *Arab Studies Quarterly*, vol. 8, no. 1 (Winter 1986), p. 6.
127 A. Dawisha, *Syria and the Lebanese Crisis* (London: Macmillan, 1980), p. 58.
128 R. Hinnebusch, "Syrian Policy in Lebanon and the Palestinians", *Arab Studies Quarterly*, vol. 8, no. 1 (Winter 1986), p. 6.
129 I. Rabinovich, "The Foreign Policy of Syria: Goals, Capabilities, Constraints and Options" in C. Tripp (ed.), *Regional Security in the Middle East* (New York: St Martin's Press, 1984), p. 41.
130 M. Ma'oz, *Syria and Israel: From War to Peace-making* (Oxford: Clarendon Press, 1995), p. 135.
131 Ibid., pp. 163–71.
132 E. Chalala, "Syrian Policy in Lebanon, 1976–1984: Moderate Goals and Pragmatic Means", *Journal of Arab Affairs*, vol. 4, no. 1 (Spring 1985), p. 70.
133 There is an excellent account of the Lebanese civil war in R. Fisk, *Pity the Nation: Lebanon at War* (Oxford: Oxford University Press, 1991). Adeed Dawisha's *Syria and the Lebanese Crisis*, (London: Macmillan, 1980) provides an in-depth analysis of Syria's decision to intervene in Lebanon in 1976.
134 For more details of the red-line agreement see Z. Schiff, "Dealing with Syria", *Foreign Policy*, no. 55 (Summer 1984).
135 P. Seale, *Asad of Syria: The Struggle for the Middle East* (London: I.B. Tauris, 1988), p. 283.
136 H. Batatu, "Syria's Muslim Brethren", *Middle East Report* (*MERIP*), no. 110 (November/December 1982), p. 20.
137 *Syria – Country Profile*, (London: The Economist Intelligence Unit, January 1979), no. 1, p. 7.
138 M. Ma'oz, *Asad: The Sphinx of Damascus* (London: Weidenfeld and Nicolson, 1988), pp. 123–34.
139 *Syria – Country Profile*, (London: The Economist Intelligence Unit, July 1978), no. 3, p. 6.
140 Ibid.
141 I. Rabinovich, "The Changing Prism: Syrian Policy in Lebanon as a Mirror, an Issue and an Instrument" in M. Ma'oz and A. Yaniv (eds.), *Syria Under Asad: Domestic Constraints and Regional Risks* (London: Croom Helm, 1986), p. 181.
142 R. Hinnebusch, "Syrian Policy in Lebanon and the Palestinians", *Arab Studies Quarterly*, vol. 8, no. 1 (Winter 1986), p. 9.

143 *Syria – Country Profile*, (London: The Economist Intelligence Unit, April 1976), no. 2, p. 3.

144 Ibid., p. 6.

145 P. Seale, *Asad of Syria: The Struggle for the Middle East* (London: I.B. Tauris, 1988), p. 270.

146 H. Agha and A. Khalidi, *Syria and Iran: Rivalry and Cooperation* (London: Pinter, 1995), p. 17.

147 L. Brand, "Asad's Syria and the PLO: Coincidence or Conflict of Interests?", *Journal of South Asian and Middle Eastern Studies*, vol. XIV, no. 2 (Winter 1990), p. 23.

148 R. Hinnebusch, "Syrian Policy in Lebanon and the Palestinians", *Arab Studies Quarterly*, vol. 8, no. 1 (Winter 1986), p. 11.

149 Ibid., p. 13.

150 L. Brand, "Asad's Syria and the PLO: Coincidence or Conflict of Interests?", *Journal of South Asian and Middle Eastern Studies*, vol. XIV, no. 2 (Winter 1990), p. 25.

151 *Syria – Country Profile*, (London: The Economist Intelligence Unit, December 1983), no. 4, p. 11.

152 *Syria – Country Profile*, (London: The Economist Intelligence Unit, August 1983), no. 3, p. 9.

153 A. Drysdale and R. Hinnebusch, *Syria and the Middle East Peace Process* (New York: Council on Foreign Relations, 1991), p. 81.

154 *Syria – Country Profile*, (London: The Economist Intelligence Unit, March 1984), no. 2, p. 11.

155 R. Hinnebusch, "Syrian Policy in Lebanon and the Palestinians", *Arab Studies Quarterly*, vol. 8, no. 1 (Winter 1986), p. 11.

156 M. Ma'oz, *Syria and Israel: From War to Peace-making* (Oxford: Clarendon Press, 1995), pp. 173–4.

157 H. Agha and A. Khalidi, *Syria and Iran: Rivalry and Cooperation* (London: Pinter, 1995), p. 15.

158 A. Ehteshami and R. Hinnebusch, *Syria and Iran: Middle Powers in a Penetrated Regional System* (London: Routledge, 1997), pp. 127–9.

159 R. Fisk, *Pity the Nation: Lebanon at War* (Oxford: Oxford University Press, 1991), p. 353.

160 A. Drysdale and R. Hinnebusch, *Syria and the Middle East Peace Process* (New York: Council on Foreign Relations, 1991), p. 126.

161 A. Ehteshami and R. Hinnebusch, *Syria and Iran: Middle Powers in a Penetrated Regional System* (London: Routledge, 1997), pp. 120–2.

162 H. Agha and A. Khalidi, *Syria and Iran: Rivalry and Cooperation* (London: Pinter, 1995), p. 20.

163 *Syria – Country Profile*, (London: The Economist Intelligence Unit, December 1983), no. 4, p. 9.

164 Ibid.

165 M. Ma'oz, *Syria and Israel: From War to Peace-making* (Oxford: Clarendon Press, 1995), p. 178.

166 Ibid., p. 179.

167 A. Norton, "Lebanon after Ta'if: Is the Civil War Over?", *Middle East Journal*, vol. 45, no. 3 (Summer 1991), pp. 457–74.

168 F. Nasrallah, "The Treaty of Brotherhood, Co-operation and Co-ordination" in Y. Choueiri (ed.), *State and Society in Syria and Lebanon* (Exeter: Exeter University Press, 1993), p. 105.

169 F. Nasrallah, "Syria after Ta'if: Lebanon and the Lebanese in Syrian Politics" in E. Kienle (ed.), *Contemporary Syria: Liberalization between Cold War and Cold Peace* (London: British Academic Press, 1994), p. 135.

170 In seeking a balance of power with Israel, Syria and Israel fitted Morgenthau's pattern of direct opposition.

171 The case of Syrian and Israeli attempts to extend their hegemony over Lebanon is an illustration of Morgenthau's patterns of competition in attaining a balance of power. The Ta'if Agreement signifies another model of Morgenthau's patterns of competition, where Syria manages to assert its hegemony over Lebanon. It was able to do so due to the new conditions, brought about by the New World Order, shaping international relations.

5

Syria and the Gulf War:
Adjusting to the New World Order

Introduction

This chapter provides an illustration of how Syria has adjusted to the New World Order which represented a change in the configuration of global power, and precipitated a new international climate. It marked the end of the Cold War, and the emergence of a global order based on the succession of global capitalism underpinned by force.[1]

Despite the fact that some observers, such as Fukuyama, saw global capitalism as the conclusive working out of historical forces – as a triumph of democracy and liberalism over tyranny – the New World Order was little altered. Force, secured by the unipolar power, remained the defining feature of international relations. Irrespective of its multipolar features, global capitalism could only be guaranteed through the military force of the US and its allies.[2]

The ascent of US political power, within the new climate, challenged the status of the former client states of the Soviet Union. The future of those states, such as Libya, Cuba, Iraq, and Syria, started to look uncertain. Nevertheless, Syria has managed to adjust to the New World Order. The combination of the state's relative autonomy from domestic forces, and its unique geopolitical position, has allowed Syria to adjust without substantial difficulty. By omnibalancing the domestic and international interests of the state, Syria has altered its regional strategy.[3]

Omnibalancing has rewarded the state with a considerable degree of autonomy. In turn, this autonomy has enabled the state to pursue a rational foreign policy, determined primarily by systemic factors, whilst domestic constraints have assumed a subordinate role. The security of the Syrian state, and the national interest, were essentially responsible for shaping Syria's decision to join the US-led coalition forces in the second Gulf War.

The second Gulf War provides us with a paradigm case for understanding the nature of the New World Order, and Syria's relationship with its central powers. Remaining within the shadows of the old order, Syria needed an opportunity to display its commitment to change. The second Gulf War provided Syria with the ideal chance to demonstrate its new strategy and its adjustment to the New World Order. Syria made a strategic decision to realign its policy towards the US.

The consequent liberation of Kuwait and the qualified destruction of Iraq allowed the New World Order to show its teeth. As the leading force in the New World Order, the US mobilised a coalition of states to repel Iraq's invasion. The action of the coalition set a precedent for future challenges to the inviolability of the state-system, and those middle powers that sought to test the durability of the hegemonic power.[4]

The Gulf War

Iraq's invasion of Kuwait on 2 August 1990, set a double challenge to the US-led New World Order. Firstly, because of the oil-dependent structure of the global economy, and the strategic relevance of the Arab Gulf to that global economy, this invasion represented a threat to the global economic order.[5] Secondly, one of the founding principles of international relations enshrined in the UN Charter of 1945, the inviolability of state borders, was threatened by Iraq's dramatic action in the Gulf. The invasion of Kuwait challenged the very foundations of the international norms contained within the UN Charter.[6]

The US-led coalition launched the second Gulf War on 17 January 1991.[7] US impatience circumvented the success of the economic sanctions and the enforced embargo,[8] favoured by Russia and the European Union, against Iraq.[9] The US-led offensive, under the banner of the UN, supported by Western powers, Saudi Arabia, Egypt, Turkey, and Syria, sought to oust Iraq from Kuwait and showed the role of force in establishing the coordinates of the New World Order.[10]

Each coalition partner was motivated by differing needs. The international justification rested on the premise that Iraq had challenged the terms of the international state-system. For many of its critics, the US-led response was indicative of the relationship between the predominant economic system and the succession of US national interest.[11] The dependency of the global economy upon a cheap and regular flow of oil was sufficient to unite the US with its economic partners in its confrontation with Iraq. The participation of the Western powers can be attributed to their defence of the international political system and the stability of the capitalist economic order.[12]

Saudi Arabia's role is self-explanatory. The cause of Saudi insecurity, a feature of domestic politics, emanated from Iraq's immediate threat to the Saudi state.[13] This created a dependency on external powers. The Arab League failed to accommodate Saudi security needs whilst the US proved a vigorous ally.

Because of its economic ties with the US, and its need to reintegrate itself into the regional political and economic system, Egypt took part in this coalition.[14] Egypt's rehabilitation in the Arab world had been completed with the restoration of relations with Syria in 1989, and the Gulf War provided it with the chance to adopt a central role in the postwar era.[15]

As a member of NATO, Turkey's participation fulfilled the needs of its Western partners. Its inclusion in the Gulf War coalition allowed the secular leaders of the state to reaffirm their commitment to the West amidst the growing sense of West-versus-East schizophrenia engulfing the country. Furthermore, the change in the world order presented a possible threat to Turkey's utility to the US and Europe; therefore Turkey sought to assert its regional and international importance.

The response of Saudi Arabia, Egypt, and Turkey, to Iraq's invasion of Kuwait is understandable as they were allied to the US and Europe prior to the advent of the New World Order and the second Gulf War. Syria's participation, however, appears to have been at odds with its professed ideological and nationalist perspective. The Syrian decision to join the Gulf War alliance appeared to contradict both its domestic and international agendas.

Syria's entry into the Gulf War coalition

The Gulf War proved to be a portentous event for Syria, as it enabled the Syrian regime to realign its global allegiance towards the US. Its global vulnerability was rapidly increasing as the influence of the Soviet Union receded, and the vacuum was filled by the US. At a regional level, on one hand, Iraq was punishing Syria's presence in Lebanon by supporting 'Aoun's war of liberation.[16] On the other hand, the PLO had recognised the right of Israel to exist, thus jeopardising Syria's coordinating role in promoting comprehensive peace.[17]

Although Syria's entry into the Gulf War coalition appeared to contradict its Arab nationalist agenda, its participation can be accounted for by the following factors:

(a) The New World Order;
(b) The peace process;
(c) The postwar regional order;
(d) Iraq's challenge to Syria's hegemony;
(e) European sanctions;
(f) Syria's economic prospects.

The New World Order

The introduction of "new thinking" into Soviet foreign policy radically altered the coordinates of international relations. The bipolar division of the world that had provided some middle powers, such as Syria, with the opportunity to exploit the vulnerabilities of their patron states, disappeared almost overnight.[18]

Syria's strategy had been devised after the Camp David Accords. Its tactics were based on coordinating the policies of the Eastern bloc of Middle Eastern states, the Mashreq, and were designed to spoil any separate peace initiatives fostered by the US or Israel. The establishment of the Steadfastness Front in 1979 in opposition to the Camp David Accords indicated the beginning of the rejectionist period. Although the fortunes of the Steadfastness Front were determined more by inter-Arab struggles than by united action, Syria's obstructionist role prevented any further progress in the Middle East peace process.[19]

Syria's role in Lebanon was characteristic of its policy of tactical rejectionism. Its long-term resistance to Israeli and international intervention in Lebanon, its active role in the intra-fratricidal Palestinian struggle, and its alleged involvement in international terrorism, were all results of its opposition to Egypt's conclusion of a separate peace.[20] Syria's rejectionist policy was endorsed by the Soviet Union as the Camp David Accords had denied the Soviet Union critical access to the region.

The rise to power of President Andropov in the Soviet Union in 1983 provided Syria with the necessary military umbrella to engage in further obstructionist policies whilst attempting to achieve a balance of power with Israel.[21] Syria's quest for strategic parity, according to the Syrian regime, was the only viable option for attaining a sufficient bargaining position to enter a more equitable peace process.[22] The introduction of perestroika in 1985 and its consequences ended Syria's post-Camp David strategy. Syria's *rapprochement* with Egypt in 1989 signalled the end of tactical rejectionism, and the acceptance of US global hegemony. In response to the changes that had taken place in the Soviet Union in the late 1980s, Syria was forced to abandon its search for strategic parity.

The revolutions that swept through Eastern Europe during the latter stages of the 1980s served to remind the Syrian regime of its own dispensability. As the political leaders and political establishments of East Germany, Romania, and Czechoslovakia were swept aside, the realities of the global environment emerged.[23] Syria's fate appeared to be precarious and dependent upon the vagaries of US foreign policy. The dissolution of the Soviet–Syrian partnership exposed Syria's regional and international vulnerability; and until the advent of Iraq's invasion of Kuwait, Syria's future looked uncertain. The US punishment of Libya in 1986 for its alleged involvement in international terrorism suggested that the same fate might await Syria.

The decline of Soviet support forced Syria to re-examine its options. These were limited as the US prepared to punish Iraq for its aggression and challenge to the New World Order. Syria's motives for participating in the US-led coalition, therefore, can be partially explained by its recognition of the need to realign its global position. The reconfiguration of global power compelled Syria to reconsider its regional strategy. The search for regional hegemony was not abandoned but a new strategy was sought to achieve its ambitions. Syria's participation in the liberation of Kuwait enabled it to gain enough diplomatic and political capital to be propelled towards the centre of a proposed international peace process.[24]

Syria and the peace process

One of the principal benefits to Syria from its participation in the US-led offensive was the convening of an international conference based upon UN Resolution 242.[25] The US administration promised Syria the prospect of peace negotiations in exchange for Syria lending the coalition legitimacy. Syria was rewarded for providing invaluable cover with an acknowledgement of its indispensability to a peaceful solution to the Arab–Israeli conflict.

As a radical state, Syria lent the US-led offensive a degree of legitimacy, which was otherwise absent from the alliance. Syria's contribution to the US-led alliance was crucial in restraining the development of a counter-alliance among the remaining radical Arab states. Syria's admission to the Gulf War coalition provided a pretext for the US to act without necessarily invoking Arab nationalist sentiments. Moreover, Asad denounced Saddam Hussein's attacks on Israel, "Nobody can drag Syria into an imposed war . . . as Saddam is trying to do with his theatrical missiles fired at Israel. Not content with dragging Iraq into the furnace, its regime is trying to embroil the whole Arab world."[26]

Syria's inclusion enabled Asad to adjust, in an expedient fashion, to the changing demands of the New World Order. The days of tactical rejectionism were consigned to the past as Syria gravitated towards the only viable and available option to pursue its regional ambitions. Syria managed to transform a potential strategic problem into a distinct advantage; the price of Syria's cover in the liberation of Kuwait was the Madrid Peace Conference, a long-term choice for Asad. A peace process would not only provide a pretext for settling the Golan Heights issue, but would also allow Syria to jostle for a pre-eminent position in the postwar regional order.

Postwar regional order

During the years of tactical rejectionism, Syria had isolated itself from the mainstream Arab states. Its support of Iran during the eight-year Gulf War translated into its exclusion from both the economic and security orders of the region.[27] The formation of the Arab Cooperation Council (ACC), with Iraq as the centre of gravity, served as a threat to Syria's claim for the leadership of the Arab nation.[28] The conclusion of the Iran–Iraq War in 1988 enabled Iraq to divert its attention towards its western borders and the balance of power in the Levant. Syria's hegemony in Lebanon was diminishing because of Iraq's growing influence through its sponsorship of General 'Aoun.[29]

Syria's entry into the second Gulf War elevated its status in the region. It extracted itself from its regional isolation whilst improving its credibility with the Gulf Arab states. The Gulf Cooperation Council

(GCC) had failed to identify Iraq as the major threat to the Gulf states whereas Syria had maintained that Iran did not constitute the principal threat in the Gulf.[30] Iraq's invasion of Kuwait vindicated Syria's support of Iran and earned it considerable diplomatic credit. The war provided Syria with an opportunity to demonstrate its utility to the Gulf Arab states. The reward for Syria was the pronouncement of the Damascus Declaration, whereby the GCC states plus Egypt and Syria agreed the new formula for guaranteeing Arab Gulf security.[31] Syria's participation guaranteed it a key role in the postwar order, with the benefits of Gulf financial aid and Gulf–US diplomatic credit.

After existing outside the regional framework throughout the 1980s, Syria was able to reintegrate itself into the regional mainstream, gaining the confidence and support of the US-friendly regimes, that is, Saudi Arabia, Kuwait, and Egypt.[32] Syria's goal of remaining at the core of Arab politics was achieved with the Damascus Declaration and the universal acknowledgement of Syria's strategic interest in Lebanon.[33] Syria's participation was also accredited in Lebanon; the US gave the Syrians the green light to extend their hegemony and remove Iraq's Lebanese client, General 'Aoun, as the last bastion of resistance to Syrian hegemony (excluding the Israeli-occupied south).[34]

Iraq's challenge to Syria's hegemony

The signing of the Iran–Iraq Peace Accord in 1988 left Iraq with a highly militarised society and made it a powerful political opponent for Syria. In the regional balance of power, Syria was outweighed in terms of population, natural resources, economic strength, and the militarisation of society. Iraq's termination of the war with Iran enabled it to re-enter the contest for regional influence. Although it was not in Syria's, or the broader Arab, interest to see Iraq destroyed, it was an advantage to witness the diminution of the threat posed by Iraq.[35]

European sanctions

After the collapse of the East European states and the reorientation of Soviet foreign policy, Syria needed to diversify its network of international support if it wished to diminish its new state of vulnerability. On 24 October 1986, the UK had suspended diplomatic relations with Syria because of the Syrian involvement in the plot to place a bomb on an El Al flight to Tel Aviv departing from Heathrow Airport, London, on

17 April 1986.[36] In addition, the European Community (EC) imposed economic sanctions on Syria on 10 November 1986. It seemed almost certain that the Syrians were involved in the plot to blow up the Israeli airliner, but the question that evaded answers was how closely the president was involved.[37]

Syria's return to European favour was achieved after its decision to join the US-led coalition forces. One dividend for participating in the second Gulf War was the restoration of diplomatic relations with the UK, and the lifting of economic sanctions by the EC.[38] However, Syria was angered at an EC vote, on 22 October 1990, taken after an exertion of British pressure, to maintain a ban on arms sales to Syria and to limit the number of Syrian diplomats and officials in Europe.[39]

Despite sending 15,000 troops to Saudi Arabia as part of its contribution to the Gulf War, Syria was still considered, by the US, as a sponsor of state terrorism.[40] Whilst acknowledging the political and diplomatic significance of Syria's participation in justifying the allied liberation of Kuwait, the US did not regard it as sufficient to warrant Syria's removal from its terrorist state list. This dichotomy still characterises the European and US attitudes to diplomatic relations with Syria. Their differences in approach, however, did not diminish the economic benefits to Syria of the lifting of economic sanctions and the windfall from the Gulf Arab states.

Syria's economic prospects

The second Gulf War provided Syria with an opportunity to compensate for the loss of the economic support of the Soviet Union through the promotion of the Syrian–Egyptian–GCC security order. Syria and Egypt were both financial beneficiaries of the second Gulf War, and were rewarded for their allegiance to the Gulf Arab states. The rewards, however, were disproportionately in Egypt's favour, which prompted Syria temporarily to review its options and suspend the deployment of its troops in Saudia Arabia.[41]

Syria received $2,000 million for its role in the liberation of Kuwait from the governments of the Gulf Arab states alone. This capital was used mainly to upgrade the Syrian military.[42] The Egyptians, on the other hand, were granted a debt write-off of $14,400 million by the US.[43] The disparities in the distribution of financial rewards reflected the differences in the relationships of the two states with the US.

The signing of the Egypt–Israel peace treaty in 1979, underpinned by economic benefits, marked the new Egyptian strategy for the recovery of the Sinai peninsula. Egypt rejected the Soviet Union and competed with Israel for US influence.[44] This strategy had been successful in disengaging Egypt from the territorial conflict with Israel[45] and had, moreover, resulted in the return of Sinai, and the cultivation of US support. However, it had also produced an economic dependency upon the US.[46]

Syria's strategy during the Cold War had rested upon Soviet support but the radical change in the world order removed the main pillar of Syria's foreign policy strategy. Syria's options were clearly limited in a US-dominated world order. Saddam Hussein's dramatic move granted Syria an unexpected opportunity to work more closely with the US.[47] Joining the US-led Gulf War coalition afforded Syria the chance to adjust to the new international climate, and pursue policies still in line with its regional objectives, but less inimical to US interests in the Middle Eastern region.

Although the decision to realign its foreign policy and join the Gulf War coalition could be considered successful for the Syrian regime, it was a difficult task justifying this change in policy to the Syrian population. The Arab credentials of the regime, a major source of legitimacy, were put under threat by the decision to lend support to the US in a war against an Arab brother. At the time of decision-making, therefore, a number of obstacles emerged that could have persuaded the political elite to adopt a pro-Iraqi position.

The Gulf War: obstacles to Syrian participation

The above explanation for Syria's joining the Gulf War coalition was examined in the light of international conditions but did not reflect the domestic constraints placed upon Syria. The following section will illustrate how Asad, although reliant upon the regime barons and sensitive to public perceptions of the regime's Arab credentials, was able to pursue a policy that appeared to be inimical to domestic and regional interests. There were few domestic constraints upon the regime as far as regards influencing its options in joining the Gulf War coalition. The two potential sources of resistance could have emerged from public discontent and from the entrenched positions of the regime barons.[48] Before discussing these factors, we should address the issue of legitimacy to be able to understand the impact of public opinion and the regime barons upon the state's foreign policy.

Legitimacy

Within the Arab world, the concept of legitimacy has undergone an evolutionary transformation over the last twenty-five years. Arab nationalism seems to have lost its appeal to the Arab population, whilst the promise of economic security may have gained in credence. Arab nationalism, therefore, may be losing its significance as a legitimising tool. The provision of economic security may provide legitimacy to a more compliant public.[49]

The Syrian case, however, is still unique within the Arab world. Regime legitimacy in Syria is not a quantifiable commodity, and it is not really possible to gauge it because of the secret nature of the regime and society. It has been traditionally measured by the Arab credentials of the state. Arab nationalism is believed to be one of the keys to understanding state–society relations in Syria.[50] As the military threat from Israel is still of paramount interest to the Syrian regime and the Syrian population, the hegemonic challenge of Israel to Syria's regional interests dominates its perception of international politics.

Arab nationalism remains a critical issue around which the Syrian population can unite behind the regime. The foreign policy gains of the regime, namely in the regional contest with Israel, have been popular and won support. The return of the Golan Heights, the liberation of the Arab territories, and the restoration of Palestinian rights have remained the central tenets of Asad's foreign policy. These goals continue to legitimise foreign policy decisions, and have not changed since Asad's seizure of power in 1970. In short, regime legitimacy has been synonymous with Arab nationalism.

Legitimacy, however, has not been a priority in the means to achieving these goals. The tactics of the Syrian regime have often seemed to be at odds with the Arab dimension in the Arab–Israeli dispute. As mentioned previously, Syria's intervention in Lebanon, its support of Iran in the Iran–Iraq War, its promotion of the anti-Arafat struggle in Lebanon, and its support of Amal in the Camp Wars of 1985, have been deeply unpopular and have been considered detrimental to the Arab cause.

Islam offers an alternative route for acquiring legitimacy. However, the Syrian regime does not possess sufficient Islamic credentials despite the public displays of religiosity by the president.[51] The violent suppression of the Islamic uprising in Hama in 1982 has stripped the regime of all pretensions of Islamic legitimacy.[52]

Although the regime of Asad is essentially unpopular, it has survived for twenty-seven years. It owes its longevity to a number of factors which can be summarised as: the Ba'th party; the armed forces; the security services; the maintenance of legitimacy. Each of these factors is independent of public opinion except for the factor of legitimacy.[53]

Public opinion

As illustrated in Chapter 4, political participation is limited in Syria. The public does not have effective access to a system of redress to challenge unpopular policy decisions. Despite the existence of an institutionalised political process, the structures in place serve more as a façade than a system of representation. Public unrest has not emerged, in any significant way, since the destruction of Hama in 1982. In this instance, the regime was dependent upon the support of its security services and Rif'at Asad's Defence Companies.[54]

It was, however, important to address public opinion before taking part in the Gulf War coalition in order to legitimise the logic of the decision. Asad found it necessary to defend his decision in a major speech on 12 September 1990.[55] Intervention, he said, was justified:

(a) To constrain the imperial powers and assure their rapid departure after the completion of the task;

(b) Because the restoration of international laws and norms would place pressure on the Western governments to implement UN Resolutions 242, 338, and 425;

(c) To ensure that an international peace process would commence after the liberation of Kuwait.

In spite of this, the public was still discontented with the decision. Public opinion during the Gulf War was expressed in covert ways, such as by the posting of seditious materials, and some demonstrations in eastern Syria, but very few Syrians were willing to challenge the regime.[56]

Syria's partnership in the alliance to liberate Kuwait, an oil-rich Gulf state, in opposition to Iraq, a fellow Ba'thist state, appeared to be contradictory to popular expression. Siding with the imperial power of the US, the long-term ally of Israel, seemed to negate the principles of Arab nationalism. Certainly, the decision to fight with the Western alliance was not determined by public sympathies with Arab nationalism. Arab nationalism and the liberation of the occupied territories remained at the centre of Asad's strategic thinking, yet abstaining from the liberation of Kuwait would have harmed Syrian interests, and intervention on the side of Iraq could have been suicidal.

Reconciliation between policy decisions and public opinion has never been critical to the state, as the regime exists largely above the influence of political interest groups. The only group that exerts real influence upon the regime can be identified as that of the regime barons. They are not, however, a coherent group for they are carefully recruited, cultivated, and removed according to the strength of the president.[57]

The Regime Barons

Although President Asad appears to be the major decision-maker in Syria, this perception is, of course, inaccurate. There is a political elite that constrains the president and represents the interests of the Ba'th party, the armed forces and the security services.

The political elite have been identified as: Vice-President 'Abd al-Halim Khaddam; Chief of Staff Hikmat al-Shihabi, and intelligence boss, 'Ali Duba. The *jama'a* around this core has been crucial to regime autonomy and stability.[58] There is little evidence that Asad encountered much resistance from the political elite, as the decision was considered to be consensual.[59] Although the decision appeared to be difficult to justify to the ideological army of Syria and the Ba'th party, Asad demonstrated the utility of his decision after the devastating defeat of Iraq.

Without the constraint of having to appease interests within the state, the Syrian elite were able to conduct and implement a policy that seemed antithetical to the traditional policies of the state. The nature of the decision-making process, and the method of implementation, did not deviate from previous patterns. Foreign policy remains the exclusive domain of the president and his coterie. High politics is still the dominant theme in Syrian foreign policy; it exists beyond the reach of any institutional framework or the vagaries of public opinion.

The relative autonomy from domestic constraint enjoyed by the state empowered the decision-makers to pursue a policy that appeared to be inimical to Arab interests and a betrayal of Syria's traditional foreign policy. Through a careful balancing of domestic and international pressures, however, the state was able to follow a rational policy founded upon national security and national interest, which owe their origins to the primacy of systemic factors in the formulation of foreign policy.

The primacy of systemic factors

Free from the impositions of constituent demands, Syria's decision to join the coalition was based upon a rational set of considerations focused on *realpolitik*. The foreign policy goals of the regime did not significantly change, but the strategy for achieving them was adapted according to the new international environment.

The rational actor model appears to offer the most appropriate analysis for Syria's decision to engage in the second Gulf War on the side of the US and its allies. The model's emphasis on national security and the national interest fit accordingly the Syrian case. The systemic factors compelled Syria to conform to a rational decision-making process. Evidently, the domestic politics models, with their focus upon the domestic arena fail to provide a convincing explanation of Syria's decision. Despite widespread domestic opposition to Syria's intervention in the second Gulf War, the state employed a policy that contravened the public mood and the interests of other influential parties.

Understanding that force was still the ultimate source of power, Asad realised that Syria needed to adapt its strategy in order to capitalise upon the changing circumstances and fortunes of international relations. Despite the talk of a New World Order based on a new morality, that order was still defined by might over right. The dominant feature of the military in international relations had not radically altered. The significance of the New World Order lay in the reconfiguration of power, which was manifested in a military unipolarity, and an economic multipolarity. As a pragmatist and a realist, Asad responded to the challenge of the New World Order. He perceived a New World Order emerging and wanted to influence it rather than be its victim. The Gulf War promised to be a watershed event in the birth of that order, and Syria's policy in the conflict would determine its status in the new order.

The calculated gamble taken by the Syrian regime vindicated its policy decision to join the US and its allies in the liberation of Kuwait. Syrian public opinion reluctantly accepted the sagacity of Asad's decision in the postwar period. It was acknowledged that Syria had been spared the ordeal of being the next victim of the New World Order, and had in the mean time elevated its status in the regional hierarchy.

Conclusion

Iraq's invasion of Kuwait afforded the US-led coalition the occasion to challenge the actions of an aggressor state (Iraq) in order to guarantee the territorial integrity of a victimised state (Kuwait). The reaction of the US-led coalition represented the nature of the New World Order, and it served to remind the world's states that international law would be upheld by the world's hegemonic powers.[60]

This perception of the New World Order is based upon international law and falls into the pluralist paradigm of international relations theory. The globalist perspective works from the assumption that the liberation of Kuwait was motivated by the need to guarantee access to cheap oil for the global economy. The action of the coalition, therefore, served the interests of the leaders of the global capitalist economy. Realists have, however, alluded to the primacy of self-interest of the members of the US-led offensive.

For realists the New World Order did not entail a break with the past. Nevertheless, it signified the next stage of world history based upon a redistribution of power. National interests remained the paramount feature of the New World Order. Realists have asserted that the liberation of Kuwait served the national interests of both the international and regional players.[61]

International actors

The destruction of an emerging middle power in the Middle East state sub-system demonstrated the nature of the New World Order. The successor to the bipolar order, either the unipolar or multipolar order, was to be reinforced by international coercion whilst conciliation and cooperation were subordinate features of the New World Order.[62] In other words, the response of the US-led coalition did not connote the ascendancy of liberal values, but the omnipresence of force in international relations.[63]

The response of the coalition served two purposes. Firstly, it illustrated the inflexible nature of the centre powers demonstrating their political and military hegemony over the world's regions. The action of the coalition set a precedent for regional middle powers. It illustrated the intolerance of the centre powers to anti-systemic forces and their readiness to mete out punishment to regional threats. As a radical force in the region, Iraq threatened to disrupt the status quo that served the interests of the US.[64]

Secondly, the coalition's response represented the collective national interests of its international members. Access to cheap oil was deemed essential to maintaining their high-tech economies and for the general servicing of the global economy. In proximity to the huge oilfields of the GCC states, Iraq's invasion posed a challenge to the continuous flow of cheap oil. As the currency of the global economy, oil is fundamental to the interdependent interests of the world's economic centres. The liberation of Kuwait, therefore, served the economic and political agenda of the international actors in the US-led offensive.[65]

Regional actors
The liberation of Kuwait also served the interests of the regional actors who took part in the US-led coalition. Saudi Arabia, Egypt, and Syria were the main Arab beneficiaries; their participation elevated their international and regional status. Saudi Arabia's acute security dilemma, incurred by Iraq's ominous presence, obliged it to seek international protection. The emergence of Iraq as a regional power after the Iran–Iraq War constituted a threat to the hegemonic interests of Egypt and Syria. Egypt's dependence upon US economic aid was partially accountable for its entry into the coalition. Syria's gravitation towards the US-centred world order was a reflection of its new strategy in foreign policy. The roles of Egypt and Syria were essentially motivated by the prominence of their national interests. Turkey's participation in the coalition forces and Israel's abstinence from attacking Iraq, despite the provocation of Iraq's Scud-missile attacks, ensured that both parties made considerable economic and diplomatic gains.[66]

From this brief observation, it is possible to suggest that Syria's decision to join the Gulf War coalition was calculated according to a set of rational decisions. The hypothesis of this chapter asserts that the primary motivation behind Syria's role in the Gulf War coalition was the necessity to realign its global position. This was not a decision taken lightly, but owed its origins to the vulnerability of Syria *vis-à-vis* Israel and the remaining superpower, the US.

There was little choice but to accept the dominant role played by the US in the world order. Unipolarity was the defining feature of international relations, and the prospect of a multipolar system emerging looked increasingly remote. Syria faced two choices: either to pursue a US-led solution, or to risk falling into isolation. Ironically, Syria was forced to adopt a strategy employed by the Egyptian government in the late 1970s; the terms of reference, however, were very different.

The reduction in Iraq's military capacity and the elimination of its political threat to Syrian hegemony in the region, and especially in Lebanon, were benefits enjoyed by Syria, but they did not constitute a major factor in the decision-making process. Moreover, the destruction of Iraq weakened the Arab balance of power with Israel, and exposed the region to more external forces. The lifting of sanctions was incidental to the decision, especially as the US failed to remove Syria from its list of terrorist states. The economic dividends accrued after the war were also negligible factors in the decision.

Adjusting to the New World Order was an essential part of Syria's foreign policy in the post-Cold War era. US–Syrian relations had reached an all-time low during the 1980s, because of the bombing of the US marine base in 1983; the episode of hostage taking; and Syria's alleged role in international terrorism.[67]

Libya paid for its activities in 1986;[68] Iraq was being prepared as the next victim in the Middle East, and Syria might have been in line for the following round of retributive action. The second Gulf War presented Syria with the opportunity to avoid this fate.

The New World Order represented a direct threat to Syria and its regime. The objectives of Syrian foreign policy were moving beyond the realms of realism; Asad, motivated by power politics, sought the first opportunity to realign Syria to the more advantageous side of the New World Order. Syria's inclusion in the US-led coalition enabled it to adjust to the environment of the New World Order.

In order to occupy a place in the postwar regional order and to achieve its regional ambitions, Syria joined the US-led coalition. This move may have appeared to have contradicted Syria's foreign policy goals of the 1970s and 1980s. But the promise of a revival of an international peace conference motivated Syria to ally itself to the conservative Gulf Arab states and their international guardians.

NOTES

1 N. Chomsky, *World Orders, Old and New* (London: Pluto Press, 1994), pp. 70–1.
2 Ibid., p. 25.
3 S. David provides an in-depth account of omnibalancing in his article "Explaining Third World Alignment", *World Politics*, vol. 43, no. 2 (January 1991), pp. 233–56.
4 K. Barhoum, "The Gulf Crisis and a New World Order", *Middle East International*, no. 391, 11 January 1991, p. 21.
5 A. Kubursi and S. Mansur, "Oil and the Gulf War: An 'American Century' or a 'New World Order'", *Arab Studies Quarterly*, vol. 15, no. 4 (Fall 1993), p. 15.
6 E. Kienle, "Syria, the Kuwait War, and the New World Order" in T. Ismael and J. Ismael (eds.), *The Gulf War and the New World Order: International Relations of the Middle East* (Gainesville: University Press of Florida, 1994), p. 384.
7 L. Freedman and E. Karsh, *The Gulf Conflict 1990–1991: Diplomacy and War in the New World Order* (London: Faber & Faber, 1993), p. 299.
8 Ibid., p. 91.
9 F. Buettner and M. Landgraf, "The European Community's Middle Eastern Policy: The New Order of Europe and the Gulf Crisis" in T. Ismael and J. Ismael (eds.), *The Gulf War and the New World Order: International Relations of the Middle East* (Gainesville: University Press of Florida, 1994), p. 81, and R. Swann, "Europe's Abortive Bridge-building", *Middle East International*, no. 391, 11 January 1991, pp. 5–7.
10 E. Hill, "The New World Order and the Gulf War: Rhetoric, Policy, and Politics in the United States" in T. Ismael and J. Ismael (eds.), *The Gulf War and the New World Order: International Relations of the Middle East* (Gainesville: University Press of Florida, 1994), p. 197.
11 N. Chomsky, *World Orders, Old and New* (London: Pluto Press, 1994), pp. 23–5.
12 L. Freedman and E. Karsh, *The Gulf Conflict 1990–1991: Diplomacy and War in the New World Order* (London: Faber & Faber, 1993), p. xxix.
13 M. Abir, *Saudi Arabia: Government, Society, and the Gulf Crisis* (London: Routledge, 1993), p. 174.
14 M. Rodenbeck, "Quiet Unease", *Middle East International*, no. 393, 8 February 1991, p. 15.
15 Egypt's central role in the postwar peace process helped to elevate its regional status. Its function as an intermediary between Syria, the PLO, and Israel has guaranteed it a role in the US-dominated regional order.
16 G. Jansen, "The Ousting of 'Aoun", *Middle East International*, no. 386, 26 October 1990, pp. 8–10.
17 M. Ma'oz, *Syria and Israel: From War to Peace-making* (Oxford: Clarendon Press, 1995), p. 206.
18 J. Bercovitch, "Superpowers and Client States: Analysing Relations and Patterns of Influence" in M. Efrat and J. Bercovitch (eds.), *Superpowers and Client States in the Middle East: The Imbalance of Influence* (London: Routledge, 1991), p. 9.
19 A. Ehteshami, "Defence and Security Policies of Syria in a Changing Regional Environment", *International Relations*, vol. XIII, no. 1 (April 1996), p. 51.

20 V. Yorke, *Domestic Politics and Regional Security: Jordan, Syria and Israel, The End of an Era?* (Aldershot: Gower, 1988), pp. 305–7.

21 E. Karsh, *The Soviet Union and Syria: The Asad Years* (London: Routledge, 1988), p. 79.

22 A. Khalidi and H. Agha, "The Syrian Doctrine of Strategic Parity" in J. Kipper and H. Saunders (eds.), *The Middle East in Global Perspective* (Boulder: Westview Press, 1991), pp. 189–91.

23 R. Hinnebusch, "State and Civil Society in Syria", *Middle East Journal*, vol. 47, no. 2 (Spring 1993), p. 243.

24 E. Kienle, "Syria, the Kuwait War, and the New World Order" in T. Ismael and J. Ismael (eds.), *The Gulf War and the New World Order: International Relations of the Middle East* (Gainesville: University Press of Florida, 1994), p. 389.

25 C. Cordahi, "Sticking to Its Principles", *Middle East International*, no. 398, 19 April 1991, p. 16.

26 J. Muir, "The PLO, Syria, and Iran", *Middle East International*, no. 392, 25 January 1991, p. 9, and *BBC Summary of World Broadcasts*, ME/0984, A/7, 31 January 1991.

27 H. Agha and A. Khalidi, *Syria and Iran: Rivalry and Cooperation* (London: Pinter, 1995), p. 26.

28 A. Ehteshami, "Defence and Security Policies of Syria in a Changing Regional Environment", *International Relations*, vol. XIII, no. 1 (April 1996), p. 61.

29 F. Nasrallah, "Syria after Ta'if: Lebanon and the Lebanese in Syrian Politics" in E. Kienle (ed.), *Contemporary Syria: Liberalization between Cold War and Cold Peace* (London: British Academy Press, 1994), p. 135, and A. Munro, *An Arabian Affair: Politics and Diplomacy behind the Gulf War* (London: Brassey's, 1996), p. 145.

30 H. Agha and A. Khalidi, *Syria and Iran: Rivalry and Cooperation* (London: Pinter, 1995), p. 29.

31 The Damascus Declaration, however, has essentially remained a paper agreement. The US and Britain have continued to provide Gulf security despite the unpopularity of an imperial presence in the region.

32 T. Shad, S. Boucher and J. Gray-Reddish, "Syrian Foreign Policy in the Post-Soviet Era", *Arab Studies Quarterly*, vol. 17, no. 1&2 (Winter/Spring 1995), p. 89.

33 H. Agha and A. Khalidi, *Syria and Iran: Rivalry and Cooperation* (London: Pinter, 1995), p. 30.

34 M. Faksh, "Asad's Westward Turn: Implications for Syria", *Middle East Policy*, vol. ii, no. 3, March 1993, p. 57, and M. Ma'oz, *Syria and Israel: From War to Peace-making* (Oxford: Clarendon Press, 1995), p. 206.

35 A. Drysdale and R. Hinnebusch, *Syria and the Middle East Peace Process* (New York: Council on Foreign Relations, 1991), p. 91, and F. Nasrallah, "Syria's Post-war Gains and Liabilities", *Middle East International*, no. 396, 22 March 1991, pp. 20–1.

36 G. Jansen, "Talking Again", *Middle East International*, no. 389, 7 December 1990, p. 15.

37 P. Seale, *Asad of Syria: The Struggle for the Middle East* (London: I.B. Tauris, 1988), p. 475.

38 F. Nasrallah, "Syria's Post-war Gains and Liabilities", *Middle East International*, no. 396, 22 March 1991, p. 21.

39 L. Marlowe, "Syria Holds the Key to UK Hostages Release", *Financial Times*, Friday 2 November 1990, p. 4.

40 E. Kienle, "Syria, the Kuwait War, and the New World Order" in T. Ismael and J. Ismael (eds.), *The Gulf War and the New World Order: International Relations of the Middle East* (Gainesville: University Press of Florida, 1994), p. 384.

41 A. Munro, *An Arabian Affair: Politics and Diplomacy behind the Gulf War* (London: Brassey's, 1996), pp. 64 and 203.

42 M. Ma'oz, *Syria and Israel: From War to Peace-making* (Oxford: Clarendon Press, 1995), p. 208.

43 R. Baker, "Imagining Egypt in the New Age: Civil Society and the Leftist Critique" in T. Ismael and J. Ismael (eds.), *The Gulf War and the New World Order: International Relations of the Middle East* (Gainesville: University Press of Florida, 1994), pp. 415–16. In the article by Y. Sadowski, "Arab Economies after the Gulf War: Power, Poverty, and Petrodollars", *Middle East Report* (*MERIP*), no. 170 (May/June 1991), p. 5, he reports that Egypt was awarded loans and grants of $1,500 million by the Saudis; moreover, Saudi Arabia and Kuwait wrote off $6,600 million worth of Egypt's debt.

44 D. Hopwood, *Egypt: Politics and Society 1945–90* (London: HarperCollins, 1991), p. 111.

45 M. Zaalouk, *Power, Class and Foreign Capital in Egypt: The Rise of the New Bourgeoisie* (London: Zed, 1989), p. 59.

46 A. Dessouki, "The Primacy of Economics: The Foreign Policy of Egypt" in B. Korany and A. Dessouki (eds.), *The Foreign Policies of Arab States: The Challenge of Change* (Boulder: Westview Press, 1991), p. 175.

47 M. Ma'oz, *Syria and Israel: From War to Peace-making* (Oxford: Clarendon Press, 1995), pp. 207–8.

48 A. Ehteshami and R. Hinnebusch, *Syria and Iran: Middle Powers in a Penetrated Regional System* (London: Routledge, 1997), pp. 179–80.

49 Interview with a Damascene businessman, 29 September 1995.

50 P. Seale, *Asad of Syria: The Struggle for the Middle East* (London: I.B. Tauris, 1988), p. 174.

51 Interview with the First Secretary of the British embassy, Damascus, 22 September 1995.

52 H. Batatu, "Syria's Muslim Brethren", *Middle East Report* (*MERIP*), no. 110 (November/December 1982), pp. 19–20.

53 R. Hinnebusch, *Authoritarian Power and State Formation in Ba'thist Syria: Army, Party, and Peasant* (Boulder: Westview Press, 1990), p. 156.

54 "Salah ed-Din al Bitar's Last Interview: The Major Deviation of the Ba'th is Having Renounced Democracy", *Middle East Report* (*MERIP*), no. 110 (November/ December 1982), p. 23.

55 G. Jansen, "Unpopular U-turn", *Middle East International*, no. 384, 28 September 1990, pp. 11–12.

56 Ibid.

57 R. Hinnebusch, "Syria: The Politics of Peace and Regime Survival", *Middle East Policy*, vol. iii, no. 4 (April 1995), p. 76.

58 Ibid., p. 77.

59 Ibid., pp. 76–7.

60 N. Chomsky, *World Orders, Old and New* (London: Pluto Press, 1994), p. 9.

61 C. Krauthammer, "The Unipolar Moment", *Foreign Affairs*, vol. 70, no. 1 (Winter 1991), p. 24.

62 Y. Kuroda, "Bush's New World Order: A Structural Analysis of Instability and Conflict in the Gulf" in T. Ismael and J. Ismael (eds.), *The Gulf War and the New World Order: International Relations of the Middle East* (Gainesville: University Press of Florida, 1994), p. 56.

63 N. Chomsky, *World Orders, Old and New* (London: Pluto Press, 1994), p. 25.

64 L. Freedman and E. Karsh, *The Gulf Conflict 1990–1991: Diplomacy and War in the New World Order* (London: Faber & Faber, 1993), pp. xxi–xxx, and N. Chomsky, *World Orders, Old and New* (London: Pluto Press, 1994), pp. 9–10.

65 N. Chomsky, *World Orders, Old and New* (London: Pluto Press, 1994), pp. 8–25.

66 *BBC Summary of World Broadcasts*, ME/0984, A/21, 31 January 1991, and L. Freedman, and E. Karsh, *The Gulf Conflict 1990–1991: Diplomacy and War in the New World Order* (London: Faber & Faber, 1993), p. 203.

67 H. Agha and A. Khalidi, *Syria and Iran: Rivalry and Cooperation* (London: Pinter, 1995), pp. 20–5.

68 N. Chomsky, *World Orders, Old and New* (London: Pluto Press, 1994), p. 23.

6

Syria and the Peace Process

Introduction

One result of the liberation of Kuwait was the convening of an international peace conference for the resolution of the Arab–Israeli conflict.
The US maintained and pursued its commitment to the peace process
despite the reluctant overtures of Shamir's government in Israel.[1] Syria's
adjustment to the New World Order, represented in its decision to join
the Gulf War coalition, was rewarded by the prospect of the peace process.

Syria's participation in the US-led peace process arose from the
change in the configuration of global power, as Asad noted: "If the New
World Order is actually to be global, then it must adhere to legitimacy
and we, along with others, must be part of it. We cannot support an
order that is biased against us and that attacks the victim."[2] The debate
about Syria's commitment to peace re-emerged as the peace process began.
Syria watchers, such as Pipes[3] and Kirkpatrick,[4] cast serious doubt on
Syria's intentions towards Israel, whilst Hinnebusch,[5] Seale, and Kienle[6]
believed that peace was a strategic option for Syria.

In this chapter I will show how Syria's engagement in the peace
process is consistent with Asad's foreign policy. Syria's entry into the
Madrid peace process was determined by the advent of the New World
Order. Prior to this shift in the global configuration of power, the prospect
of a solution based upon a comprehensive formula remained elusive.
Syria's exclusion from the separate peace tracks, which had included Egypt
and Lebanon, had encouraged Syria to develop tactical rejectionism. The
New World Order produced a climate conducive to a more comprehensive
peace formula. Hence, Syria's path of rejectionism was discarded as peace
became a strategic option for Syria.[7]

Syria's foreign policy has been consistent since 1974. It has been
motivated by the quest for a comprehensive solution to the Arab–Israeli
conflict based upon UN Resolutions 242 and 338.[8] More recently,
however, the terms of a peace settlement for Syria have become more

fluid. Since Jordan and the PLO have signed separate peace deals with Israel, Syria has been left at liberty to settle the issue of the Golan Heights without reference to the Palestinian question, which has been the central feature of the Arab–Israeli conflict since its inception.

The Palestinian question has also been central to the legitimacy of the Syrian state. The regime's Arab credentials, obtained from its vociferous defence of the Arab territories, have served to justify foreign policy and unpopular domestic policies. Deviation from the Palestinian agenda, therefore, could be deemed to be betraying pan-Arabism, thereby risking regime legitimacy.

I contend that this idea is outdated. The Syrian population has carried the burden of Palestine for the last fifty years; furthermore, it attributes the absence of democracy within Syrian society to the omnipresent threat of the Israelis.[9] Peace with Israel, irrespective of the Palestinians, would liberate Syria from its security dilemma and decompress the domestic political system. From this perspective, it is more likely that the Syrian population perceives the separate PLO–Israel deal as an opportunity to pursue state or domestic interests over Arab interests.[10]

Traditionally, Syria has been depicted as an enemy of peace. In this chapter, I intend to refute this assumption and show that peace has been a realistic option for Syria since Asad took power. Peace has been conceived of in terms of a comprehensive option, thus universally satisfying Arab needs and ambitions. Before presenting this hypothesis, I intend to analyse the major events that characterised Syrian foreign policy throughout the 1970s and 1980s. The main focus of this chapter is to present an understanding of Syria's role in the current peace process.

Syria and the peace process

The collapse of the Soviet Union and the succession of the US, as the architect of the New World Order, swept away the status quo and precipitated a change in the Middle Eastern regional order. The invasion of Kuwait provided the optimum moment for collating the interests of the US allies in the region, and for incorporating Syria into the formula.

> With these trends reinforced by the crumbling of East European regimes and the disintegration of the Soviet Union, the radical regimes in the Middle East concluded that they had been left to the

mercy of the only remaining superpower, the United States, and its lackeys, of which Israel was first and foremost.[11]

The changes in the world order presented a window of opportunity for Israel and the Arab states to find a resolution to the Arab–Israeli conflict. The structural determinants, namely, the emergence of the US as the world's superpower, together with a weakened Arab world, created a context in which the US could impose a peace upon the region. The Madrid Peace Conference, which commenced in October 1991, initiated an irreversible process in which Jordan, with a Palestinian delegation, Lebanon, and Syria participated in bilateral talks.

At this stage of the negotiations, Syria was the linchpin of the Arab camp; it persuaded the other Arab parties to conform to a united policy. Realising that a separate peace had weakened the Arab position after Egypt had accepted the terms of Camp David in 1979, Syria sought to coordinate the policies of the Arab parties. Before attending the Madrid Peace Conference on 31 October 1991, Syria convened a coordinating session in Damascus on 23 October 1991.[12] This was one opportunity to confront Israeli ascendancy through a unified position.

This chapter has been divided into two main sections: the history of the peace process, and the state of the current peace process. The first section will summarise Syria's conceptualisation of peace in the 1970s and 1980s. The second section will examine Syria's role in the peace process with reference to the changes in the New World Order.

History of the peace process
The map of the contemporary Middle East, which was essentially drawn up after World War I, set the structural precedents for the region's future. The dismemberment of Greater Syria into individual states administered by the mandatory powers sought to disfigure the political and geographical orientation of the region. The deliberations of the Sykes–Picot Agreement and the issue of the Balfour Declaration in 1917, accompanied by the subsequent creation of Israel, generated structural fault lines that dragged the region irrevocably towards war.[13]

The Arab states of the region did not accept the existence of the state of Israel. It was believed to be a revocable state without indigenous roots. It owed its existence and allegiance to the Western powers.[14] Hence, the objective of the regional powers has been to eliminate the state of Israel in their pursuit of regional influence. Israel provided a nexus for the newly formed Arab states to unite behind a single cause and to search for their own trans-state schemes. The Iraqi and Transjordanian schemes to re-create the Fertile Crescent and Greater Syria provide examples of how the trans-state objectives of the newly independent states dominated the region's politics.[15] One political manifestation of the Arab nationalist movement was the rising Ba'th party.

The Ba'th party and Israel

The Ba'th party, founded in 1940, represented a more aggressive and visionary form of Arab nationalism. Its appeal as a revolutionary movement far exceeded the chivalrous objectives of the early leaders of Arab nationalism, whose acceptance of the Arab state-system and acquiescence to the creation of Israel were habitually denounced.[16]

As an ideology, Ba'thism called for the renaissance of Arabism, a regeneration of the great Arab empires, and the expulsion of all occupying powers. The attitude to the state of Israel was the focal point of Ba'thi philosophy and served to unify the objectives of Ba'thism.[17] The anti-Israeli rhetoric of the Ba'th regime after 1963 had called for the destruction of Israel, and the breakup of the Arab state sub-system. According to these principles, in conjunction with the expansionist tendencies of the Israeli state, conflict between Syria and Israel was an inevitable feature of the contemporary Middle East.[18]

Syria and Israel

Syria has long been regarded by the West as an ardent opponent of peace. This understanding has been based upon the military confrontations and vocal antipathy between Syria and Israel. The creation of Israel has been the source of Syria's enmity; its creation marked the demise of the Greater Syrian region as a single political and cultural unit. Viewed as an imperial and alien state, Israel symbolised the failure of evolutionary Arab nationalism to resist the imposition of another successive period of occupation.[19]

Although the creation of Israel affected the entire Arab world, because of its geographic proximity, its most immediate impact was felt in the Levant. It challenged Syrian influence in Lebanon, Jordan, and Palestine, and at the same time undermined the legitimacy of the Syrian state. As a result, Syria's domestic politics after 1948 were necessarily determined by the existence of Israel. The preoccupation of Syrian foreign policy was the challenge that Israel had set before it. The Syrian leadership has owed its credentials to the success of its Arab nationalist agenda, and its opposition to Israeli statehood.[20]

As previously mentioned, the 1967 war was a defining moment in contemporary Middle Eastern history. It signalled the permanence of Israel's presence in the region as the combined Arab effort to destroy Israel had failed. The structural faults remained, but Israel's existence was an inescapable fact.

The details of the struggle between Syria and Israel during the period 1948–70 are not strictly relevant here, as we are mainly concerned with the Asad years. But it is important to understand that the struggle derived from the structural factors that shaped the Middle Eastern region after World Wars I and II.[21] With a change of leadership in Egypt and Syria in 1970, the next phase of the regional conflict moved away from the destruction of Israel and focused on the liberation of the territories occupied in 1967.[22]

Asad and Sadat: a new direction

Asad's rise to power was accompanied by a brand of realism that recognised the durability of Israel. At the time, neither Egypt nor Syria recognised the state of Israel, but their changing behavioural patterns acknowledged the contemporary realities. The ambitions of Syrian and Egyptian foreign policy, as displayed in the October War of 1973, were confined to liberating the territories occupied during the June 1967 War.[23]

The October War

The June War of 1967 contributed to a fundamental change in the military arena in the Arab–Israeli conflict. Asad gained invaluable experience during that war and understood the limitations of Syria's military capabilities. Success had to be determined in the air, and the Israeli air force enjoyed the supremacy afforded by the US military edge.[24] This reality played a significant part in shaping the military coordination of Egypt and Syria in the October War.

The unity between Egypt and Syria in the war campaign of 1973 led to development of the two-front strategy to liberate the occupied territories. Committed to the principle and utility of unity, Asad was aware that the Arabs were weak and ineffectual when divided against the rapidly consolidating state of Israel. The war of 1973 was a war to liberate the Arab territories, and to give the front-line Arab states the diplomatic advantage in postwar negotiations. In effect, the October War was a war for peace.

The war provided a moral and psychological victory for the Arab states. The notion of Israeli supremacy had been severely challenged, and the Arab states had seized the diplomatic advantage.[25] The war initiated a process that produced a watershed in the Arab–Israeli conflict. However, the unity between Syria and Egypt, already fractured through a breakdown in military coordination,[26] dissipated as Egypt pursued a separate peace deal with Israel.[27]

The October War of 1973 illustrated the precedence of Egypt's national state interest over Arab interest. Egypt's political and cultural homogeneity allowed for the creation of a more particular foreign policy,[28] whilst Syria's national interests were intricately tied to the broader Arab agenda.[29] The first and second disengagement agreements between Israel and Egypt led to the signing of the Camp David Accords. The conclusion of that peace treaty rejected Syria's aim of achieving comprehensive peace.[30]

Arab unity had preoccupied the Syrian and Egyptian leaderships since the 1950s.[31] Their foreign policies had been determined by the projection of regional competition with Israel. In 1973, President Sadat's ambitions appear to have deviated from those of the Arab majority in order to satisfy Egypt's national interest. Egypt's domestic problems took priority over its foreign policy commitments and Sadat entered into US-brokered talks. The US induced Egypt to enter into a peace agreement with Israel through the offer of financial assistance and the promise of annual aid.[32] Because of the primacy of the economic crisis, the role of the economy became the distinguishing feature of Egyptian foreign policy in the late 1970s.[33]

Egypt's abandonment of the Syrian–Egyptian formula had significantly weakened Syria's negotiating position with Israel. Despite its isolation, Syria maintained a steadfast commitment to comprehensive peace. For Asad, it was necessary for Syria and Egypt to coordinate their activities in order to achieve a real peace – a peace that satisfied all parties. Syria remained consistent in its objectives, and demanded a total withdrawal from the occupied territories in return for peace. Contained within the language it used was a tacit recognition of Israel's existence. In 1974, Asad remarked in an interview:

> For our part we look upon peace in its true sense . . . a peace without occupation, without destitute peoples, and without citizens whose homeland is denied them . . . Anyone who imagines that the peace process can be a piecemeal process is mistaken . . . We may now say as we have always said – that peace should be based on complete withdrawal from the lands occupied in 1967 and on the full restoration of the rights of the Palestinian people.[34]

During the early stages of the second disengagement talks, Syria had been willing to attend an international conference if it was based on the land-for-peace formula contained within UN Resolutions 242 and 338. These conditions were not acceptable to either Israel or the US. For Israel, any conference taking place under international aegis, particularly one based upon UN Resolutions, could carry binding obligations that were unacceptable to the Israeli state.[35] At the same time, for the US, an international conference would have incorporated the Soviet Union, which would have elevated the status of the latter in the peace process and in particular in the Middle East. The US acquisition of Egypt as a client state from the Soviet Union had already won it a major advancement in the zero-sum game; an international conference held the possibility of awarding the Soviet Union an undeserved extension of its sphere of influence.[36] Syria's effective exclusion from the Geneva conference in 1977, then, was based on the procedural arrangements favoured by the US and Israel.[37]

During the period 1974–8 it appears that Syria was prepared to enter a peace process based on the principles of UN Resolutions 242 and 338. Syria's options, however, were limited. As a consequence of the separate Egyptian peace deal, Syria became the only belligerent front-line state, and found itself in a vulnerable position. It had the capacity to join a US-sponsored peace process, yet it demanded a comprehensive solution to the Arab–Israeli conflict. The US insistence on separate peace deals served to exclude Syria from any peace process. Peace could not be achieved in isolation; it was no longer an option. Rejectionism became the key to Syrian policy, and the pursuit of strategic parity became the strategy of its foreign policy.[38]

1980s: tactical rejectionism[39]

Strategically, Syria signed over its future to the vagaries of Soviet fortune; the avenues for peace looked bleaker as Syria embraced tactical rejectionism,[40] and Israel's expansionist tendencies were reinforced by an ideologically driven US administration.[41] The polarisation of US–Soviet relations after the signing of the Camp David Accords and the election of President Reagan was reflected in the escalating animosity between the Israelis and the Syrians.

Syria's tactics changed after the withdrawal of Egypt from the Arab–Israeli conflict. From a position of isolation, Syria attempted to remedy the inequality in the balance of power between itself and Israel. The pursuit of strategic parity depended upon the strategic support of the Soviet Union and Soviet compliance with Syrian objectives.[42] The structural determinants of the region and the international environment pushed Syria to embrace tactical rejectionism and a Treaty of Friendship with the Soviet Union in 1980. Structural forces created the need, but the decisions were forged from a limited number of pragmatic options available to the Syrian elite.[43]

Syria's era of rejectionism commenced with the rejection of the Fahd Plan in 1981, on the pretext that it represented another partial peace settlement.[44] Syria actively sought to derail all possible peace initiatives in the 1980s which attempted to conclude a peace settlement without Syria. The old adage that the Middle East cannot go to war without Egypt, or create peace without Syria, gained credence throughout the 1980s.

Syria used all available means to prevent the PLO and Jordan from reaching an understanding in their conflicts with Israel. Assassinations, military manoeuvres along the Jordanian border, encouragement of the rebellion among the PLO factions, and suicide bombings in Lebanon, were devices employed by the Syrian regime to destroy all efforts at conciliation with Israel.[45]

Syria's decade of rejectionism ended in 1989 when it restored relations with Egypt and attempted to reintegrate into the emerging global order. As previously mentioned, the transformation of Soviet foreign policy forced Syria to moderate the terms of its international relationships, and to engage in the New World Order.

Despite Syria's decade of tactical rejectionism in the 1980s, Asad had continually indicated his willingness to enter into a peace process committed to achieving comprehensive peace. The pursuit of comprehensive peace had remained Syria's goal despite the tactical manoeuvres employed to destroy separate peace initiatives.

The current peace process

The peace process has undergone a number of transformations since its inception in Madrid in October 1991. There have been two presidential elections in the US and two elections in Israel. Shamir's reluctance to attend the Madrid Conference appeared to have produced a stalemate during the talks. The election of the Rabin–Peres team, in June 1992, produced an era of optimism, as both men had discussed the concept of land for peace and territorial compromise. The election of US President Clinton, in November 1992, and his assumption of office in January 1993 were greeted with hesitation in the Arab world, as the former Bush administration had been less pro-Israeli than previous US administrations.[46] Notably, there were no leadership changes within the Arab world during this period.

The Clinton administration and the Rabin government cooperated closely through the offices of the US secretary of state, Warren Christopher. The US endorsement of Israeli policies within the region has led some observers to charge the Clinton team with having lost sight of objectivity.[47] The Syrians denounced the Clinton administration after it used its veto to prevent the condemnation of further Israeli annexation of East Jerusalem.[48]

The assassination of Rabin in November 1995 caused the international community to reflect upon the role played by the Israeli leader and the momentum of the peace process itself. The peace process, created by the structural forces of the post-Gulf War order, had survived the numerous changes of administrations and governments. The prospect of Netanyahu becoming Israeli prime minister, however, appeared to threaten the fabric of the peace process.[49]

The achievement of a comprehensive peace settlement has been the ambition of the Syrians since 1974, but the loss of the PLO and Jordan as negotiating allies has left Syria diplomatically isolated once again. Syria's isolation in the 1990s is unlike that of the 1980s as it has not retracted its commitment to peace, despite the obstacles placed in the path of progress. Syria's participation in the US-sponsored peace process has remained resolute, although its demands have decreased incrementally according to necessity.[50]

The twists and turns of the peace process

The peace process has taken a number of different routes since it began in October 1991. Each event in the region has had an impact on the rate and nature of negotiations. The US has, wherever possible, tried to apply pressure on the participating parties to maintain the momentum. The process has, however, been beset with problems, from Israeli reluctance to attend the Madrid Conference to the re-writing of the Oslo Accords in order to accommodate the demands of Netanyahu and the Hebron settlers.

In this section, I will examine Syria's role in the current peace process. Since the commencement of the Madrid Conference, the PLO and Jordan have followed Egypt's example and have signed separate peace treaties. There have been many developments in the path of peace since October 1991, but neither Syria nor Lebanon have concluded peace treaties with Israel. Syria's function in the peace process cannot, of course, be studied in isolation as all the components of the peace process are ultimately interconnected.

In examining the peace process, I shall use the following events as signposts:

The Madrid Peace Conference;
the multilateral talks;
the election of Rabin;
the expulsion of 415 Palestinians;
Operation Accountability;
the Oslo Accords;
the Hebron massacre;
the Jordanian peace deal;
the Wye Plantation talks;
Operation Grapes of Wrath.

These events seem to present themselves as natural obstacles or catalysts to the process.

The Madrid Peace Conference

The Madrid Peace Conference presented the states of the Middle East with an opportunity to reach a peaceful settlement to their historic conflict.

The international environment and the ensuing political conditions were ripe for a settlement and the US was in a position to exert its international and regional influence.

In the New World Order, the US could pursue its interests in the Middle East without the explicit cover of the UN. Thereupon, the formula for the peace process was not conducted under the aegis of the UN. The UN was reduced to observer status, and the Soviet Union/Russia played only a nominal role in the negotiations.[51] The regional conditions have also provided the US with enough leverage to persuade the main adversaries of the conflict to attend the conference for the regional players were all weakened after the demise of the Soviet Union and the invasion of Kuwait.

The PLO's decision to support Saddam Hussein proved to be disastrous for its international legitimacy and financial income. Irrespective of the international support it had gained throughout the *intifada*, the PLO lost its credibility through its support of Iraq.[52] Arafat's unequivocal backing of Saddam Hussein provided the US with the pretext to exclude the PLO from direct representation at the Madrid Peace Conference. This gave the US administration sufficient flexibility to persuade the Israelis to attend.[53]

The Jordanian decision to abstain from pledging support to either side in the conflict left it vulnerable to regional and international pressures. Through this process, Jordan had alienated itself from the US and the Gulf Arab states. As a long-term supporter of Jordan, the US felt betrayed by King Hussein's option, and was intent on punishing Jordan. Jordan's acquiescence in attending the Madrid Peace Conference was indicative of its weakness; its conciliatory role towards the US also illustrated its desire for international rehabilitation.[54]

Through Syria's participation in the liberation of Kuwait, Asad managed to accumulate sufficient diplomatic capital to occupy a prime position in the peace process.[55] For Syria, the invitation to attend the conference was a recognition of its centrality to the peace process. After years of patience and tactical manœuvring, Asad had achieved his goal of engaging in an international conference whose foundation was built upon UN Resolutions 242, 338 and 425.[56] In an interview with the newspaper *Al-Akhbar*, Asad noted his appreciation of the way the regional and international attitudes had changed: ". . . the opportunities for peace have become better than at any other time before because of the current international climate and also because of the development and increase in the number of those desiring peace even inside Israel itself."[57]

Unlike the positions of Jordan and the PLO, Syria's regional position improved during the tactical reorientation of the second Gulf War.[58] However, this did not negate its vulnerability to the regional hegemony of Israel, or the international hegemony of the US.[59] Syria's attendance at the Madrid Conference, under less than ideal conditions, was a consequence of the change in the world order; and Syria's participation signified its adjustment to the New World Order.[60]

Syria's participation in the conference
Secretary of State Baker travelled to Damascus in July 1991 in order to secure the Syrian seal of approval for the conference proposal. Syria was the first state to accept Baker's proposals for the Madrid session.[61] After Syria's acceptance of the conference proposal, the rest of the Arab states followed suit and agreed to attend.[62]

For Syria, its diplomatic capital was at its maximum level; the second Gulf War had helped to ingratiate the regime with the US administration, and the diplomatic weight of Egypt and Saudi Arabia helped it to counterbalance the strategic alliance between Israel and the US. Israel had the upper hand in the balance of power; Syria's pursuit of strategic parity was over. Henceforward, Syria sought a new strategy based upon the Egyptian experience.

In order to combat US pressure, Syria conducted a coordinating session in Damascus on 23 October 1991.[63] Asad attempted to dissuade the other Arab parties from attending the multilateral round of talks. Their participation in the talks, Asad argued, would form the first stage of normalisation of relations with Israel before the latter had committed itself to peace.[64] The Syrian view was that the Arab delegations could resist US diplomatic pressure only from a united platform. Asad had paid the price for Egypt's separate peace treaty in 1979; another separate peace deal would leave Syria isolated and regionally weakened.

For five decades, the public in the Arab world had been fed anti-Israeli propaganda. Since the legitimacy of the Syrian regime rested on its Arab credentials, Syria's agreement to participate in the peace process required public justification. The Syrian public had to be prepared for the language of peace; such a move demanded an incremental introduction of new notions, such as those of "honourable peace", and "the peace of the brave". Nevertheless, it was crucial for Syria to appear tenacious and courageous in negotiating with the Israelis. The opening ceremony of the Madrid Peace Conference illustrated this point, with the Syrian public being treated to a demonstration of Syrian strength through the medium of rhetoric.[65]

Before the Madrid Peace Conference started, Syrian Foreign Minister Farouq al-Shara', had announced his refusal to shake hands with the Israeli delegate. He said:

> This hand that you would like me to shake is very guilty, because it is a hand which occupies our land, ignores Palestinian national rights and we have been suffering from this occupation, and the Palestinians in the occupied territories have been suffering from constant repression.[66]

The exchanges between Foreign Minister al-Shara' and the Israeli prime minister, Shamir, were acrimonious as each delegate accused the other of acts of tyranny and terrorism.[67] Although the charges were made, they were most probably created for public consumption to satisfy both countries' domestic constituencies.

During the opening sessions in Madrid, Shamir refused to commit Israel to the land-for-peace formula demanded by the Syrians. The Syrians believed that Shamir's intransigence was designed to edge the Syrians out of the peace process. The inauguration of a new settlement on the Golan,[68] and the Knesset's timely approval of a non-binding resolution declaring the Golan non-negotiable, were also believed to have been measures to frustrate the Syrians.[69] Syrian withdrawal from the peace process would have served the international interests of the Israeli state, and satisfied the perception of the Israeli public.

Syria's tolerance of these acts of belligerency demonstrated its regional and international vulnerability. The significance of the peace process to Syria's regional position was becoming apparent. In the past, Syria had enjoyed enough leverage from its partnership with the Soviet Union to remain steadfast in its demands. Without the backing of a major patron, Syria's diplomatic position was much more fluid and susceptible to pressure. An exit from the peace process was not a realistic option, but points of substance remained non-negotiable.[70]

Procedures

Asad made a number of concessions on the issue of procedure, but the substance of the peace process remained the same. He considered the terms of reference as balanced; they did not fulfil all of Syria's demands, but they reflected the political realities of the time. This was deemed to be the optimum moment for reaching an agreement satisfactory to all parties involved.[71]

At the expense of procedural details, Syria attended the Madrid Peace Conference. Asad had been calling since 1974 for an international conference conducted under the auspices of the UN, with binding resolutions based on UN Resolution 242 and the principle of land for peace. Attendance at the conference required Syria to rescind this position. President Asad received a letter of assurance from the US stipulating that the Madrid Peace Conference, and ensuing peace process, would be based upon UN Resolutions 242 and 338, but adding that this letter of assurance was not a binding commitment.[72]

Although the Madrid Peace Conference was not an international conference, the presence of representatives of Europe and the UN as observers added to the prestige of the event. Asad commented:

> As for the UN role, it took me some time before I was convinced that the group of elements together constituted an adequate UN role – the observers and the Resolutions through which the UN exists [in the process], and that any agreements would be ratified by the Security Council. Also calling the UN an observer just means it has no vote and this is not a voting conference; an observer takes part in discussions and activities.[73]

The absence of direct PLO representation was accepted by Asad as he commented: "everything will be done in agreement with the Palestinians and nothing will be done in isolation from them."[74] Asad added in a US television interview on 18 September 1991 that Israel would not have peace without settling the Palestinian problem: "If we leave any part of the problem unresolved, there will be no stable peace in the region . . . The Arab problem is basically a single problem, dividing it will not help."[75]

Palestinian participation

The Palestinian issue was crucial to Syria's role in the peace process. As part of the comprehensive solution, the simultaneous resolution of the

Palestinian issue was essential to the fulfilment of Syrian interests. The liberation of Golan was also contingent upon the liberation of all the occupied territories, and the restoration of Palestinian rights. The issues were all interdependent, and a separate Syrian peace was not part of the agenda. Asad commented: "Had Syria thought of its own interest only . . . it would have achieved a unilateral solution . . . But it did not and will not do this. The Golan was originally occupied in a battle waged for Palestine."[76]

The absence of independent Palestinian participation from previous peace schemes had traditionally prevented Syria from engaging in regional or international peace discussions. Syria, in its aim of maximising its regional power, needed to incorporate the Palestinian issue within its sphere of influence. The inclusion of Palestinian interests under the umbrella of Jordan, especially in the form of the Arafat–Hussein Accord in 1985,[77] militated against Syrian hegemony over Mashreq affairs. In the context of Syria's wish to extend its influence, and its need to acquire legitimacy from its pan-Arab role, the Palestinian issue remained central to Syrian foreign policy.

The demands of the New World Order, however, forced a change in Syria's perception of the Palestinian role. The US acceptance of Israel's demand that the PLO could not represent the Palestinians was imposed on the peace formula. Because of the prevailing international conditions, Syria was unable to resist this imposition. The inclusion of Palestinian delegates in the Jordanian negotiating team signified another procedural concession from the Syrians.[78]

The structure of the peace process, built upon the concept of bilateral discussions, produced sufficient space for the Israelis to pursue separate peace deals. The Syrians were bargaining for a final status agreement whilst the Palestinians, under the ambit of the Jordanian team, were negotiating for an interim agreement. This in-built discrepancy set structural fault lines that the Palestinians and Syrians were unable to reconcile.[79]

The first round of talks, which began on 30 October 1991 in Madrid, served as an introduction to the peace process. It represented the first stage of the US-led initiative, and for the first time brought delegates from Israel, Syria, Jordan and Lebanon to the same negotiating table.[80]

The perennial rift between Asad and Arafat was bridged at a meeting held to coordinate Palestinian and Syrian positions on 19 October 1991.[81]

The meeting was a necessary part of the reconciliation between the two leaders; their last meeting had been in 1983 after Syria had encouraged the Abu Musa faction to seize control of Fatah and depose Arafat as its leader. Although the PLO was not officially attending the peace process, the Palestinian delegation was coordinating its stance with Arafat.[82] During his visit to Damascus, Arafat had pledged his support for Syria's position in the multilateral talks.[83]

The multilateral talks

Although Syria had made procedural concessions to attend the first round, it had refused to commit itself to attending the multilateral round of talks unless Israel announced its willingness to return the Golan Heights to Syria. In an interview with Syrian Arab Television, Muwaffaq al-'Allaf, the head of the Syrian negotiating team, pointed out the incongruity of the multilateral talks: "While Israel is occupying the Golan Heights, Jerusalem, the West Bank and Gaza and southern Lebanon, it wants to sit down for talks with Syria, Lebanon, Jordan and the Palestinians to discuss economic cooperation, water-sharing, and the environment."[84]

The multilateral round of talks was designed to include the GCC states and Egypt in a round of regional talks. It was to focus on economic cooperation and the issues of water and security. Syria considered the multilateral talks constituted normalisation of the relations between the region's states before the advent of peace. Syria thus refused to attend the multilateral talks on the grounds that regional cooperation could not be discussed before Israel made a commitment to peace.[85]

Despite Syria's attempt to discourage the Arab parties from joining the multilateral talks, eleven states attended them in Moscow when the second round took place in January 1992.[86] The unity Syria deemed necessary for a strong bargaining position dissipated as the Jordanians and the Palestinians joined the multilateral talks. The process towards normalisation without a firm commitment to the nature of peace had started. This division among the Arab ranks caused the Syrians great consternation, and indicated the fractured nature of the Arab policy.

Understanding the inequitable pressure placed upon those front-line states attending the talks, Syria chose to criticise the US for not putting pressure on the Israelis to accept a UN role in the talks. The Israelis were able to attend the multilateral talks without making concessions to

UN participation in the regional discussions, or compromising on their principles on the selection of Palestinian candidates for the discussions. Syria recognised an emerging scenario where it would be excluded from the peace process. It continued to refuse to participate in the multilateral talks as Asad argued that such talks acknowledged Israel's legitimacy without achieving any form of peace.[87]

Syria refused to attend the Casablanca Conference in November 1994,[88] the first regional economic conference to include Israel, on the basis that it legitimised Israel's regional role before a comprehensive peace had been established. Shara' justified Syria's refusal by stating:

> If we are not going to attend the Casablanca Conference, it is because we care about regional co-operation and development, and we believe that holding such conferences, holding multinational, multilateral talks before achieving genuine peace in the region, would not give the results these multilateral talks and international conferences would yield after being 100% sure that peace is going to be established in the region.[89]

The election of Rabin

The election of Yitzhak Rabin as Israeli prime minister in June 1992 was welcomed by the Arab delegations in the peace process.[90] The Israeli Labour Party had been associated with the land-for-peace formula, and was thought to have a less obstructionist attitude to the peace process. However, it had been a Likud government that had concluded peace with Egypt in the 1970s; moreover, Rabin's reputation had been built upon his *intifada*-crushing personality.[91] The election of Rabin was accompanied by widespread speculation about a Syrian–Israeli deal. It is easy in retrospect to say that the rumours were false, but diplomatic gossip emanated from a variety of sources.[92] Conclusion of a separate peace deal ran against the Syrian national interest, however. It would have precluded Syria from extending its sphere of influence over its Arab neighbours by isolating Syria from the remaining peace process, and annulling its influence over the Palestinian, Jordanian, and Lebanese tracks. Syria's role as the hegemonic leader of the Greater Syrian states could have been contained in a similar manner to Egyptian hegemony in the Middle East. The Syrians believed that inequitable progress could be made in the bilateral talks, but pledging itself to comprehensive peace meant that a peace treaty could not be concluded until all diplomatic tracks were satisfied.[93]

The sixth round of talks of the Madrid Peace Conference opened on 24 August 1992 with Rabin as Israel's prime minister. There was a considerable reduction in pre-talk animosity between the Syrian and Israeli sides. Syria's spokeswoman, Bushra Kanafani, told the press that the word "comprehensive" was more acceptable to the Rabin team, but the substance of the talks had not significantly altered.[94] Israel's chief negotiator with the Syrians, Itamar Rabinovich, also noted a change in atmosphere and a reduction in tension between the two sides – the peace talks were then assuming a businesslike tone.[95]

In spite of its conflicting and ambivalent references to the Golan Heights, the diplomatic language of the new Labour government suggested that there was room for manœuvre. This feature had been lacking in the previous rounds of talks.[96] A major difference between the approaches of the Likud and Labour governments was the acceptance, by Rabin's team, of the applicability of UN Resolution 242 to the talks.[97] Although there was no agreement on the meaning of Resolution 242, the Golan was included in its ambit, which constituted a movement from the Israeli side.

Both the Israeli and Syrian negotiating teams had to satisfy their domestic constituencies. The Israelis had to placate the settlers in the Golan who were predominantly Labour supporters, and who stood to challenge the policies of the state.[98] The credibility of the Syrian state rested upon the total unequivocal liberation of Golan; Asad had built his reputation upon the attainment of this objective.

The second half of the sixth round of the bilateral talks opened with a Syrian proposal that offered a peace treaty in return for the total evacuation of the Golan Heights.[99] Israel demanded to know the terms of the peace treaty, displaying its desire for normalisation of relations which would include an exchange of embassies and open borders. Israel's response disappointed the Syrian negotiating team which considered the requests unreasonable as Israel had not committed itself to total withdrawal from the Golan.[100]

In an interview with Voice of Israel radio, Rabinovich, the chief negotiator of the Israeli negotiating team, reiterated Israel's reluctance to discuss the extent of withdrawal from the Golan:

We neither voiced nor hinted at any willingness to accept the Syrian demand for a full withdrawal from the Golan Heights. We came to the current round of talks with renewed formulations. These contain Israel's clarification that our acceptance of Resolution 242 means that the withdrawal element would be included in the context of a peace treaty, if and when it is signed, when Israel's demands are met. However, Israel accepts Resolution 242 as talking about a withdrawal from territories, rather than a withdrawal from the territories.[101]

The Israelis refused to follow the Sinai formula for the Golan. In particular, they wanted to avoid the "cold peace" (peace without normalisation) inherited from the Egyptian–Israeli peace treaty of 1979.[102] The chief Syrian negotiator, al-'Allaf, expressed his frustration with the Israeli negotiating team: "They are not talking at all about withdrawal . . . we are not ready to discuss any further point with Israel unless Israel discusses with us the question of total withdrawal from our territory."[103]

The nature of the peace remained uncertain at this stage of the discussion as the Syrians refused to speculate on the prospect of "warm peace" (peace with normalisation). According to Jansen, the Syrians had admitted in private that partial withdrawal would be acceptable if Syrian sovereignty was acknowledged over the entire Golan. An international buffer force and demilitarised zones would be a prerequisite for this form of agreement. The statements were disclosed behind closed doors and only fuelled expectations.[104]

Israel repeated its demand for Syria's acceptance of the principle of a separate peace treaty but this was not an issue of discussion for the Syrians. Prior to the seventh round of talks on 29 October 1992, amidst endless rumours and speculation, Arafat expressed his concern that Syria and Israel were moving towards a separate peace treaty, and hence leaving the Palestinians at the mercy of the Israelis.[105] Asad responded to Arafat's apprehensions by reassuring the Palestinian leader that Syria was committed to total peace and total withdrawal. Comprehensive peace based on the formula of land for peace remained the objective of Syria. As a gesture to Rabin, Asad used the expression the "peace of the brave" to illustrate Syria's intention of achieving peace. It was through unity that the peace of the brave would be attained. As an encouragement, during the seventh round of talks, Rabin conceded, "We will negotiate withdrawal in the Golan, but not withdrawal from the Golan."[106]

Syria's determination to fulfil its pledge to support the Palestinians was demonstrated by the convening of a rejectionist conference in Damascus in January 1992 at which ten Palestinian factions criticised the Palestinian delegation for attending the multilateral talks.[107] Syrian and Palestinian interests were ultimately linked and could not be divorced from each other. Asad's accommodation of the rejectionist factions served to strengthen his bargaining position with both the Arabs and the Israelis. Use of proxy groups had long formed part of Syria's tactic for extending its influence beyond its limited resource base.[108]

The expulsion of 415 Palestinians

The expulsion of 415 Palestinians, alleged Hamas supporters, from the occupied territories to Lebanon in December 1992 without regard to international law stalled the peace talks. The accused were deported without trial and left to face the hardship of the Lebanese winter in tents and temporary shelters. Israel's actions contravened the Universal Declaration of Human Rights and the Fourth Geneva Convention to which it was a signatory.[109] International condemnation came from the UN Security Council, the European Union, and the International Committee of the Red Cross. Lebanon's response was to deny entry to the deportees, thus exerting pressure on Israel to accept UN Resolution 799, which called on Israel to allow the return of the deportees.[110] The expulsion produced many more contradictions to the peace process. The Arab states refused to continue the talks until the 415 expelled Palestinians were allowed to return to the occupied territories.[111]

In the midst of the deportee crisis, Bill Clinton assumed the presidency of the US. In selecting his team, Clinton appointed Warren Christopher as secretary of state in place of Baker. The intervention of Clinton's new administration seems to have added a new impetus to the peace process at a time when the Israeli deportation of Palestinians could have derailed it.[112]

The new US team pushed for Syria to return to the negotiating table; it was also successful in bringing the Palestinians back to the table, as they were fearful of being excluded from the process. Syria displayed uncharacteristic ambivalence in its attitude towards the plight of the deportees and called for the resumption of talks. For Syria, the peace process had developed a momentum of its own and isolated incidents, such as the expulsion of the Palestinians, were not sufficient to halt the process.[113]

After meeting Christopher in Damascus on 21 February 1993 the Syrian foreign minister, al-Shara', said: "the goal of the peace process is broader and more important than the issue of the Palestinian deportees in Lebanon."[114] This suggested that the process itself was more important than the constituent parts. Syria's insistence on incorporating all parties, and its policy of coordinating Arab diplomatic unity, appeared to have been abandoned.

A potential change in Syrian foreign policy presented a direct threat to the Palestinian negotiating team. Syria's diplomatic weight could have persuaded the other participants to attend the talks despite the Palestinian absence. In the twists and turns of the peace process, Syria denied that it was making progress with Israel on the fast track. Al-Shara' replied to the rumours in an interview published in the French newspaper *Le Figaro*, on 26 February 1993: "If we wanted a separate peace, we could have done it years ago. If more attention is paid to the Syrian–Israeli negotiations than to the others, that is because there can be no peace without Syria."[115]

Rabin and Clinton

Rabin's first visit to the White House guaranteed continued US support for Israel. More importantly, Rabin announced his commitment to peace based on the principles of UN Resolutions 242 and 338. The change in both administrations seemed to presage a more active role for the US in the peace process. Clinton appointed many pro-Israel candidates to his administration; the US role in the peace process thus looked less favourable to the Arab side than under the Bush administration. The Syrian–Israeli peace was placed on the fast track by both Rabin and Christopher, whilst the Palestinian track received less attention as it stagnated over the issue of the deportees.[116]

In an apparent change of US and Israeli policy, the peace process started to assume characteristics once displayed by the Egyptian–Israeli peace process. Israel targeted Syria for a separate peace; it believed that peace with its northern neighbour would prevent further Palestinian progress.[117] Rabin acknowledged that a fundamental change had taken place in Syrian–Israeli relations. Asad's commitment to peace was becoming more credible, and his stand against Islamic militancy made the prospect of peace with Syria even more attractive.

Syria's insistence that the Palestinians attend the ninth round of talks, before the fulfilment of UN Resolution 799, demonstrated the intensity of its commitment to the peace process.[118] The Americans and the Syrians encouraged the Palestinians to take part in the talks. The structural determinants seemed to push the Palestinian delegation towards peace although the deportees felt betrayed, and the supporters of Hamas in the territories deplored the official Palestinian position.

Operation Accountability

Operation Accountability was the code-name for Israel's response to Hizbollah activities in south Lebanon. Retaliation for the Katyusha rockets, fired into northern Israel by Hizbollah, was severe.[119] It took the form of collective punishment, and was inflicted on the civilians living in the south Lebanon region. The response was characteristic of Israeli reprisals. It was estimated that, in the Israeli bombing raids, at least 130 people were killed and 450 wounded, whilst 400,000 fled their homes.[120]

Israel's objective was to eliminate the Hizbollah threat, and to challenge the cohesion of the Lebanese state. Israel sought to exploit the divisions within the Lebanese state by challenging its sovereignty over south Lebanon. The Lebanese government, however, was resolute in its response to Israel as it permitted Hizbollah to continue its resistance to the Israeli occupation of south Lebanon.[121]

The south Lebanese border provides Syria and Israel with an arena for confrontation whereas the Syrian–Israeli border along the Golan Heights is governed by the disengagement agreements of 1974.[122] As an instrument of Syrian political pressure, Hizbollah's activities have been a bargaining chip in Syria's negotiations with Israel.[123]

If a peace agreement is reached between Syria and Israel, Hizbollah may lose its utility to Syria. Realising this, it has started to integrate itself into the constitutional politics of Lebanon's economic and political reconstruction. Until a peace agreement is signed, however, Hizbollah will remain one of the Syrian regime's bargaining chips in regional politics and in the peace process.

Hizbollah, as a revolutionary organisation, has proved to be very useful to Syria's regional goals, and Syria has been effective in persuading the organisation to act according to its interests, by controlling arms supplies to it. Syria's special relationship with Hizbollah, orchestrated through the offices of Iran, has enabled it to influence the group's behaviour.[124] As a proxy of Syria and Iran, Hizbollah exerts timely pressure on Israel; its revolutionary philosophy, emboldened by resistance, acts as a continuous irritant to the Israelis.[125]

Notwithstanding the growing Syrian–Iranian tensions as Syria sought to constrain Hizbollah, Asad had sufficient leverage over the organization to assist US mediation between it and Israel. Despite the death of Syrian soldiers from Israel's reprisal raids, Asad exercised restraint, and exerted pressure on Hizbollah to suspend its attacks on northern Israel. Syrian intervention produced a climate in which a cease-fire agreement was reached through the offices of the US.[126]

Syrian diplomatic intervention achieved three objectives:

(a) It subdued the conflict;
(b) It helped to produce an understanding between Hizbollah and Israel;
(c) It allowed Asad to gain diplomatic credit with the US.[127]

Syrian mediation was rewarded by a more constructive US role, albeit temporary, which brought about a change in the content of the Syrian–Israeli dialogue. Syria's constraining role in south Lebanon had indicated its readiness to control Hizbollah; moreover, this role also gained the Syrian state credit with both the US administration and the Israeli government.

The prospect for progress on the Syrian-Israeli peace track was beginning to improve. Syrian and Israeli intransigence was incrementally and symmetrically receding, whilst both sides jostled for diplomatic advantage. The continuing ambivalence in their public statements was most probably aimed at satisfying public opinion in both countries. These contradictions between public statements and the steps taken on the peace track served to minimise public criticism as the two sides drew closer to each other.

Although it was not openly admitted, the concepts of normalisation and withdrawal had been used simultaneously. Neither side was willing to concede the extent of normalisation or withdrawal, but a formula for promoting Syrian–Israeli peace was in the making.

Meanwhile, Syria was careful not to contradict its pledge to achieve comprehensive peace, and stated that any such agreement would not be signed or implemented until the Palestinian, Jordanian, and Lebanese tracks had reached their natural conclusions.[128] However, the announcement of the Oslo Accords and the Declaration of Principles, conceived in private talks between the PLO and Israel under Norwegian guidance in August 1993, abruptly halted progress on the Syrian–Israeli track.[129]

The Oslo Accords

The announcement that the PLO had reached a secret agreement with the Israelis stunned the Arab world. The world media greeted the news with applause and praised Rabin and Arafat for their courage in striking such a deal. The Syrian president remained mute. The Gaza–Jericho First Plan came at a time when the Palestinian delegation was dissatisfied and increasingly losing faith in the leadership of the PLO. Furthermore, the PLO's decision to support Saddam Hussein during the second Gulf War had been financially disastrous. Wracked by acute leadership and financial crises, the PLO was losing its authority and legitimacy among its members and constituency.[130]

The Oslo Accords transformed Arafat's precarious position as leader of the Palestinian struggle for statehood into that of a victor and popular leader again. The contents of the deal, although deficient in numerous areas, were perceived to be the first step towards achieving statehood. Arafat's constituency within the occupied territories initially pledged its support for the Accords. The PLO, particularly Arafat's Fatah, had regained its legitimacy among the West Bank and Gazan population.[131]

Prior to the signing of the Accords, the PLO and Israel agreed formally to recognise each other. The Gaza–Jericho First Plan granted the Palestinians self-rule in the occupied territories at the beginning of a five-year interim period. At the beginning of the third year, the issue of Jerusalem, the status of Israeli settlements, and the fate of the Palestinian refugees were to be negotiated.[132]

After the PLO–Israel deal had become public knowledge, Arafat and his foreign minister, Farouq Qaddumi, visited Syria to seek Asad's approval. The move made by the Palestinian leader and his team had shocked the Syrian government.[133] The decision to reach a separate agreement through secret discussions was reminiscent of Sadat's style of negotiating. Asad had once again been circumvented in the peace process, and left as a spectator with a diminishing sense of influence and importance.

This time, Syria could not afford to adopt rejectionism, as it had done after the conclusion of the Camp David Accords. Syria's options were no longer so durable; the nature of the New World Order, and the predominance of the US in the Middle East, militated against Syrian rejectionism. In addition, the collapse of the East European political systems, and Iraq's crippled condition, stood as constant reminders to Syria that power politics determined the coordinates of the New World Order.

The PLO–Israeli accord marked a defining moment in Syria's perception of the Palestinian question. Firstly, it showed the potency of the New World Order and its impact upon the Syrian state. In particular, it indicated Syria's inability to resist the conclusion of another separate peace deal. Secondly, the Syrian public, after five decades of supporting the Palestinian cause, was ready to accept a separation of Syrian and Palestinian interests.[134] The burden of supporting the Palestinians had levied a heavy toll upon the Syrian population, in terms of personal sacrifice and material wealth.[135]

Until this moment, Asad had referred to the Palestinians as "southern cousins", and believed that the Palestinian cause belonged to the Arab nation, and not exclusively to Arafat or Fatah. Since 1970, the nature of Syrian-Palestinian relations had been determined by the competition between the pro-Arafat factions within the PLO, and Syria's attempt to assert its influence over PLO foreign policy. Syria's policy in Lebanon during 1983 provides an example.

As referred to in Chapter 4, Syria's encouragement of the fratricidal conflict between the pro-Arafat and anti-Arafat Palestinian factions in Lebanon was justified as part of Syria's strategy to unify the Arab position. Syria's means to control and influence Palestinian activities were frequently justified by the ends.

Syria's regional credibility as the coordinator of Arab affairs was under review after the PLO had signed a separate deal. Syrian influence over Jordan and Lebanon was believed to be unequivocal. On 27 December 1993, the Syrian foreign minister delivered a message to Jordan's King Hussein from President Asad, stressing the necessity for the coordination of action between Jordan, Lebanon, and Syria with the aim of isolating Arafat. Al-Shara' was also reported to have issued a warning to Jordan to refrain from embarking on a separate peace process. King Hussein had agreed not to sign any agreement with Israel before the Syrians and the Lebanese were ready to conclude peace with the Israelis.[136]

The Palestinian deal may have served the interests of the Palestinians within Gaza and the West Bank, but it emasculated the collective Arab bargaining position. The Palestinian issue had been central to the peace process. The Arab–Israeli conflict, irrespective of the Golan Heights and south Lebanon issues, was based on the creation of the Israeli state and the displacement of the Palestinian population. Arafat had tried to secure the future of a Palestinian state through an autonomy agreement that was disconnected from the other bilateral tracks in the peace process.

Israel, according to the Syrians, had successfully divided the existing unity between the Arab states. With the conclusion of Arafat and Rabin's deal, the issue of Palestine was no longer an Arab issue, but became a PLO one. The PLO had acted on behalf of the Palestinian population and was, therefore, responsible for the Gaza–Jericho First Plan.[137]

The Syrian press started to use familiar idioms to set a distance between the Palestinian and Syrian struggle with Israel. An incisive idiom suggested that the Syrians could not be more royal than the king.[138] Syrian Foreign Minister al-Shara' said:

> Syria's stance has never changed. Syria insisted and continues to insist on withdrawal from all the Arab lands occupied in 1967. However, the others, or some of the others, have broken away and negotiated for the West Bank, Jerusalem and the Jordanian territories. Thus Syria does not wish to be more royal than the king.[139]

In other words, the Palestinians had determined their own future and the Syrians were no longer responsible for their southern cousins.

According to members of the Syrian public, Arafat's move provided the Syrian regime with a pretext to reach a peace settlement with Israel divorced from the Palestinian issue.[140] The return of the Golan, in this instance, would be disengaged from the fate of the West Bank and Gaza. Syrian state interests started to acquire an importance of their own, but regional hegemony and national security still dominated the Syrian agenda.[141]

The only oppositional course to the Oslo Accords open to Asad was to allow the ten Palestinian rejectionist groups to reside in Syria. Just as Hizbollah has been a playing-card among Asad's deck of options, "the group of ten" became another sensitive card. It gave the Syrian regime access to the Palestinian political arena, and the potential to disrupt the implementation of the peace deal in the occupied territories.[142] Courting the rejectionist groups gave Asad important leverage over his adversaries. As one Syrian official observed, "These groups can be held on a tight leash or let loose. They feel obliged to Syria and they can be persuaded to change course."[143] After all, dirty tricks (or operations considered illegal according to international norms), had enabled Syria to promote its regional interests beyond the scope of its natural resources.[144]

The Palestinian groups in Damascus had been aware of the limitations placed on them by the Syrians. The relationship between the Syrian state and the Palestinian factions was one of patron and client. The determinants of the relationship were explicit as Syrian interests took precedence over factional interests, and, therefore, subjugated the activities of the groups to Syrian approval.[145]

The Palestinian groups, especially the Communist Party (PPP) and the PFLP, had been punished by the Syrian regime for contradicting the policies of the Syrians. The alliance between the Islamic and secular groups, under Syrian tutelage, bore many limitations as their collective partnership was based on tactical motives rather than any ideological affinity.[146]

Syria's international interests prevented the rejectionist groups from sabotaging the peace process within the occupied territories.[147] It remained, however, a potential source of power for Asad, as Cohen observed:

> Although Damascus now represents no substantial military threat to Israel, its control of Lebanon and its ability to unleash radical and fundamentalist Palestinian forces opposed to a negotiated settlement of the conflict gives it a measure of veto power over the peace talks.[148]

Thus, one could argue that the Syrian state was paying Arafat, Israel, and the international community a service by containing the potential threat of the rejectionist factions.

Although the Syrian regime expressed its dismay at Arafat's separate deal, and the method by which it was achieved, the regime did not condemn it. Asad outlined the basis of Syria's response as being one guided by the determinants of the New World Order. He said:

If Syria wanted to obstruct the agreement it would have foiled it, and if it becomes clear to us that this agreement will create major damage, we will do so. But we do not believe it constituted a threat and was just a step along a long road.[149]

Syria commenced a waiting game as Arafat entered negotiations over the fine details of the Oslo Accords. Asad spelled out Syria's position in a speech made to the People's Council:

> From the beginning [of the current peace process], our decision was clear: coordination with Arab parties participating in the peace process . . . when we raised the matter of coordination, we did so on the premise that the other Arab parties, which were involved in a negotiating process in an unequal manner with the Israeli side, should benefit from Syria's situation – its negotiating strength and its various capabilities on the battlefield – in addition to the fact that Syria is the basic element for peace in the region.[150]

Convinced that Syria would achieve a real peace, Asad was insistent that the time-scale was not an issue.

The Clinton–Asad meeting

The Syrian–Israeli track fell apart after the Oslo Accords and Syria's refusal to attend another round of talks. Clinton's meeting with Asad in Geneva on 16 January 1994 was designed to give the Syrian–Israeli track a fillip.[151] The meeting itself did not produce any significant progress, but it did draw Syria closer to the epicentre of the New World Order.

Asad's meeting with Clinton in Geneva sent a signal to the international community that Syria was gravitating towards the norms of the hegemonic global power. Syria achieved its aims from the meeting, which were, notably, to push the peace process forward, to improve bilateral US–Syrian relations and to discuss Syria's regional role.[152]

During their press conference, President Clinton acknowledged that Syria was the key to a wider settlement.[153] Syria, however, was not removed from the US terrorist state list, which would have made it eligible for American investment, loans, and procurement of advanced technologies;[154] but the meeting gave Asad international prestige, and Syria a platform from which to promote its regional agenda.

Asad punctuated his public address in Geneva with the following phrase: "In honour we fought. In honour we shall negotiate. In honour we shall make peace."[155] He stated that Syria saw "peace with Israel as a strategic choice to secure Arab rights", and which enabled "all peoples in the region to live in security".[156]

Syria's commitment to achieving comprehensive peace, despite the PLO–Israeli separate deal, formed part of Asad's platform, as indicated by the following statement:

> I hope that our meeting today will contribute to the realisation of the aspirations of the people of the region . . . that this new year will be the year of achieving the just and comprehensive peace which puts an end to the tragedies of violence and wars endured by them for several decades.[157]

Asad did not commit Syria to the normalisation of relations, as required by the Israelis, in return for withdrawal in the Golan. The Syrian president did refer to Syria's acceptance of the principle of normal relations, but this would be a feature of the second phase of the peace process, he said, when full withdrawal had been completed.[158]

Syria's commitment to peace as a strategic choice indicates how the New World Order has impinged upon Syria's option for regaining the Golan and liberating the rest of the occupied territories. With the demise of the Soviet Union and the advent of the New World Order, peace had become a strategic option for Syria. In its pursuit of its goals, Syria showed its readiness to improve bilateral relations with the US, but not at the expense of its regional status.[159]

The Hebron massacre

The Clinton–Asad meeting prompted the Syrians and Israelis to resume their negotiations. On 25 February 1994, before the talks began, Baruch Goldstein, an Israeli settler from Khan Yunis, had shot 48 Palestinian Muslims praying in the Ibrahim mosque in Hebron. Hence, the following round of talks in the peace process was suspended by the Arab parties.[160]

Although the Syrian–Israeli track stopped simultaneously with the talks of the PLO, Jordan, and Lebanon, Syria worked towards easing Syrian–Israeli tensions. In order to facilitate such a move, a confidence-building gesture was made when 57 Israeli Arabs visited Syria between

7 and 10 March 1994. The delegation was led by 'Abd al-Wahhab Darawsha from the Arab Democratic party.[161]

As in the case of the expelled Palestinians in the winter of 1992–3, after the Hebron massacre the Syrians had been waiting to return to the negotiating table, and so persuaded the Jordanians and Lebanese to circumvent Palestinian resistance to resuming the talks. This revealed Syria's readiness to proceed with the negotiations, and also demonstrated Syria's dismissive attitude towards the interests of the PLO.

The Jordanian peace deal

Maintaining the momentum of the peace process became a priority for Syria. The Palestinians had chosen their own route, but Syria's commitment was constant though the terms of reference were unclear. Separate peace was not an acceptable option, but progress on the bilateral talks was the aim. The comprehensive outcome would be completed through the simultaneous signing of treaties between Israel and Syria, Jordan, and Lebanon. Syria, in this context would hold the key to "setting the new structure of the peace into concrete".[162]

Just as Syria's quest for strategic parity was pursued with vigour, Syria's strategic choice for peace acquired the same momentum. Syria could not desert the peace process after the announcement of the Oslo Accords, nor could it change its strategy after Jordan and Israel reached a separate peace deal of their own.

On 25 July 1994 at the White House in Washington, D.C., King Hussein and Prime Minister Rabin signed the Washington Declaration[163] ending the state of war between the two states.[164] This did not constitute a full peace treaty, but signalled that a treaty was within reach. Despite the Washington Declaration, it was considered very unlikely that Jordan could sign a separate peace treaty without the support or consent of Syria. Such a move, it was thought, could provoke the Syrians into escalating a crisis with the Jordanian government.

In a move aimed at preventing Syria's isolation, Asad was given prior warning of the Jordanian–Israeli summit by the US president. The Syrian president apparently gave a discreet nod of acceptance, understanding that progress in the bilateral talks was appropriate as long as a peace treaty had not been concluded.[165]

Jordan's new position did not produce any major shock waves within the region.[166] Relations between Israel and Jordan had existed covertly for many years, and seemed to be common knowledge among journalists and Middle Eastern observers. The reported collusion between Israel, Jordan, and the US during Black September in 1970 had suggested that an implicit understanding existed between the Israeli and Jordanian leaderships.[167]

Jordan's decision to pursue its own national agenda was not revelationary either, as the PLO's signature of the Oslo Accords had provided the Jordanian government with a pretext for focusing on its own problems. The announcement of the PLO's government in exile in 1988, and the revocation of Jordan's claims to the West Bank, formally separated the political and geographical jurisdiction of Jordan and the PLO.[168] The PLO's agreement to Oslo further relieved Jordan of its commitment to the Palestinians, and removed any structural obstacles to conclusion of a peace treaty. The only remaining obstacle to an Israel–Jordan peace accord was Syria.

The inter-Arab rivalry between Syria and Jordan had produced many permutations of support within the region, and numerous combinations of punishment and reproach. Both states were alleged to have participated in clandestine operations against each other over the years; they had, in the light of new global and regional realities, found a *modus vivendi*. The collapse of the old world order and Jordan's disastrous decision to support Saddam Hussein exposed Jordan's vulnerabilities to the policies of the Gulf Arab states, in particular Saudi Arabia, and to the recriminatory policies of the US.[169]

Jordan and the PLO found refuge in Syrian diplomatic support. Syria's comprehensive approach, encompassing Jordan's weakness, enabled Jordan to maximise its relative strength within the forum of a united position. Syria's own position was emboldened, as it adopted its familiar role as the guardian of Arab interest.[170]

The PLO's engagement in secret peace talks with Israel, and the resulting Oslo Accords, weakened the unity of the Arab diplomatic front. Jordan enjoyed a distinct advantage from the Palestinian–Israeli initiative, whilst for Syria the result brought ambiguity and uncertainty.

In its desperate bid for international rehabilitation, Jordan charted a course towards the US. With a poor resource base, the imposition of international and regional economic sanctions, and growing domestic militancy, Jordan desperately needed the benefits of rehabilitation which included a critical financial package designed to placate the overburdened populace. For Jordan, the Oslo Accords produced the optimum moment to complete this period of rehabilitation. The price for rehabilitation was peace with Israel.[171]

As in Egypt's case, economic crisis precipitated the need for a change in foreign policy; the US, meanwhile, was the party willing to reduce Jordan's debt.[172] King Hussein and Prime Minister Rabin addressed the US Congress on 27 July 1994, stating that the war between Israel and Jordan was over. As an inducement for Jordan to sign a separate peace treaty, the Congress pledged to reduce Jordan's $700 million debt to the US to $220 million.[173]

Jordan's decision to sign a separate peace treaty with Israel on 26 October 1994 reflected the changes within the regional and international climate. Syria was unable to contest the decision or prevent the implementation of the peace treaty. Syria's response was confined to condemnation of King Hussein and his government. The Syrian regime charged the Jordanian regime with betraying the Arabs. In his speech to the People's Council, on 10 September 1994, Asad said:

> For decades, Syria waged the Arabs' battle against the Israeli occupation, to liberate the land and recover the [Arabs'] rights. Our people carried the principal burden in the confrontation and we offered great sacrifices in lives and suffering, and the conflict was reflected in the country's public life . . . I do not want to discuss what they [the Palestinians and Jordanians] arrived at, but reality makes unambiguously clear the enormity of the damage that unilateralism has inflicted on the core of the causes for which we have long fought and struggled.[174]

Syria's comprehensive policy had essentially failed. The Israelis and the Americans had managed to persuade the Palestinian and Jordanian governments to abandon the joint Arab stance. The prospect of concluding a separate peace treaty was more attractive than waiting for the Syrians to reach a settlement and then coordinate the final round of multilateral talks.

The arrival of the New World Order signified a diminution in Syria's regional power projection. The redistribution of global power led to a reduction in Syria's ability to influence the decision-making process within the Middle East region. Whereas Syria had challenged the PLO and the Jordanians in the past, the hegemonic role played by the US in the Middle East seemed to grant both actors more freedom from Syrian tutelage in their decision-making processes.

The Syrian government looked as if it had become a casualty of the New World Order. After following the option of strategic peace and engaging in the Madrid Peace Conference, Syria had been circumvented as the Jordanians and Palestinians signed separate peace treaties. Syria looked increasingly isolated from the successes of the peace process, and its regional hegemony appeared under threat from Israel.

Through the peace policy, Rabin and Peres had aimed to shape the new Middle Eastern order. Their new order was determined by the primacy of economics; Israel's desire to extend its economic hegemony in the region underpinned its commitment to peace.[175] Peace with Syria was crucial to eliminating the risk of war and enhancing Israel's chance of integrating itself into the region. Peace was a desirable objective for both Syria and Israel, but their terms of reference were very different.

The mode of direct and private discussion provided the potential for Syria and Israel to reconcile their differences. The Syrian and Israeli chiefs of staff met in Washington to discuss security issues.[176] The failure of Amnon Shahak and Hikmat al-Shihabi, respectively the Israeli and Syrian chiefs of staff, to find common ground in their meeting of December 1994, however, led to the drawing up of the Aims and Principles of Security Arrangements, and the resumption of discrete talks in June 1995.[177] This new formula for discussion was unable to accommodate the polarised positions of the chiefs of staff and required the offices of the Syrian and Israeli chief negotiators and aides. This resulted in the private talks at the Wye Plantation, Maryland, US, during December 1995.[178]

The Wye Plantation talks

US Secretary of State Christopher encouraged Syria and Israel to break their deadlock through private discussions at the Wye Plantation in Maryland. The Camp David and Dayton Accords (the US-sponsored agreement to end the struggle over Bosnia) had been achieved through US-engineered talks, and had therefore set a precedent for the resolution of the Syrian–Israeli conflict. The first round of talks took place on 27–9 December 1995 and the second round on 3–5 January 1996.[179]

The issue under discussion was that of the Golan Heights. Israel's interest in the Golan Heights has been attributed to their location as a strategic buffer between Syria and Israel. The Golan Heights' substantial water reserves, and biblical significance are also cited as justification for the Israeli annexation of this land in 1981.[180] For the Syrians, the Golan Heights have become symbolic of their regional national struggle with Israel. The return of the Golan would relieve the state of its responsibility for the 1967 débâcle, and recover some of the lost honour of the Ba'th regime.[181] The return of the Golan would also give Syria a defensive buffer zone, which is of particular importance because Damascus is just forty miles from the Golan Heights.

Formerly, Syria's commitment to peace with Israel had been based upon a full withdrawal from all the occupied territories. This position had changed during the peace process; because of the separate peace deals of the PLO and the Jordanians, Syria's concept of comprehensive peace had been modified. Walid Moualem, Syria's chief negotiator and ambassador to the US, commented:

> We still want comprehensiveness – comprehensiveness was one basis of the Madrid process. Our foreign minister in Madrid went around to the various Arab delegations to insist on the same venue and timing for the negotiations, and here in Washington we had regular coordinating meetings for the heads of Arab delegations . . . But we were taken by surprise by Oslo – we did not know about the secret talks until the agreement was announced. We were also surprised by the Jordanian treaty.[182]

Syria's inability to restrain the PLO and Jordan from concluding their peace deals caused the leadership to review its negotiating position.

The separate PLO and Jordanian peace deals had struck the Syrians a double blow. On the one hand, they had relieved Syria from the burden of its historical legacy, and presented the state with the opportunity to strike a deal in accord with its self-interest. The fatigue of the Syrian public, in supporting the Palestinian people, allowed the Syrian state to alter its official position vis-à-vis the Palestinian cause. The unconditional return of the Golan Heights, therefore, offered the state the prospect of a new source of legitimacy. Full withdrawal from the Golan would also vindicate Asad's authoritative domestic policy, and accentuate his foreign policy successes. On the other hand, Israel was successful in isolating Syria from the peace process by its peace accords with the PLO and Jordan. Syrian hegemony in the Levant was diminishing as Israel had grown in regional stature. The economic dynamism of Israel stood to erode Syria's influence further. The new Middle Eastern order, based on the unipolar intervention of the US and the success of its client state, ensured that the region was subordinated to the prevailing regional and international hegemonic orders, and its Arab character effaced.

A peace treaty with Israel, focused solely upon the Golan, held the possibility of de-linking Syria from its spheres of influence as the regional competition with Israel assumed an economic character. However, Lebanon could not be uncoupled from Syria's sphere of influence, nor could a Lebanese–Israeli peace be durable without Syrian compliance. Walid Moualem said:

> We said that comprehensive peace from our perspective includes Syria and Lebanon together at the same time. We sign together, and Israel withdraws both from south Lebanon and the Golan Heights.[183]

The Syrians were free to pursue a peace deal with Israel based upon the total liberation of the Golan Heights for full peace. The discussions at the Wye Plantation were designed to propel the process towards a hasty conclusion. Apparently, in July 1994, Israel agreed to a full withdrawal to the 4 June 1967 lines.[184] This paved the way for the negotiations to address the cumulative issues of a peace treaty, which included: the meaning of withdrawal; the timetable of withdrawal; normalisation of relations; security arrangements.

Meaning of withdrawal
Withdrawal, Syria argued, meant an Israeli return to the 4 June 1967 borders, which left Syria some access to Lake Tiberias.[185] Israel insisted that the international boundary meant the pre-1948 borders, which placed the lake entirely in its territory: Syria could not be allowed to return to the northern shore of Lake Tiberias, Israel's water reserve.[186] After the election of Netanyahu as Israel's prime minister in May 1996, President Asad disclosed that Rabin had conceded a full withdrawal from the Golan in accordance with Syria's conditions.[187] The talks at the Wye Plantation were based on this premise, and were, therefore, invested with the potential to produce a peace treaty. The claim that Israel had conceded full withdrawal was first made public in Hebrew in a publication, and then by Egypt's president, Hosni Mubarak, in an interview with *al-Hayat* newspaper.[188]

Timetable of withdrawal

The timing of withdrawal remained a problem. Syria wanted full withdrawal with a reasonable time frame of about a year.[189] Pointing to Israel's reluctance to fulfil the Oslo Accords, Asad rejected any agreement that left the outcome to Israel's discretion and refused normalisation prior to full withdrawal.

During Rabin's premiership, Israel proposed a three-stage Golan withdrawal over a period of five years. After the inception of the process, Syria would have to establish diplomatic relations with Israel, and implement the policy of normalisation. Withdrawal would be linked to normalisation. The assassination of Rabin catapulted the Syrian–Israeli peace process to the forefront of Israeli foreign policy.

With an impending election, it appeared that Shimon Peres was intent on concluding a quick deal. Unlike Rabin, Peres was a professional politician and not a military man. He needed to assert his strong leadership through a show of force to impress upon the public his ability to guarantee Israeli security. Incorporating Syria into the peace process offered Peres the chance of re-election, but the assassinations of the leader of Islamic Jihad, Shaqaqi, in Malta in October 1995, and of Yahya 'Ayyash (the infamous Palestinian bomber from Gaza) on 4 January 1996, changed the course of the peace process.[190]

Normalisation

The issue of normalisation divided the Syrian and Israeli negotiating teams, though Syria had confirmed its commitment to normalisation.[191] Normalisation would follow the conclusion of the withdrawal of Israel from the Golan and the signing of a peace treaty. As al-Shara' said: "Let us put things in the proper sequence. We do not want to have loopholes or snags here and there, which would be counter-productive."[192]

Barak, the Israeli foreign minister, included the free flow of goods, services and people, joint water and trade projects and the integration of the two countries' electricity grids, into the concept of normalisation.[193] Syria, however, was reluctant to agree to economic normalisation, as the Syrian ambassador to the US, Moualem, explained.

> They wanted open borders, open markets for their goods, and so on. This would have an obvious effect on our own economy. Our economic regulations are not against them; we do open our markets

to any country. And how can you integrate two economies when one has a per capita income of $900 per year and the other has a per capita income of $15,000 per year? Such integration is not possible, so we discussed a transitional period during which we could raise our economy to the level where there can be competition without undue hardship on our society.[194]

Security arrangements

As Israel inched closer to agreeing to a full withdrawal from the Golan, it insisted on security substitutes for territory. Its maximum position included dismantling Syrian chemical weapons and a radical reduction in the Syrian standing army. Since Syria's regular army is much larger than Israel's regular army, such demands would demolish Syria's deterrent ability, given Israel's nuclear monopoly and Syria's inability to mobilise reserves rapidly.[195]

Israel also wanted a limited forces zone requiring a Syrian pull-back almost as far as Damascus. Syria accepted demilitarisation of the Golan but wanted equal limited forces zones on both sides of the border, which Israel refused.[196] The negotiations stalled over an Israeli demand for an early-warning station on Mount Hermon.[197] Syria insisted that aerial or satellite surveillance was adequate, and that a continued Israeli presence there would be an affront to Syrian sovereignty.[198]

Missed opportunities

The Wye Plantation talks produced the opportunity for a Syrian–Israeli peace deal. It had become known in retrospect that Rabin had agreed to full withdrawal in return for full peace. This agreement formed the basis of the Wye Plantation talks. The assassination of Rabin accelerated the peace process as his successor, Peres, aimed to achieve a rapid solution to the conflict. Both parties were intent on securing peace; the issues of normalisation were within reach.

The intransigence of both parties had been broken. The prospect of peace, although a secret, appears to have been an option. Peres' decision to hold an early election, and his need to establish security credentials, shattered the progress of the Wye Plantation talks.

Operation Grapes of Wrath

After the assassination of Rabin on 4 November 1995, the prospective

Israeli elections dominated the regional political scene. The speculation over Rabin's successor, Peres, had produced some hope for a Syrian–Israeli peace deal, yet the Syrian–Israeli track remained in the background in discussions.[199]

Peres had been the Israeli architect of the Oslo Accords, and its more progressive dimensions were attributed to him. Peres, portrayed as a dove to the hawk Rabin, seemed to promise hope for the Syrians and the disenchanted Palestinians. But the election procedure took precedence over the peace process, and the contest of electioneering distorted the political views of both the Labour and Likud parties.

Rabin had been the military and political component of the partnership, whilst Peres played the diplomatic role. Despite their antipathy towards each other, they had managed to complement each other's substance and style of leadership. Peres lacked the military stature of Rabin; Rabin's military successes, particularly in the 1967 War, had been carved into Israeli folklore, and his leadership skills were legendary. Peres, as a trained diplomat, could not compete with Rabin's security credentials.[200]

The assassination of Shaqaqi in Malta, in October 1995, by Mossad, and of 'Ayyash on 4 January 1996 by Shin Bet,[201] created a fundamental problem that looked set to derail the peace process. The retaliatory moves came in the form of a series of devastating suicide bombings targeting civilian population centres within Israel. Islamic Jihad and Hamas had, until the assassinations of Shaqaqi and 'Ayyash, reached an informal agreement with the Palestinian Authority to refrain from violent opposition to the peace process.[202]

The assassinations provoked a violent response which halted progress on all of the peace tracks. President Asad refused to condemn publicly the suicide missions, and as a result the Israeli government unilaterally suspended the negotiations on the Syrian–Israeli track. Therefore, Peres faced the prospect of a general election with distinct disadvantages which included: increased domestic insecurity; an ailing Palestinian–Israeli interim agreement; no significant progress on the Syrian–Israeli track; no personal record of military integrity.

The spate of suicide bombings had started to divide public opinion until Peres' apparent failure to protect the security of Israeli citizens produced a new consensus of public opinion. The sympathy vote, derived from Rabin's assassination, was rapidly diminishing as the national obsession with security started to gain priority among the public.

Peres' response to Labour's receding support was dramatic; it came in the form of an excessive military retaliation against Hizbollah.[203] The latter's activities had not diminished in intensity as they were governed only by the verbal understanding reached between Hizbollah and Israel after Operation Accountability in July 1993.

Operation Grapes of Wrath was launched in April 1996 with two objectives:

(a) To provide an election platform for Peres and the Labour Party;
(b) To pressurise Syria and Lebanon into returning to the peace talks.

The Clinton administration was firmly committed to the re-election of Peres; accordingly it lent Israel its unequivocal support in Operation Grapes of Wrath.[204] Both the US and Israeli administrations had presided over the critical stages of the peace process, and had invested enormous political capital into it, although one could argue that Clinton's role had remained peripheral and possibly ceremonial.

It is not possible to gauge the intention of the operation, but Grapes of Wrath seemed to have spun out of control and proved to be far more devastating than was originally anticipated. The mission was dominated by the supremacy of Israeli air power, which exceeded the range and capabilities of Hizbollah's Katyusha rockets. It was estimated by UN peacekeepers that there were 3,000 aerial sorties by fighter bombers and helicopter gunships over 17 days; 30,000 artillery shells were fired, plus hundreds of shells from ships. Hizbollah's arsenal was not so impressive; it was estimated to consist of 1,100 Katyusha rockets.[205]

Peres' sanctioning of military action appears most likely to have been motivated by his desire to increase his prospect of re-election. Security had not been the exclusive preserve of Israel's generals, since the military was ultimately responsible to the civilian government, as the highest authority in Israel. The escalation of the Israeli assault, and the resulting massacre at Qana, brought international condemnation on Peres' government and discredited it in the eyes of the Israeli public. On 18 April 1996, 102 sheltering refugees were killed by Israeli self-propelled artillery as they sought refuge in the UN base of Qana.[206]

What appeared to be a bid for re-election turned out to be a domestic and international disaster for Peres, Israel, and the US. The excessive use of force and the consequent human devastation undermined Peres' stature as a sagacious politician. It also allowed the Syrians, Lebanese, and French to assert their influence in the implementation of the cease-fire and its arrangements.[207]

The Israeli military initiative was partially designed to eliminate the pernicious threat of Hizbollah from northern Israel, thereby terminating one of Syria's principal sources of pressure. Without the option of Hizbollah as a persistent irritant to the Israelis, it was estimated that the Syrians would be forced to return to the peace talks. Ironically, the Syrians were the main beneficiaries, in terms of accumulating diplomatic credit and exercising control over Hizbollah.

A consequence of Operation Grapes of Wrath was the propulsion of Syria towards the epicentre of the cease-fire process. By taking a back seat, the Syrian president played a fundamental role in achieving the cease-fire. As the Americans tried to formulate their own proposals, the French and the Syrians negotiated the terms and conditions of the cease-fire between Israel and Lebanon. On 26 April 1996, Israel and the US accepted the terms of the cease-fire, which were based on the existing terms reached after Operation Accountability in July 1993.[208]

Instead of remaining a verbal agreement, the parameters of behaviour were set out in a document. This included the following stipulations:

(a) Armed groups were not to attack Israel with any type of weapons;
(b) Israel was prohibited from attacking Lebanese civilians or civilian targets in Lebanon;
(c) Attacks on civilian infrastructure were banned, as was the launching of attacks into Israel's occupation zone from areas of civilian habitation;
(d) The parties would retain the right of legitimate defence within stipulations of the understanding.[209]

On 16 May 1996, Israel and the US agreed to the establishment of a monitoring committee composed of Israel, Lebanon, Syria, the US, and France; the rotating chair belonged to the US and France, thus elevating the role of France in the region.[210]

This episode demonstrated Syria's ability to survive in the New World Order. In an attempt to persuade the Israeli public of his security credentials, Peres had lost the political and diplomatic advantage gained through the separate peace agreements with the PLO and Jordan. Operation Grapes of Wrath had also failed to eliminate Syria's political, diplomatic, and military manœuvrability.

Syria's influence over Hizbollah, and therefore its access to northern Israel by proxy, has continued to provide an opportunity to exert pressure on the Israelis. Syria's access, indeed, had improved after Operation Grapes of Wrath, as the terms of the cease-fire legitimised Hizbollah's attacks within the security zone. Syria's regional influence was also enhanced because of the special role it played in brokering the cease-fire.

Emerging from yet another period of political isolation, Syria managed to elevate its regional status through its dominance in Lebanon. Throughout the 1980s, during its period of tactical rejectionism, Syria had fought its campaign through Lebanon. Lebanon had become the last stronghold of Syrian influence; its matrix of confessions and propensity for violence had provided Syria with a context within which it could resist Israeli and US intervention. In the 1990s, Israel had formally removed the PLO and Jordan from Syria's influence, and in turn focused its attention on Lebanon and Hizbollah.

The environment of the New World Order took away Syria's option for rejecting peace after Jordan and the PLO had signed separate agreements. Syria's actions were conditioned according to the new distribution of power within the world system. On the other hand, Lebanon has remained a Syrian stronghold, and Asad has remained a key player in its orientation. In the 1980s, through persistence and a sustainable loss of life, Syria had managed to defeat the Israelis and the US in Lebanon. Operation Grapes of Wrath provided another chance for Syria to achieve such a victory, but in the 1996 case, the success was diplomatic rather than military.

In yet another twist of the peace process, Syria had managed to avoid regional isolation and a capitulating return to the peace negotiations on Israel's terms. Israel's escalation of the conflict has failed to reduce Syria's influence in Lebanon and its ability to pressurise Israel through the activities of Hizbollah.

Operation Grapes of Wrath failed to persuade the Israeli public to re-elect the Labour party. After the first direct election of an Israeli prime minister, Benyamin Netanyahu assumed office in June 1996. The change of government within Israel and the election of Netanyahu have compounded the problems for the Palestinians. The Oslo Accords and the accompanying agreements have subsequently been amended to accommodate the demands of Israel's settlers.[211] The Jordanian peace is also showing signs of weakness as the process of normalisation has not been embraced by the Jordanian population,[212] and the US Congress has not approved the cancelling of the Jordanian debt promised by the Clinton administration as an inducement to peace.[213] The platform on which Netanyahu was elected denied Syria's sovereignty over the Golan, and has therefore appeared to end the prospects for a Syrian–Israeli peace deal during his term of office.[214]

Conclusion

It has been argued throughout this chapter that Syria's commitment to peace has been constant since 1974. Achieving comprehensive peace between the Arab states and Israel would serve the national interests of Syria in its struggle for regional hegemony with Israel. Comprehensive peace would enable Syria to extend its sphere of influence over its Levantine neighbours without invoking the prospect of military confrontation with Israel.

The concept of comprehensive peace has entailed the liberation of the occupied territories, including the West Bank, Gaza, south Lebanon, and the Golan Heights. The restoration of Palestinian rights has also been a component of the comprehensive peace.[215] Shara', the Syrian foreign minister, had made the Syrian position on peace very clear when he stated: "What we want is to implement UN Resolutions, in particular, UN Security Resolutions 242 and 338. These resolutions call for Israel's withdrawal from the occupied Arab lands and safeguarding the Palestinian national rights."[216]

The Syrian commitment to comprehensive peace was asserted by President Asad in an interview with CNN on 28 October 1991.

> No one in the region, or outside the region, Europe, the USA, Eastern Europe, or other areas of the world has interest in the absence of a comprehensive peace in this region. Any separate or partial peace process will not achieve peace, security and stability in the region and any party continuing the state of war with Israel will bring back complicated circumstances to the region which will lead to comprehensive wars in the future.[217]

The conclusion of separate peace deals has become the greatest of Syria's fears. Syria's disdain of separate peace formulas had been displayed throughout the 1980s. The creation of the Steadfastness Front to undermine Egypt's separate peace with Israel, and Syria's tactical rejection of the Lebanese–Israeli Accord, illustrated its conviction of the need to spoil formulas which excluded it from the peace process.

The end of the Cold War and Iraq's invasion of Kuwait offered an opportunity for Syria to present itself at the centre of a more comprehensive solution to the Arab–Israeli conflict. The Madrid Peace Conference provided the forum for an international resolution to the Arab–Israeli conflict. Syria's agreement to attend the Madrid Peace Conference was based on its foundation of UN Resolutions 242, 338, and 425. Syria showed its flexibility, a concession to the New World Order dominated by the US, by modifying some of its demands for participating in the peace process.

During the Madrid Peace Conference, Syria tried to coordinate the policies of Jordan, Lebanon, and the PLO. Diplomatic unity offered the Arab states the potential to resist Israeli pressure in the negotiating process. The bilateral talks, however, set the Palestinians and Jordanians down a different track. The PLO and Jordanian acquiescence to the Oslo Accords and the Jordan–Israel peace treaty, respectively, represented a serious set-back for the Syrians.

The Palestinians and Jordanians were motivated by the opportunity to achieve short-term gains in their national interest. Rousseau's fable of the stag hunt provides an apposite explanation for their behaviour.[218] If applied to this case, it would suggest that existing in an anarchic state of nature, where self-help governs the behaviour of states, the PLO and Jordan have made rational decisions based upon their immediate concerns. The hunt for the stag (comprehensive peace) was flawed from the outset, as the hare (separate peace) held the prospect of short-term gratification. The pursuit of the hare has weakened the potential of the pack, and allowed the stag to escape to the safety of the folkloric forest.

The short-term satiation of the hare has left the PLO hungry as the winter sets in; meanwhile, the lion of Syria has kept his sights on the stag. The inherent problems contained within the Oslo Accords have justified Syria's search for a comprehensive peace, and its reluctance to settle for a separate peace deal. The issues of Jerusalem, the Israeli settlements, and the refugees, for example, have yet to be resolved, whilst

Israel continues to build settlements in the West Bank, and to annex East Jerusalem.[219]

The separate peace deals signed by the PLO and Jordan have undermined Syrian influence in the Levant, and weakened its position in the balance of power with Israel.[220] Geopolitically isolated, Syria has remained an observer as Israel concluded separate peace treaties with the PLO and Jordan. However, the limited nature of the peace treaties has left Syria with some leverage in the peace process.

Since the PLO and Jordan have signed separate peace deals, Syria has two choices:

(a) To conclude a separate peace deal with Israel, where Israel withdraws from the Golan in exchange for peace and normalisation;

(b) To wait to conclude a comprehensive peace in the aftermath of the Oslo Accords.

Comprehensive peace is no longer an option in the near future. The PLO and Jordan have signed separate peace treaties with Israel; the Gulf Arab states have suspended their secondary boycott of Israel. Syria may hold some Palestinian cards, in the form of the rejectionist Palestinian groups, but these groups do not constitute a bridge to peace. At most, Syria can try to spoil the PLO–Israel peace agreement, but the details of Oslo I, Oslo II, the policies of the Likud government, and the corruption of Arafat's regime, are tending to this objective.[221]

To conclude, there has been little progress on the Syrian–Israeli track. Numerous obstacles have served to prevent either side from making concessions. The balance of power, in diplomatic terms, has continued to determine the stalemate between the two adversaries. Each event has empowered one player at the expense of the other.

The contest between Syria and Israel for regional hegemony found a new expression in the Madrid Peace Conference. Attending the conference, however, did not prevent the old enemies from engaging in their struggle in Lebanon. Operation Accountability and Operation Grapes of Wrath, two Israeli assaults upon Hizbollah, were attempts at weakening Syria's hand in the peace negotiations.

The determinants of a comprehensive peace held the possibility of Syria containing Israel's hegemony. Israel has always been aware of this fact, and, therefore, followed a separate peace approach, which had been designed to incorporate the Levantine states into its orbit of influence.

The prospect of peace had attracted the Arab parties, and convinced them to engage in separate peace deals with Israel.

Evidently Israel's regional hegemony, together with its integrated relationship with the US, have impinged upon Syria's options. In the aftermath of the second Gulf War, the pursuit of peace through the US-led peace process gave Syria its only opportunity to find a solution satisfying its minimal requirements. Peace under the auspices of the US presented itself as a strategic choice; Syria was not in a political or military position to resist the encompassing features of the New World Order.

NOTES

1 S. Cohen, "The Geopolitics of a Golan Heights Agreement", *Focus*, vol. 42, 1 June 1992, p. 15.
2 *BBC Summary of World Broadcasts*, ME/1351, A/9, 9 April 1992.
3 D. Pipes, "Syria's People May Not Want Peace", *Jewish Exponent*, 25 November 1994, pp. 1–3.
4 J. Kirkpatrick, "We Shouldn't Risk US Dollars on Unreliable Arafat and Assad", *Human Events*, vol. 51, 28 July 1995, p. 10.
5 A. Drysdale and R. Hinnebusch, *Syria and the Middle East Peace Process* (New York: Council on Foreign Relations, 1991), pp. 201–7.
6 E. Kienle, "Syria, the Kuwait War, and the New World Order" in T. Ismael and J. Ismael (eds.), *The Gulf War and the New World Order: International Relations of the Middle East*, (Gainesville: University Press of Florida, 1994), p. 390.
7 C. Richards, "Assad Adds His Weight to Middle East Peace Talks", *The Independent*, 17 January 1994, p. 1.
8 *BBC Summary of World Broadcasts*, ME/1402, A/1, 9 June 1992.
9 Interview with Syrian businessman, 25 June 1994.
10 This assumption is based on a number of interviews undertaken in Syria during October 1995.
11 E. Karsh, "Peace in the Middle East", *The Oxford International Review*, vol. 5, no. 1 (Winter 1993), p. 39.
12 G. Butt, "Asad the Coordinator", *Middle East International*, no. 411, 25 October 1991, p. 7.
13 E. Karsh, "Peace in the Middle East", *The Oxford International Review*, vol. 5, no. 1 (Winter 1993), p. 37.
14 J. Galvani, P. Johnson and R. Theberge, "The October War: Egypt, Syria, Israel", *Middle East Report (MERIP)*, no. 22 (November 1973), p. 15.
15 T. Petran, *Syria* (New York: Praeger, 1972), pp. 97–105.
16 M. Ma'oz, "The Emergence of Modern Syria" in M. Ma'oz and A. Yaniv (eds.), *Syria under Assad: Domestic Constraints and Regional Risks* (London: Croom Helm, 1986), p. 21.

17 T. Petran, *Syria* (New York: Praeger, 1972), pp. 89–92.
18 M. Ma'oz, *Syria and Israel: From War to Peace-making* (Oxford: Clarendon Press, 1995), pp. 82–4.
19 A. Ben-Meir, "The Israeli–Syrian Battle for Equitable Peace", *Middle East Policy*, vol. iii, no. 1 (January 1994), p. 74.
20 For more details of the theoretical approach consult F. Lawson, *Why Syria Goes To War: Thirty Years of Confrontation* (London: Cornell University Press, 1996).
21 For more details of the early Syrian–Israeli struggle see: M. Ma'oz, *Syria and Israel: From War to Peace-making* (Oxford: Clarendon Press, 1995); T. Petran, *Syria* (New York: Praeger, 1972); P. Seale, *The Struggle for Syria: A Study of Post-War Arab politics 1945–1958*, (London: Oxford University Press, 1965), and A. Rathmell, *Secret War in the Middle East: The Covert Struggle for Syria, 1949–1961* (London: I.B. Tauris, 1995).
22 E. Karsh, "Peace in the Middle East", *The Oxford International Review*, vol. 5, no. 1 (Winter 1993), p. 37.
23 M. Ma'oz, *Syria and Israel: From War to Peace-making* (Oxford: Clarendon Press, 1995), pp. 120–30.
24 P. Seale, *Asad of Syria: The Struggle for the Middle East* (London: I.B. Tauris, 1988), p. 140.
25 The use of the oil weapon by the Gulf Arab states provided economic, political, and diplomatic leverage for the Arab states.
26 P. Seale, *Asad of Syria: The Struggle for the Middle East* (London: I.B. Tauris, 1988), pp. 194–201.
27 J. Lorenz, *Egypt and the Arabs: Foreign Policy and the Search for National Identity* (Oxford: Westview Press, 1990), p. 51.
28 For more details of Egyptian and Syrian identity see E. Kienle, "Arab Unity Schemes Revisited: Interest, Identity, and Policy in Syria and Egypt", *International Journal of Middle East Studies*, vol. 27, no. 1 (February 1995), pp. 53–71.
29 J. Galvani, P. Johnson and R. Theberge, "The October War: Egypt, Syria, Israel", *Middle East Report (MERIP)*, no. 22 (November 1973), p. 10.
30 D. Hopwood, *Egypt: Politics and Society 1945–90* (London: HarperCollins, 1991), p. 110.
31 E. Kienle, "Arab Unity Schemes Revisited: Interest, Identity, and Policy in Syria and Egypt", *International Journal of Middle East Studies*, vol. 27, no. 1 (February 1995), pp. 54–6.
32 A. Dessouki, "The Primacy of Economics: The Foreign Policy of Egypt" in B. Korany and A. Dessouki (eds.), *The Foreign Policies of Arab States: The Challenge of Change* (Boulder: Westview Press, 1991), p. 175.
33 Ibid., p. 156, and R. Burrell and A. Kelider, *Egypt the Dilemmas of a Nation – 1970–1977: The Washington Papers*, vol. v, no. 48 (London: Sage, 1977), p. 61.
34 P. Seale, *Asad of Syria: The Struggle for the Middle East* (London: I.B. Tauris, 1988), p. 256.
35 A. Ehteshami and R. Hinnebusch, *Syria and Iran: Middle Powers in a Penetrated Regional System* (London: Routledge, 1997), p. 158.
36 R. Burrell and A. Kelider, *Egypt the Dilemmas of a Nation – 1970–1977: The Washington Papers*, vol. v, no. 48 (London: Sage, 1977), p. 65.
37 E. Zisser, "Asad of Syria – the Leader and the Image", *Orient*, vol. 35, no. 2 (June 1994), p. 256.

38 A. Khalidi and H. Agha, "The Syrian Doctrine of Strategic Parity" in J. Kipper and H. Saunders (eds.), *The Middle East in Global Perspective* (Boulder: Westview Press, 1991), pp. 186–218.

39 This term has been borrowed from A. Drysdale and R. Hinnebusch, *Syria and the Middle East Peace Process* (New York: Council on Foreign Relations, 1991), p. 129.

40 A. Drysdale and R. Hinnebusch, *Syria and the Middle East Peace Process* (New York: Council on Foreign Relations, 1991), p. 129.

41 *Syria – Country Profile*, (London: The Economist Intelligence Unit, May 1981), no. 2, p. 25.

42 R. Freedman, "The Soviet Union and Syria: A Case Study of Soviet Policy" in M. Efrat and J. Bercovitch (eds.), *Superpowers and Client States in the Middle East: The Imbalance of Influence* (London: Routledge, 1991), p. 164.

43 Ibid.

44 E. Karsh, "Peace in the Middle East", *The Oxford International Review*, vol. 5, no. 1 (Winter 1993), p. 38.

45 Ironically, Begin's government shared Syria's disdain for PLO and Jordanian initiatives, especially those that included references to territorial compromise. See A. Drysdale and R. Hinnebusch, *Syria and the Middle East Peace Process* (New York: Council on Foreign Relations, 1991), p. 131.

46 T. Seelye, "Syria and the Peace Process", *Middle East Policy*, vol. ii, no. 2 (1993), pp. 104–9.

47 J. Kagian, "More of the Same at the UN", *Middle East International*, no. 544, 21 February 1997, p. 6.

48 G. User, "Land Confiscation in Arab Jerusalem", *Middle East International*, no. 500, 12 May 1995, pp. 3–4; P. Kidron, "Rabin Caves in on Land Confiscations", *Middle East International*, no. 501, 26 May 1995, p. 3, and D. Neff, "The 30th Veto to Shield Israel", *Middle East International*, no. 501, 26 May 1995, pp. 5–6.

49 L. Drake, "A Netanyahu Prime Minister", *Journal of Palestine Studies*, no. XXVI, no. 1 (Autumn 1996), pp. 58–69, and G. Usher, "Picture of War", *Middle East International*, no. 535, 4 October 1996, pp. 3–5.

50 R. Hinnebusch, "Does Syria Want Peace? Syrian Policy in the Syrian–Israeli Peace Negotiations", *Journal of Palestine Studies*, vol. XXVI, no. 1 (Autumn 1996), pp. 48–9.

51 M. Diab, "Have Syria and Israel Opted for Peace?", *Middle East Policy*, vol. iii, no. 2 (1994), p. 83.

52 E. Karsh, "Peace in the Middle East", *The Oxford International Review*, vol. 5, no. 1 (Winter 1993), p. 39.

53 D. Neff, "Settlements and Guarantees: The US Threatens Linkage", *Middle East International*, no. 409, 27 September 1991, pp. 3–4; P. Kidron, "Consternation in Israel", *Middle East International*, no. 409, 27 September 1991, pp. 4–5, and P. Kidron, "Sullen Acceptance", Middle *East International*, no. 411, 25 October 1991, pp. 9–10.

54 G. Hawatmeh, "Still in Two Minds", *Middle East International*, no. 409, 27 September 1991, p. 8, and S. Islam, "Hussein's Plea for Jordan", *Middle East International*, no. 409, 27 September 1991, p. 9.

55 A. Ehteshami and R. Hinnebusch, *Syria and Iran: Middle Powers in a Penetrated Regional System* (London: Routledge, 1997), p. 158.

56 D. Butter, "Asad Treads Cautiously", *Middle East Economic Digest*, vol. 37, no. 40, 8 October 1993, p. 3.
57 Ibid.
58 L. Freedman, "Syrian Initiative Increases Regional Risks for Assad", *The Times*, Monday 17 January 1994, p. 10.
59 A. Ehteshami and R. Hinnebusch, *Syria and Iran: Middle Powers in a Penetrated Regional System* (London: Routledge, 1997), p. 157.
60 Ibid., p. 158.
61 *BBC Summary of World Broadcasts*, ME/1125, A/8, 16 July 1991.
62 *BBC Summary of World Broadcasts*, ME/1126, A/1, 17 July 1991.
63 *BBC Summary of World Broadcasts*, ME/1213, A/2, 26 October 1991.
64 R. Hinnebusch, "Does Syria Want Peace? Syrian Policy in the Syrian–Israeli Peace Negotiations", *Journal of Palestine Studies*, vol. XXVI, no. 1 (Autumn 1996), p. 49.
65 G. Hawatmeh, "The Pluses and the Minuses", *Middle East International*, no. 412, 8 November 1991, p. 5.
66 D. Neff, "The Make-or-Break Process Begins in Madrid", *Middle East International*, no. 411, 25 October 1991, p. 3.
67 *BBC Summary of World Broadcasts*, ME/1220, E/17, 4 November 1991.
68 *BBC Summary of World Broadcasts*, ME/1225, A/1, 9 November 1991.
69 J. Muir, "Syrians Refuse the Bait", *Middle East International*, no. 413, 22 November 1991, pp. 5–6.
70 V. Yorke, "Prospects for Peace: The Syrian Dimension", *Middle East International*, no. 414, 6 December 1991, pp. 16–17.
71 *BBC Summary of World Broadcasts*, ME/1126, A/3, 17 July 1991.
72 *Mid-East Mirror*, 15 October 1991.
73 *BBC Summary of World Broadcasts*, ME/1128, A/1–A/2, 19 July 1991.
74 J. Muir, "The Arabs Fall into Line", *Middle East International*, no. 405, 26 July 1991, pp. 4–5.
75 G. Hawatmeh, "Still in Two Minds", *Middle East International*, no. 409, 27 September 1991, p. 8.
76 *Foreign Broadcast Information Service*, 8 May 1990, p. 31.
77 L. Brand, "Asad's Syria and the PLO: Coincidence or Conflict of Interests?", *Journal of South Asian and Middle Eastern Studies*, vol. XIV, no. 2 (Winter 1990), pp. 23–5.
78 A. Ehteshami and R. Hinnebusch, *Syria and Iran: Middle Powers in a Penetrated Regional System* (London: Routledge, 1997), pp. 160–1.
79 Ibid., p. 159.
80 *BBC Summary of World Broadcasts*, ME/1218, E/13–E/24, 1 November 1991.
81 L. Andoni, "A Leap into Darkness", *Middle East International*, no. 411, 25 October 1991, p. 4.
82 See H. Ashrawi, *This Side of Peace: A Personal Account* (New York: Simon & Schuster, 1995).
83 *BBC Summary of World Broadcasts*, ME/1209, A/4, 22 October 1991.
84 *BBC Summary of World Broadcasts*, ME/1226, A/9, 11 November 1991.
85 R. Hinnebusch, "Does Syria Want Peace? Syrian Policy in the Syrian–Israeli Peace Negotiations", *Journal of Palestine Studies*, vol. XXVI, no. 1 (Autumn 1996), p. 49.

86 G. Butt, "Flagging Arab Spirits", *Middle East International*, no. 418, 7 February 1992, pp. 4–5.
87 R. Hinnebusch, "Does Syria Want Peace? Syrian Policy in the Syrian–Israeli Peace Negotiations", *Journal of Palestine Studies*, vol. XXVI, no. 1 (Autumn 1996), p. 49.
88 L. Dajani, "The Casablanca Conference – Winners and Losers", *Middle East International*, no. 488, 18 November 1994, p. 18.
89 G. Nader, "Syrian Foreign Minister Farouk al-Sharaa Reaffirms Peace for Golan Withdrawal", *Middle East Insight*, vol. xi, no. 1 (November/December 1994), p. 17.
90 G. Nader, "Imagining Peace with Syria: Changes Show the Country and Regime are Prepared for Peace", *Middle East Insight*, vol. xi, no. 1 (November/December 1994), p. 10.
91 P. Kidron, "Yitzhak Rabin, 1922–1995", *Middle East International*, no. 513, 17 November 1995, p. 4.
92 See below.
93 J. Neriah, "Progress and Challenges on the Syrian Track: An Israeli Perspective on the Negotiations", *Middle East Insight*, vol. xi, no. 4 (May/June 1995), p. 11.
94 M. Hallaj, "Round Six: Hope then Disappointment", *Middle East International*, no. 433, 11 September 1992, p. 3.
95 J. Neriah, "Progress and Challenges on the Syrian Track: An Israeli Perspective on the Negotiations", *Middle East Insight*, vol. xi, no. 4 (May/June 1995), p. 10.
96 *BBC Summary of World Broadcasts*, ME/1465, A/2–A/3, 21 August 1992, and ME/1469, A/1–A/2, 26 August 1992.
97 A. Ehteshami and R. Hinnebusch, *Syria and Iran: Middle Powers in a Penetrated Regional System* (London: Routledge, 1997), p. 165.
98 P. Kidron, "242 But not an Inch", *Middle East International*, no. 433, 11 September 1992, pp. 4–5.
99 A. Ehteshami and R. Hinnebusch, *Syria and Iran: Middle Powers in a Penetrated Regional System* (London: Routledge, 1997), pp. 165–6.
100 M. Hallaj, "Peace Talks: The Illusion of Optimism Exposed", *Middle East International*, no. 434, 25 September 1992, p. 3.
101 *BBC Summary of World Broadcasts*, ME/1522, A/2, 27 October 1992.
102 G. Jansen, "Syria's Bottom Line", *Middle East International*, no. 434, 25 September 1992, p. 5.
103 M. Hallaj, "Peace Talks: The Illusion of Optimism Exposed", *Middle East International*, no. 434, 25 September 1992, p. 3.
104 G. Jansen, "Syria's Bottom Line", *Middle East International*, no. 434, 25 September 1992, p. 5.
105 M. Hallaj, "The Seventh Round of the Bilateral Peace Talks", *Middle East International*, no. 437, 6 November 1992, p. 5.
106 Ibid.
107 G. Butt, "Flagging Arab Spirits", *Middle East International*, no. 418, 7 February 1992, p. 4.
108 Syria's support of the ten rejectionist Palestinian groups, Hizbollah, Amal, and allegedly the PKK, has given Syria a leverage over its powerful enemies.
109 H. Baram, "The Expulsion of the Palestinians: Rabin Shows His True Colours", *Middle East International*, no. 441, 8 January 1993, p. 3.
110 "An Act of Heartless Cruelty", *Middle East International*, no. 441, 8 January 1993, p. 2.

111 J. Kagian, "Retreat from 799: Security Council Bends to US Pressure", *Middle East International*, no. 444, 19 February 1993, p. 3.

112 A. Ehteshami and R. Hinnebusch, *Syria and Iran: Middle Powers in a Penetrated Regional System* (London: Routledge, 1997), p. 166.

113 Ibid.

114 *BBC Summary of World Broadcasts*, ME/1620, A/1, 23 February 1993.

115 G. Butt, "Speaking with Two Voices", *Middle East International*, no. 445, 5 March 1993, pp. 7–8.

116 D. Neff, "Clinton, Rabin, and a Deal with Syria", *Middle East International*, no. 446, 19 March 1993, p. 3.

117 D. Neff, "Clinton Dangles Carrots for the Palestinians", *Middle East International*, no. 448, 16 April 1993, p. 3.

118 G. Butt, "Arab Intentions Unclear", *Middle East International*, no. 448, 16 April 1993, p. 5.

119 S. Edge and D. Butter, "Can the US Pull Peace from War?", *Middle East Economic Digest*, vol. 37, no. 32, 13 August 1993, pp. 2–3.

120 J. Muir, "Rabin's Revenge Exacts an Appalling Toll", *Middle East International*, no. 456, 6 August 1993, p. 3.

121 *BBC Summary of World Broadcasts*, ME/1755, A/5, 31 July 1993.

122 J. Moore, "An Israeli–Syrian Peace Treaty: So Close and yet So Far", *Middle East Policy*, vol. iii, no. 3 (1994), pp. 61–2.

123 M. Ma'oz, *Syria and Israel: From War to Peace-making* (Oxford: Clarendon Press, 1995), p. 225.

124 H. Agha and A. Khalidi, *Syria and Iran: Rivalry and Cooperation* (London: Pinter, 1995), pp. 19–21.

125 S. Edge and D. Butter, "Can the US Pull Peace from War?", *Middle East Economic Digest*, vol. 37, no. 32, 13 August 1993, pp. 2–3.

126 H. Baram, "The Crime and its Reward", *Middle East International*, no. 456, 6 August 1993, p. 4.

127 Ibid., pp. 4–5.

128 *Washington Report on Middle Eastern Affairs*, vol. XII, no. 2 (August 1993), p. 6.

129 P. Seale, "Asad's Regional Strategy and the Challenge from Netanyahu", *Journal of Palestine Studies*, vol. XXVI, no. 1 (Autumn 1996), pp. 34–5.

130 L. Andoni, "Arafat and the PLO in Crisis", *Middle East International*, no. 457, 28 August 1993, p. 3.

131 G. Usher, "Why Gaza Mostly Says Yes", *Middle East International*, no. 459, 24 September 1993, pp. 19–20.

132 G. Butt, "The Deal That Could Change the Middle East", *Middle East International*, no. 458, 10 September 1993, pp. 3–4.

133 Interview with vice-minister of foreign affairs, Raslan Allush, 27 June 1994.

134 A. Ehteshami and R. Hinnebusch, *Syria and Iran: Middle Powers in a Penetrated Regional System* (London: Routledge, 1997), p. 178.

135 Interview with a Syrian journalist in Damascus, September 1995.

136 G. Hawatmeh, "Hussein Stands by the PLO", *Middle East International*, no. 466, 7 January 1994, p. 9.

137 G. Butt, "The Deal that could Change the Middle East", *Middle East International*, no. 458, 10 September 1993, pp. 3–4.

138 Interview with a Damascene bureaucrat, 5 October 1995.
139 *BBC Summary of World Broadcasts*, ME/2503, MED/10, 8 January 1996.
140 Interview with a Damascene bureaucrat, 5 October 1995.
141 Interview with a Damascene bureaucrat, 5 October 1995.
142 A. Ben-Meir, "The Israeli–Syrian Battle for Equitable Peace", *Middle East Policy*, vol. iii, no. 1 (1994), p. 75.
143 Ibid.
144 P. Seale, *Asad of Syria: The Struggle for the Middle East* (London: I.B. Tauris, 1988), pp. 459–91.
145 Interview with the Press Secretary of the DFLP, Maher Hamdi, Damascus, 10 October 1995.
146 Interview with the Press Secretary of the DFLP, Maher Hamdi, Damascus, 10 October 1995.
147 Interview with Press Secretary of the PFLP, Damascus, 4 October 1995.
148 S. Cohen, "The Geopolitics of a Golan Heights Agreement", *Focus*, vol. 42, 1 June 1992, p. 15.
149 *BBC Summary of World Broadcasts*, ME/1799, MED/16, 21 September 1993, and ME/1802, MED/1–ME/3, 24 September 1993.
150 D. Gold, "The Syrian–Israeli Track – Taking the Final Step: What Sacrifices Will Assad Make to Get Back the Golan?", *Middle East Insight*, vol. x, no. 6 (September/October 1994), pp. 16–17.
151 G. Butt, "Asad Gains Maximum Benefits for Minimal Concessions", *Middle East International*, no. 467, 21 January 1994, p. 3.
152 C. Richards, "Clinton Wooed by Syrian President", *The Independent*, 17 January 1994, pp. 11.
153 Ibid.
154 A. Ben-Meir. "The Israeli–Syrian Battle for Equitable Peace", *Middle East Policy*, vol. iii, no. 1 (1994), p. 80.
155 L. Graz, "How It Looked Close Up", *Middle East International*, no. 467, 21 January 1994, p. 6.
156 C. Richards, "Assad Adds His Weight to Middle East Peace Talks", *The Independent*, 17 January 1994, p. 1.
157 Ibid.
158 Ibid.
159 R. Dergham, "Assessing Assad", *Middle East Insight*, vol. xii, nos. 4&5 (May/August 1996), p. 13.
160 H. Baram, "Has Hebron Sounded Oslo's Death-knell?", *Middle East International*, no. 470, 4 March 1994, pp. 3–4.
161 M. Jansen, "An Unusual Delegation", *Middle East International*, no. 471, 18 March 1994, p. 11.
162 E. Ya'ari, "Syria Next vs. Damascus Last", *Middle East Insight*, vol. xi, no. 1 (November/December 1994), p. 20.
163 A. Ehteshami and R. Hinnebusch, *Syria and Iran: Middle Powers in a Penetrated Regional System* (London: Routledge, 1997), p. 219.
164 D. Neff, "Hussein and Rabin Make Their Declaration", *Middle East International*, no. 481, 5 August 1994, pp. 3–4.
165 G. Hawatmeh, "Jordan's Dramatic Peace Gestures", *Middle East International*, no. 480, 22 July 1994, pp. 3–4.

166 Interview with Asad's former adviser (1985–9), George Jabbour, 7 October 1995. According to Jabbour Syria had anticipated such a move.

167 P. Seale, *Asad of Syria: The Struggle for the Middle East* (London: I.B. Tauris, 1988), p. 161.

168 *BBC Summary of World Broadcasts*, ME/0467, A/1, 26 May 1989.

169 L. Andoni, "Sigh of Relief", *Middle East International*, no. 389, 7 December 1990, p. 7; L. Andoni, "Cutting the Strings", *Middle East International*, no. 394, 22 February 1991, pp. 10–11, and Hawatmeh, G. "Fissured Opinion", *Middle East International*, no. 395, 8 March 1991, pp. 14–15.

170 D. Neff, "Syria is the Key Issue", *Middle East International*, no. 480, 22 July 1994, p. 4.

171 G. Hawatmeh, "Jordan's Dramatic Peace Gestures", *Middle East International*, no. 480, 22 July 1994, pp. 3–4.

172 D. Neff, "Hussein and Rabin Make Their Declaration", *Middle East International*, no. 481, 5 August 1994, pp. 3–4.

173 Ibid.

174 H. Asad, "We Want a Just Peace Because We Want Stability", *Middle East Insight*, vol. x, no. 6 (September/October 1994), p. 16.

175 P. Seale, "Asad's Regional Strategy and the Challenge from Netanyahu", *Journal of Palestine Studies*, vol. XXVI, no. 1 (Autumn 1996), p. 36.

176 *Syria – Country Report*, (London: The Economist Intelligence Unit), 1st Quarter 1996, p. 10.

177 L. Butler, "Fresh Light on the Syrian–Israeli Peace Negotiations: An Interview with Ambassador Walid al-Moualem", *Journal of Palestine Studies*, vol. XXVI, no. 2 (Winter 1997), p. 92.

178 P. Seale, "Asad's Regional Strategy and the Challenge from Netanyahu", *Journal of Palestine Studies*, vol. XXVI, no. 1 (Autumn 1996), p. 36.

179 *BBC Summary of World Broadcasts*: ME/2496, MED/1–MED/3, 29 December 1995; ME/2497, MED/1–MED/3, 30 December 1995; ME/2498, MED/1–MED/5, 31 December 1995; ME/2500, MED/7–MED/11, 3 January 1996; ME/2501, MED/1–MED/3, 4 January 1996, and ME/2502, MED/4–MED/7, 4 January 1996.

180 This view has since been discounted. For more information see: I. Shahak, "The Real Problem between Israel and Syria", *Middle East International*, no. 523, 12 April 1996, p. 19, and M. Muslih, "The Golan: Israel, Syria, and Strategic Calculations", *Middle East Journal*, vol. 47, no. 4 (Autumn 1993), pp. 611–32.

181 R. Hinnebusch, "Does Syria Want Peace? Syrian Policy in the Syrian–Israeli Peace Negotiations", *Journal of Palestine Studies*, vol. XXVI, no. 1 (Autumn 1996), pp. 50–1.

182 L. Butler, "Fresh Light on the Syrian–Israeli Peace Negotiations: An Interview with Ambassador Walid al-Moualem", *Journal of Palestine Studies*, vol. XXVI, no. 2 (Winter 1997), pp. 88–9.

183 Ibid.

184 Ibid., pp. 84–5.

185 H. Baram, "Asad Waits for 1997", *Middle East International*, no. 517, 19 January 1996, pp. 5–6.

186 J. Moore, "An Israeli–Syrian Peace Treaty: So Close and yet So Far", *Middle East Policy*, vol. iii, no. 3 (1994), pp. 76–7.

187 H. Asad, "Syrian President Hafiz al-Asad, Interview with CNN, Damascus, 25 September 1996", cited in *Journal of Palestine Studies*, vol. XXVI, no. 2 (Winter 1997), pp. 151–2.

188 L. Butler, "Fresh Light on the Syrian–Israeli Peace Negotiations: An Interview with Ambassador Walid al-Moualem", *Journal of Palestine Studies*, vol. XXVI, no. 2 (Winter 1997), p. 83.

189 *BBC Summary of World Broadcasts*, ME/2504, MED/1–MED/2.

190 See below: "Operation Grapes of Wrath".

191 E. Ya'ari, "Syrian Foreign Minister Addresses Israeli Public", *Middle East Insight*, vol. xi, no. 1 (November/December 1994), p. 19.

192 Ibid.

193 D. Neff, "Christopher's Final Goal", *Middle East International*, no. 518, 2 February 1996, p. 7.

194 L. Butler, "Fresh Light on the Syrian–Israeli Peace Negotiations: An Interview with Ambassador Walid al-Moualem", *Journal of Palestine Studies*, vol. XXVI, no. 2 (Winter 1997), pp. 86–7.

195 J. Moore, "An Israeli–Syrian Peace Treaty: So Close and yet so Far", *Middle East Policy*, vol. iii, no. 3 (1994), pp. 76–9.

196 Ibid., pp. 78–9.

197 P. Seale, "Asad's Regional Strategy and the Challenge from Netanyahu", *Journal of Palestine Studies*, vol. XXVI, no. 1 (Autumn 1996), p. 36.

198 D. Neff, "Christopher's Final Goal", *Middle East International*, no. 518, 2 February 1996, p. 7.

199 J. Ozanne, "Police Seize Arms Stockpile at Home of Rabin's Assassin", *Financial Times*, 10 November 1995, p. 16.

200 J. Ozanne, "Struggle to Hold It All Together: Shimon Peres, The Acting Israeli Leader Faces Formidable Challenges in Keeping the Peace Process Going", *Financial Times*, 11 November 1995, p. 6.

201 K. Amayreh, "The Killing of Yahya 'Ayyash", *Middle East International*, no. 517, 19 January 1996, p. 4.

202 G. Usher, "Hamas and the Bus Bomb", *Middle East International*, no. 506, 4 August 1995, pp. 4–5.

203 G. Jansen, "The Giant's Failure", *Middle East International*, no. 525, 10 May 1996, p. 7.

204 Ibid.

205 Ibid.

206 "What Happened at Qana?", *Middle East International*, no. 525, 10 May 1996, p. 5.

207 M. Jansen, "Lebanon Cease-fire Terms", *Middle East International*, no. 525, 10 May 1996, p. 5, and R. Swann, "Trying Not to Gloat", *Middle East International*, no. 525, 10 May 1996, pp. 7–8.

208 M. Jansen, "Lebanon Cease-fire Terms", *Middle East International*, no. 525, 10 May 1996, pp. 5–6.

209 Ibid., p. 6.

210 Ibid.

211 K. Amayreh, "Sabre-rattling Settlers", *Middle East International*, no. 541, 10 January 1997, p. 4, and G. Usher, "Unfinished Struggle – Arafat after Hebron", *Middle East International*, no. 542, 24 January 1997, pp. 3–4.

212 S. Kamal, "Hussein's Sorrow and Shame", *Middle East International*, no. 546, 21 March 1997, p. 9.

213 E. Ya'ari, "Syria Next vs. Damascus Last", *Middle East Insight*, vol. xi, no. 1 (November/December 1994), p. 23.

214 D. Gardner, "Syria Rejects Israeli Demand to Restart", *Financial Times*, 28 November 1996, p. 4.

215 A. Ehteshami and R. Hinnebusch, *Syria and Iran: Middle Powers in a Penetrated Regional System* (London: Routledge, 1997), pp. 160–1.

216 *BBC Summary of World Broadcasts*, ME/1402, A/1, 9 June 1992.

217 *BBC Summary of World Broadcasts*, ME/1215, A/3, 29 October 1991.

218 E. Haas, "Obscurities Enshrined: The Balance of Power as an Analytical Concept", in P. Viotti and M. Kauppi (eds.), *International Relations Theory: Realism, Pluralism, and Globalism* (New York: Macmillan, 1987), p. 106.

219 See P. Kidron, "Har Homa: The Price of Netanyahu's Showmanship", *Middle East International*, no. 545, 7 March 1997, pp. 3–5.

220 E. Ya'ari, "Syria Next vs. Damascus Last", *Middle East Insight*, vol. xi, no. 1 (November/December 1994), pp. 20–3.

221 D. Hirst, "Shameless in Gaza", *The Guardian*, 21 April 1997, pp. 8–9.

Conclusion

Introduction

In an increasingly complex world of interdependence and dependence, the paradigm of realism has fallen from grace. Its analysis has been deemed to be ill-fitted to the globalisation of the world economy, and the advancement in global communications. The spread of information technology, and the accompanying communications' revolution, have helped to deconstruct the myths of an anarchical world order. Furthermore, the globalisation of interests has helped to reduce threats to national security as national interests have become increasingly interdependent.

The integration of the world's economies, based on an international division of labour, has diffused power throughout the global economy. Power has become a much more diffuse commodity, and no longer relates exclusively to military power. This has made international capital and information important sources of power.

The succession of global capitalism, and the advent of the information revolution have challenged the primacy of the state as the principle actor in international relations. Pluralists propose that the state has started to lose its significance as the adjudicator of international relations. The proliferation of the transnational actors, international agencies, and the establishment of transnational governmental bodies, have all contributed to the erosion of state autonomy.

Globalists work from a less optimistic base. They refute the premise of interdependence among states. Alternatively, they perceive international relations through a world-systems theory. The relations between the states of the core and the periphery of the global economy are characterised as dependent. Integration, it is argued, has not led to a universal improvement in the livelihoods of the global population. On the contrary, global capitalism has exacerbated the impoverishment of the states in the periphery of the global economy.

It has been argued in this book that realism and neo-realism are the most appropriate models for explaining Syria's adjustment to the New

World Order. Realism is an ahistorical paradigm of international relations theory. Realism, and its sister neo-realism, highlight the uniformity of states' foreign policies. Foreign policy is the product of the anarchical system where states compete in a self-help environment. With their focus on the international political system, both paradigms have stressed the central role played by the state in conducting international relations.

The state is the principal actor in Syria. In the anarchical environment of the international political system, and the penetrated Middle Eastern sub-system, Syria has sought to accumulate power, preserve its national security, and attain a regional balance of power with its hegemonic foe. It has attempted to insulate itself both from the external and domestic environments.

The author recognises that realism, however, has some flaws. Alongside pluralism and globalism, realism appears to be the most primitive paradigm of international relations theory. It cannot adequately account for the rise of TNCs, or the dependency of the Third World upon the centre states of the global economy. Moreover, it concentrates only on the international political system, and does not pay attention to the domestic process. Nevertheless, domestic politics are a crucial factor when considering states of the Third World.

The deficit of state consolidation in the Third World has exposed foreign policies to the irrational impulses of state elites attempting to appease their domestic constituencies. As in all Third World states, the lack of a dynamic institutional framework in Syria suggests that the state has been open to the interests of dominant social groups. Thus, there is a need to examine the domestic politics of Syria.

As we have seen, the post-independence Syrian state was fraught with instability. The permeability of the state, a feature accentuated by the French authorities, had been exploited by other regional and international actors. Their interference in Syrian affairs challenged the sovereignty of the state; the state, therefore, lacked insulation from the combination of domestic and international actors.

The arrival of Asad at the helm of the Syrian state has led to the transformation of Syria's fortunes. He has injected a dose of realism into Syria's foreign policy, and engaged in the old art of statecraft. Through a process of state consolidation, Asad has skilfully transformed Syria from a weak fractious state into a convincing regional player. He has managed to elevate the role of the state in Syrian affairs. Under Asad's rule, the state has become the principle actor, and has been unequivocally in control of foreign policy.

The Syrian state has been forged through its struggle with Israel. After 1970, the competition between Syria and Israel changed course. Dispensing with guerrilla warfare tactics, Syria has engaged in a balance-of-power game. The ideology of Arab nationalism has been relegated to legitimising Syrian foreign policy, whilst the politics of power accumulation has been used to consolidate the power potential of the state. Power within the state has been consolidated through a national programme of state-building. The state, through a complex of corporations, reordered state–society relations. In principle, the state assumed a monopoly of power, and built its base upon the foundations of the military and the Ba'th party.

In reordering state–society relations, the Syrian state has aimed to gain relative autonomy from the domestic forces within society. The state resides above all the forces within society by balancing the interests of competing groups. Those groups owe their allegiance to the state, though they have limited access to the decision-making process, according to the levels of patronage. The regime barons, for instance, have participated in the affairs of high politics with the president. The state, however, is constrained neither by the economic interests of the business class, nor by the ideological interests of the Ba'th party.

The patrimonial system is still prevalent in Syria and militates against the implementation of institutional processes in decision-making. The patrimonial system purchases valuable legitimacy for the state which is otherwise lacking in the political system. The substituting of the institutional for the patrimonial system would enable the state to formalise its relations with society. At present, the state is still dependent on the armed forces and security services to guarantee its survival. Although the state exists above society, its legitimacy base is weak, and its formal institutions lack authority. In other words, although the Syrian state is unitary, its status is perpetually in question.

The absence of institutional depth within Syria has led us to consider omnibalancing as a model for examining Syria's foreign policy. Realism operates from the assumption that states are the principal actors in international relations, and that their behaviour is governed by the international political system, rather than the domestic arena. States are considered to be unitary, and their internal politics are deemed to be irrelevant. This element of the paradigm may be applicable to Western countries, where state consolidation has taken place over a period of two or three centuries, but in the new states of the Third World it loses its pertinence. Therefore, omnibalancing, with part of its focus on the domestic scene, has afforded us the opportunity to examine domestic politics and the international political systems that impinge upon state behaviour.

Omnibalancing has allowed us to incorporate aspects of realism and domestic politics models. By using the omnibalancing model, it has been possible to gauge the array of influences on the formulation of Syrian foreign policy. In particular, omnibalancing has presented itself as the best model for explaining Syria's adjustment to the New World Order.

The New World Order

The definition of the New World Order has been critical to this study. It has been identified, by the author, as the redistribution of power throughout the international political system. The collapse of the Soviet Union in the autumn of 1991 led to the diffusion of its power into the system of states. Examined away from the utopian visions, the New World Order has been presented as a transformation in the structure of the international political system from bipolarity to unipolarity.

The structure of the international political system has been defined by the balance of power. The fluctuation in the structure of the system is not yet complete and the world order is still in transition. This transition has been attributed to the diverse nature of global power. Rosecrance has suggested that the five great bases of power (the US, Russia, the European Union, Japan, and China) control the organisation of the world order.[1] Krauthammer, however, has contested this concert of powers view:

> Only a few months ago it was conventional wisdom that the new rivals, the great pillars of the new multipolar world, would be Japan and Germany (and/or Europe). How quickly a myth can explode. The notion that economic power inevitably translates into geopolitical influence is materialist illusion.[2]

Nye has combined these two analyses and compared the New World Order to a multi-layered cake, where the US is the dominant military power, Japan, Europe, and China are the emerging economic centres, and the rest of the world's states prop up the system. The nature of the New World Order was soon revealed after the invasion of Kuwait.

The second Gulf War

Iraq's invasion of Kuwait on 2 August 1990 was the first challenge to the New World Order. The second Gulf War created the opportunity for the utopians to observe their New World Order. The end of the Cold War had removed the prospect of superpower conflict and competition. Soviet compliance with the US, albeit token support, signified the arrival of a new era in international relations. The international community had the opportunity to resolve the situation through peaceful and diplomatic means.

On 17 January 1991, diplomacy gave way to military power. High-technology armaments, and pervasive information systems, dominated the spectacle of war. The coalition of interests, represented in the *upper layers of the cake*, achieved their aspirations, through the exercise of military power; they committed themselves to the US-led world order.

Although there is room for debate when defining the world order, two points of clarity have emerged since the dissolution of the Soviet Union:

(a) The balance of power remains the most useful analytical tool for examining the international political system;
(b) The Middle Eastern sub-state system is dominated by the unipolarity of the US.

The balance of power

The balance of power continues to provide the most appropriate description of the international political system. Despite the spread of transnationalism, and the effects of the globalisation of production, states remain the sovereign units in international relations. The power of TNCs and international agencies may be on the increase, but states are still the principal referents of the international political system.

States exist in an anarchical arena, and the systemic forces that derive from this environment impinge upon the behaviour of states. In order to survive, states are compelled to function according to a self-help principle, hence producing a uniformity of state behaviour. States adopt rational foreign policies based upon their national interest. The balance of power provides the mechanism for producing world order; the absence of an international hierarchy militates against any other mechanism for regulating world order.

The structure of the New World Order has taken on a unipolar form for the immediate future, but the rise of new economic centres, such as those of China, Japan, and Europe, will gradually transform this unipolar structure into a multipolar one.

Unipolarity in the Middle East

Located at the crossroads between the Occident and the Orient, the Middle East region has found itself unduly subjected to the pressures of the international political system. As a regional system, the Middle East has been highly penetrated by international actors and, in consequence, remains vulnerable to external factors.

During the 1980s, Libya, Iran, and Syria had refused to accommodate US interests in the area; accordingly they were labelled as terrorist states. As they were enemies of the emerging dominant hegemonic order, their futures had become uncertain. Libya had already faced US recrimination in 1986 prior to the dissolution of the Soviet system.

Throughout the bipolar era, Syria had been a pernicious thorn in America's side. With the rise of US hegemony in the region, Syria has been forced to adjust its policy orientation. In order to counter the perennial threat from Israel, Syria had to leave the eclipsing shadow of the Soviet Union, and seek shelter on the periphery of US influence.

The Gulf War provided Syria with an opportunity to traverse from the collapsing world order to the unipolar world order. The force of the hegemonic world order pushed Syria towards international rehabilitation, and an acceptance of US domination of the world order. This realignment has allowed Syria to invest in a new regional order. Instead of becoming a victim of the New World Order, Syria extracted itself from the policies formulated in the climate of the Cold War, and adjusted to the demands of the unipolar configuration of global power.

The demise of Soviet influence in world affairs, and the fluctuation in the international reconfiguration of power, enhanced the role of the US as the world's only superpower. When Iraq invaded Kuwait on 2 August 1990, the US found itself in a unique position; it was able to adopt an instrumental role in shaping the policies of the new Middle Eastern order.

The US-led coalition

Iraq's invasion of Kuwait led to the Saudi invitation to the US-led coalition forces to launch an offensive on Iraq from Saudi soil. The stationing of US troops in Saudi Arabia gave the US unprecedented access to the region. It became the unipolar force in the region, and represented a threat to the client states of the former Soviet Union. The destruction of Iraq, one of the region's large military powers, established the credentials of the new regional order and the potency of the New World Order. The unipolarity of US hegemony in the Middle East became dangerous for the "pariah" states of the region.

Syria's participation in the liberation of Kuwait, therefore, was an expression of a rational choice. The decision was justified to the Syrian population in Arab nationalist terms; yet by observing the structural factors of the international and regional systems, one is able to identify a policy based upon the determinants of power politics.

Syria's decision to join the Gulf War coalition was formulated in accordance with its national security objectives. It was not hampered by ideology, nor constrained by Arab nationalism. It was arrived at through a careful calculation of costs and benefits. The US dominance of the international political system, namely, the transformation in the international configuration of power, impinged upon Syria's options. The political survival of the state, in an environment of self-help, rested upon its ability to accommodate the change in the international political environment, and to insulate itself from domestic repercussions.

The Syrian state enjoyed sufficient autonomy to pursue a policy that contravened the public mood. This does not, however, eliminate the vulnerability of the Syrian state. The centrifugal forces that tore the East European states apart are a constant reminder of the vulnerability of states resting upon façade institutions and coercion. The rewards for Syria's participation were an important source of vindication for the political elite, and a necessary sweetener for the regime barons, who had been uncertain about the prudence of Asad's course of action.

Syria's decision to join the US-oriented liberation of Kuwait has empowered the Syrian state to avoid the punitive fate of Iraq, and gave it a chance to participate in the postwar regional order. Syrian complicity with the coalition forces was based on a rational decision-making process. The systemic factors pushed Syria towards adopting a policy founded upon self-help. The international balance of power of the Cold War era no longer offered Syria protection from the hegemonic ambitions of Israel and the US. National security, which is a primary constituent of a rational foreign policy decision-making process, compelled the Syrian elite to choose a US-friendly path.

The reward for Syria's rational decision to enter the war, in collusion with an imperial force, against its Ba'thi neighbour, was a role in the postwar regional order, and the convention of an international peace process.

Syria and the peace process

The New World Order had changed the structure of the international political system, and the coordinates of the region. With the dissolution of Soviet power, the US has been empowered to enforce a peace process upon the region, a process flexible enough to include Syria.

Syria's entry into the Madrid Peace Conference in October 1991, and its participation in the following rounds of the peace process, have demonstrated Syria's commitment to peace. It has been the assertion of the author that Syria's commitment to peace has been consistent since 1970.

The fulfilment of comprehensive peace has held the prospect of terminating the state of war between the Arab states and Israel. Comprehensive peace for Syria, where Gaza, the West Bank, southern Lebanon, and the Golan Heights were to be returned for peace, according to the land-for-peace formula, contained the possibility of extending Syrian influence throughout the Levant in return for peace. In other words, peace would not mean a conclusion of the struggle between Syria and Israel. Peace would only move the contest onto another plane of competition. The structural determinants of the region have ensured that both states are locked in an interminable regional struggle for hegemony.

The US understood the centrality of Syria to the Levant, and that its exclusion from the peace process would prove to be disruptive. Syrian compliance, meanwhile, was also based on the US-led war with Iraq, which had provided a portent for Syria. Rationality dictated a policy grounded in national interest.

The fluctuation in the configuration of global power had left Syria in a vulnerable state. The pursuit of strategic parity was essentially over; Syria's strategies were exhausted, and the dominance of the US in world affairs meant that "pariah" status was dangerous without the umbrella of the Soviet Union. The structural forces of the international political system pushed Syria towards the peace process. Attending the Madrid Peace Conference was, therefore, based on a rational decision.

Syria's position has not been ideologically driven, but based on an understanding of power politics, and the regional balance of power. The Levant Security Doctrine had catered for Syrian security through the incorporation of the foreign policies of Lebanon, Jordan, and the PLO into a unified policy. Comprehensive peace had the same goals.

Although Syria had been required to make procedural concessions, in attending the Madrid conference, it remained resolute in its demand for the land-for-peace formula. Comprehensive peace formed the bedrock of its negotiating position. President Asad stressed the coordination among the Arab states, and Syria's determination to resist separate peace.

The Syrian state sought to sell the peace to its population. The years of indoctrination had fostered a deep disdain for the Israeli state and its citizens, and the Syrian state needed to modify this residual base of mistrust in order to justify its peace negotiations. The peace was made easier to sell after Israel and the PLO had announced the results of their secret talks.[3]

Despite attempting to coordinate the positions of the Arab parties, in their negotiations with the Israelis, Syria was unable to restrain the PLO and Jordan from concluding separate peace deals with Israel. Their separate peace deals undermined the Syrian position and, in effect, isolated it from the peace process. Unity had provided the Arab states with a semblance of balance with the Israelis. Asad's commitment to securing the Levant Doctrine moved from the field of confrontation to the peace process.

Syria's response revealed the extent of its regional and international vulnerability. The impact of the New World Order had taken its toll on Syria's ability to resist the imposition of separate peace deals. In the past, tactical rejectionism had empowered Syria in its disruption of separate peace formulas, but Syria's hands were tied by the New World Order. Adjusting to the New World Order entailed exercising restraint.

As a rational actor, the Syrian state quietly accepted the *fait accompli* of Arafat's secret talks. Asad had been outmanoeuvred by the Israelis. They had employed the classic divide-and-rule policy of the former imperial powers. Syria observed the events and promised not to interfere unless its interests were directly harmed. Asad, however, maintained a deck of negotiating cards in Syria, the Damascus 10 (the ten Palestinian groups based in Damascus who reject the Oslo Accords), but they were confined to the bottom drawer of diplomacy.

The conclusion of the PLO and Jordanian peace deals presented the Syrians with the opportunity to seal a separate deal of their own. Prior to the PLO move, Syria's self-interest came under the spotlight after Rabin had become Israeli prime minister in 1992. It is unwise to speculate in the field of politics, but we can be certain that Syria would have acted according to its perceived long-term interests. We cannot be certain whether it would have signed a separate peace before the PLO, but if one looks at history, Syria's rejection of separate peace was in line with its national interests.

These have been interwoven with Lebanon, Jordan, and the Palestinians since the dismemberment of Bilad al-Sham, and the creation of Israel. The rise of Asad to his self-styled presidential monarchy marked a transition in Syrian history. Through the politics of power accumulation, the preservation of national security, and the promotion of national interest, Syria has extricated itself from regional vulnerability, and, in turn, projected itself as the keystone of regional stability.

Until the metamorphosis of the world order, Syria's foreign policy had been based on a strategy of attaining a balance of power with Israel. Lebanon, Jordan, and the Palestinians formed a critical part of the strategy, but its Achilles' heel had remained the possibility of separate peace which would destabilise Syria's influence in the region, thus harming its national interests.

The separate peace deals of the PLO and Jordan thus harmed Syria's national interest by significantly impairing Syria's ability to thwart Israel's hegemony. Syria was compelled, however, by the determinants of the international political system, to remain in the peace process. Exclusion would have meant regional and international isolation and would have entailed the disengagement of Syria's interests with Jordan and the PLO. Hence, a new peace was pursued, one pertaining to the liberation of the Golan and southern Lebanon.

Syria's adjustment to the New World Order required a downgrading of its ambitions. The PLO and Jordan have undermined Syria's stature as the repository of Arab power in the Levant. Comprehensive peace drained the channels of the separate peace tracks, and left Syria with the residue of a Golan and Lebanon deal. Syria's terms of reference on the Golan, however, have remained unequivocal: full withdrawal for full peace.

The Wye Plantation talks were designed to resolve the Syrian–Israeli impasse over the Golan Heights. In the light of the problems emanating from Oslo I and Oslo II, the Israeli government aimed to secure a peace deal with the Syrians. The talks showed how both Syria and Israel had reached an understanding of each other's concerns and needs.

We have learnt in retrospect that Israel had accepted the principle of complete withdrawal for full peace. The decision had been *deposited* with the US administration along with the incremental concessions attained during the process of talks. With this admission by the Syrians, we are able to see how close Syria and Israel had moved to peace. Peres was eager to conclude a deal on the Golan to enhance his political prestige, and to advance Israel's hegemonic interests in the region. Asad held sufficient power to broker a peace deal without generating domestic opposition groups.

The structural determinants of the international political system, and the vagaries of the Middle Eastern sub-system have pushed Syria and Israel towards concluding a peace deal. But the opportunity slipped through the fingers of both leaders, as Asad played for time, and Peres sought an early election victory.

Adjusting to the New World Order

In conclusion, Syrian foreign policy has been determined by the international political system. Foreign policy has been based upon securing national security, conceived within the terms of the Levant Security Doctrine, in an anarchic arena. Attaining a balance of power with Israel, its historic foe, has determined the policy initiatives of the state.

Syria's foreign policy has been consistent since 1970. The maximisation of power has been the guiding principle behind containing the threat of Israel, and extending its own hegemony over the Levant. Syria's commitment to peace has been concomitant to its foreign policy goals, namely, the recovery of the Arab territories seized in 1967 by Israel.

Since 1970, three identifiable strategies have been employed, whilst a myriad of tactics have been discernible. Each strategy and tactic has been justified by Syria's consistent foreign policy goals. The prospect of separate peace has proved to be the nemesis of Syria, but comprehensive peace ("cold", or without normalisation) has been a long-term objective of the Syrians. Throughout the 1970s and 1980s, the structural determinants of the international political system militated against progress on the comprehensive track.

The collapse of the Soviet Union and the birth of the New World Order have opened a window of opportunity for Syria and the Middle East region. The second Gulf War offered Syria the optimum moment to realign itself with the US, and to seize the peace initiative. Comprehensive peace offered Syria the possibility of containing Israel's hegemonic ambitions, but separate peace represented a challenge to Syria's own hegemonic ambitions.

Without a major patron, Syria had become more vulnerable; thereupon, it was compelled to adjust to the New World Order. Syria's adjustment to the New World Order has been based upon a rational set of criteria and included balancing the interests of its domestic groups against the constraints of the international political system. Syria had witnessed, and experienced the heat at the epicentre of the New World Order's authority; courting an alternative axis existed beyond the realms of rationality. Assimilation to the dominant hegemonic order, even if partial, provided Syria with a lifeline of survival in the anarchic and hostile state of nature.

Domestically, Syria was able to accommodate its adjustment to the New World Order without incurring undue damage to the state. By balancing the interests of the social forces within the Syrian Bonapartist state, Syria has managed to place the area of high politics far from the public eye. The autonomy from domestic forces, therefore, has invested the Syrian state with the ability to formulate foreign policy decisions away from internal constraints. The decision to reorient Syria's foreign policy towards the US was sufficiently insulated from domestic censure.

Thus, Syria's adjustment to the New World Order entailed man-œuvring from the bipolar to the unipolar world order and transferring its struggle with Israel from the battlefield to the negotiating room.

NOTES

1 R. Rosecrance, "A New Concert of Powers", *Foreign Affairs*, vol. 71, no. 2 (Spring 1992), p. 65.
2 C. Krauthammer, "The Unipolar Moment", *Foreign Affairs*, vol. 70, no. 1 (Winter 1991), p. 24.
3 After talking to a number of Syrian businessmen, bureaucrats, and *shabab* in Damascus, it started to become clear that the actions of the PLO had relieved the Syrian population of its commitment to Palestine. The Syrian youth were not really interested in Palestine; consumerism had arrived in Damascus – music, fashion, and Western interests were more important than politics.

Bibliography

Articles in periodicals

"After Assad?", *The Middle East,* no. 232 (March 1994), p. 5.

"An Unlikely Dynasty", *The Middle East,* no. 218 (December 1992), p. 18–19.

"A Peaceful Pounce, and the Prey Got Away – Syria/Iran Relations", *The Economist,* 4 June 1988, p. 37.

"Arabs Threaten Ties with US", *Middle East Economic Digest,* vol. 17, no. 44, 19 November 1973, pp. 1973–5.

"Boom in Syrian Trade", *Middle East Economic Digest,* vol. 17, no. 21, 25 May 1973, pp. 587–90.

"Dialogue with ME Replaces Crisis Fears", *Middle East Economic Digest,* vol. 19, no. 52, 26 December 1975, pp. 3–4.

"Dynastic Disappointment", *The Middle East,* no. 232 (March 1994), pp. 12–13.

"Euphrates Dammed in Syria", *Middle East Economic Digest,* vol. 17, no. 28, 13 July 1973, p. 793.

"Exit Lebanon: New US Ally Syria's De Facto Annexation of Lebanon with Massacre at French Embassy", *The New Republic,* vol. 203, no. 20, 12 November 1990, p. 7.

"Fresh Light on the Syrian–Israeli Peace Negotiations: An Interview with Ambassador Walid al-Moualem", *Journal of Palestine Studies,* vol. XXVI, no. 2 (Winter 1997), pp. 81–94.

"Hafez Assad: Land before Peace", *Time,* vol. 140, no. 22, 30 November 1992, p. 49.

"In from the Cold: Kuwait–Iraq Conflict Promotes Alliance between US and Syria", *The Economist,* 13 October 1990, p. 42.

"Oil Wealth May Counter War Setbacks – But Can Never Repair the Human Tragedies on Both Sides", *Middle East Economic Digest,* vol. 17, no. 42, 19 October 1973, pp. 1209–13.

"Oklahoma Bombing Incident", *Financial Times,* 11 August 1995, p. 4.

"PLO Accord Riles Arab Partners", *Middle East Economic Digest,* vol. 37, no. 36, 10 September 1993, p. 9.

"Salah ed-Din al Bitar's Last Interview: The Major Deviation of the Ba'th Is Having Renounced Democracy", *Middle East Report (MERIP),* no. 110 (November/December 1982), pp. 21–3.

"Shame: Criticism of George Bush's Meeting with Syria's Hafez Assad", *National Review,* vol. 42, no. 24, 17 December 1990, p. 13.

"Syria Accepts What It Once Rejected", *Middle East Dialogue,* no. 2, 27 January 1994, p. 1.

"Syria Has to Choose: Relations with Iran and Lebanon", *The Economist,* 21 May 1988, p. 16.

"Syria Hopes for Big Oil Finds", *Middle East Economic Digest,* vol. 19, no. 52, 26 December 1975, pp. 32–3.

"Syria Stays Put", *The Middle East,* no. 212 (June 1992), pp. 14–15.

"Syria", *Middle East Economic Digest,* vol. 18, no. 52, 27 December 1974, p. 1618.

"Syria: Asad Weighs New Israeli Proposals", *Middle East Economic Digest,* vol. 37, no. 39, 1 October 1993, p. 22.

"Syria: Assad's Uncertain Future", *The Middle East,* no. 208, February 1992, pp. 9–10.

"Syria: Budget Cuts Are the Price of Foreign Policy Successes", *Middle East Economic Digest Annual Review 1976,* vol. 20, no. 52, 31 December 1976, pp. 53–5.

"Syria: Don't Leave me in the Lurch", *The Middle East,* no. 212 (June 1992), pp. 11–12.

"Syria: Smuggling Crackdown Punishes Smokers", *Middle East Economic Digest,* vol. 37, no. 27, 9 July 1993, p. 20.

"Syrian Executions Concern Amnesty", *Financial Times,* 17 November 1994, p. 6.

"Syrian Industrial Exports Up", *Middle East Economic Digest,* vol. 17, no. 29, 20 July 1973, pp. 819–22.

"Syrian Social National Party: Interview with Abdullah Saidi", *Middle East Report (MERIP),* no. 61, October 1977, p. 17.

"The ME in the World Economic Crisis", *Middle East Economic Digest,* vol. 18, no. 52, 27 December 1974, p. 1589.

"The Myth of the Powerless State", *The Economist,* 7 October 1995, pp. 15–16.

"The October War and its Aftermath", *Middle East Economic Digest Annual Review 1973,* vol. 17, no. 52, 28 December 1973, pp. 1498–506.

"The Odd Man Out in Syria: Hafez Assad's Approach to Middle East Peace Process", *The Economist,* 23 October 1993, p. 50.

"Two Shot Dead at US Abortion Clinic", *Financial Times,* 31 December 1994, p. 1.

"Ungovernment-in-Exile: Syria, Iran Want to Forge Alliance Capable of Unseating Saddam Hussein", *The Economist,* 13 October 1990, p. 42.

"US Moves on Protesters", *Financial Times,* 25 January 1994, p. 5.

"War and Oil Crisis", *Middle East Economic Digest Annual Review 1973,* vol. 17, no. 52, 28 December 1973, p. 1497.

"War Threatens Oil Output", *Middle East Economic Digest,* vol. 17, no. 41, 12 October 1973, pp. 1181–3.

"What Happened at Qana?" *Middle East International,* no. 525, 10 May 1996, p. 5.

"When a Car Costs as Much as a House", *The Middle East,* no. 217, November 1992, pp. 36–7.

"Why Syria Invaded Lebanon", *Middle East Report (MERIP),* no. 5 (October 1976), pp. 3–10.

Ahrari, M. "Moscow and the Middle East: The Future of Strategic Relationships", *Journal of South Asian and Middle Eastern Studies,* vol. XVII, no. 4 (Summer 1994), pp. 1–20.

Ajami, F. "The Summoning", *Foreign Affairs,* vol. 72, no. 4 (September/ October 1993), pp. 2–9.

Alexander, I. "The Fire Next Time: Concerns over Syrian and Iranian Motives to Reject the Israeli–PLO Peace Treaty", *National Review,* vol. 45, no. 22 (15 November 1993), p. 26.

Amayreh, K. "Sabre-rattling Settlers", *Middle East International,* no. 541, 10 January 1997, p. 4.

—"The Killing of Yahya 'Ayyash", *Middle East International,* no. 517, 19 January 1996, p. 4.

Andoni, L. "Arafat and the PLO in Crisis", *Middle East International,* no. 457, 28 August 1993, p. 3.

—"A Leap into Darkness", *Middle East International*, no. 411, 25 October 1991, pp. 3–4.

—"Cutting the Strings", *Middle East International*, no. 394, 22 February 1991, pp. 10–11.

—"Sigh of Relief", *Middle East International*, no. 389, 7 December 1990, p. 7.

"An Act of Heartless Cruelty", *Middle East International*, no. 441, 8 January 1993, p. 2.

Asad, H. "Syrian President Hafiz al-Asad, Interview with CNN, Damascus, 25 September 1996", cited in *Journal of Palestine Studies*, vol. XXVI, no. 2 (Winter 1997), pp. 151–2.

—"We Want a Just Peace Because We Want Stability", *Middle East Insight*, vol. x, no. 6 (September/October 1994), p. 16.

Atkeson, E. "The Middle East: A Dynamic Military Net Assessment for the 90s", *Washington Quarterly*, vol. 16, no. 2 (Spring 1993), pp. 115–33.

Atlas, Y. "Syria Gets a Free Pass: US Reluctance to Confront Syria's Role in International Terrorism, Drug Trafficking and Arms Shipments", *Insight*, vol. 9, no. 35 (30 August 1993), p. 6.

Ayoob, M. "Security in the Third World: The Worm about to Turn", *International Affairs*, vol. 60, no. 1 (Winter 1983/84), pp. 41–51.

Baram, H. "Asad Waits for 1997", *Middle East International*, no. 517, 19 January 1996, pp. 5–6.

—"Has Hebron Sounded Oslo's Death-knell?", *Middle East International*, no. 470, 4 March 1994, pp. 3–4.

—"The Crime and its Reward", *Middle East International*, no. 456, 6 August 1993, pp. 4–5.

—"The Expulsion of the Palestinians: Rabin Shows His True Colours", *Middle East International*, no. 441, 8 January 1993, p. 3.

Barhoum, K. "The Gulf Crisis and a New World Order", *Middle East International*, no. 391, 11 January 1991, pp. 21–2.

Bartley, R. "The Case for Optimism: The West Should Believe in Itself", *Foreign Affairs*, vol. 72, no. 4 (September/October 1993), pp. 15–18.

Batatu, H. "Syria's Muslim Brethren", *Middle East Report* (*MERIP*), no. 110 (November/December 1982), pp. 12–23.

—"Some Observations on the Social Roots of Syria's Ruling Military Group and the Causes for its Dominance", *Middle East Journal*, vol. 35, no. 3 (Summer 1981), pp. 331–44.

BBC Summary of World Broadcasts, several issues.

Beeston, R. "Geneva Summit Boosts Hopes of Middle East Peace", *The Times,* 17 January 1994, p. 10.

Ben-Aharon, Y. "But Syria Should First Be Defanged", *Moment,* 28 February 1995.

—"Negotiating with Syria", *Global Affairs,* vol. 8, no. 1 (Winter 1993), pp. 141–7.

Ben-Meir, A. "In Search of Security Guarantees: What's Preventing Israel and Syria from Concluding an Agreement", *Middle East Insight,* vol. xi, no. 4 (May/June 1995), pp. 13–18.

—"The Israeli–Syrian Battle for Equitable Peace", *Middle East Policy,* vol. iii, no. 1 (January 1994), pp. 70–83.

Beyer, L. "The Agony of Victory: By Reuniting Beirut, Syria's Hafez Assad Is the First Clear Cut Winner of the Gulf Crisis. The Lebanese May Not Fare as Well", *Time,* vol. 136, no. 18 (29 October 1990), p. 51.

Binyan, L. "Civilization Grafting: No Culture an Island", *Foreign Affairs,* vol. 72, no. 4 (September/October 1993), pp. 19–21.

Booth, K. "Security in Anarchy: Utopian Realism in Theory and Practice", *International Affairs,* vol. 67, no. 3 (July 1991), pp. 527–45.

Brand, L. "Economics and Shifting Alliances: Jordan's Relations with Syria and Iraq, 1975–81", *International Journal of Middle East Studies,* vol. 26 (1994), pp. 393–413.

—"Asad's Syria and the PLO: Coincidence or Conflict of Interests?", *Journal of South Asian and Middle Eastern Studies,* vol. XIV, no. 2 (Winter 1990), pp. 22–44.

Brown, C. "Aftermath of Bloodshed Mars Peace Talks", *The Guardian,* 19 April 1994, p. 11.

Budiansky, S. "Saying Hello to a New Era? The Decade of Hostage-taking may be Ending as MidEast Political Arrangements Begin to Shift", *US News and World Report,* vol. 111, no. 8, 19 August 1991, p. 22.

Butler, L. "Fresh Light on the Syrian–Israeli Peace Negotiations: An Interview with Ambassador Walid al-Moualem", *Journal of Palestine Studies,* vol. XXVI, no. 2 (Winter 1997), pp. 83–92.

Butt, G. "Asad Gains Maximum Benefits for Minimal Concessions", *Middle East International,* no. 467, 21 January 1994, pp. 3–4.

—"The Deal That Could Change the Middle East", *Middle East International,* no. 458, 10 September 1993, pp. 3–4.

—"Arab Intentions Unclear", *Middle East International*, no. 448, 16 April 1993, pp. 5–6.

—"Speaking with Two Voices", *Middle East International*, no. 445, 5 March 1993, pp. 7–8.

—"Flagging Arab Spirits", *Middle East International*, no. 418, 7 February 1992, pp. 4–5.

—"Asad the Coordinator", *Middle East International*, no. 411, 25 October 1991, p. 7.

Butter, D. "Special Report: Syria", *Middle East Economic Digest*, vol. 39, no. 39, 29 September 1995, pp. 8–15.

—"Special Report: Syria", *Middle East Economic Digest*, vol. 38, no. 46, 18 November 1994, pp. 8–14.

—"Syria Edges Closer to a Deal with Israel", *Middle East Economic Digest*, vol. 38, no. 32, 12 August 1994, pp. 2–3.

—"Syrian Business Makes a Comeback", *Middle East Economic Digest*, vol. 38, no. 20, 20 May 1994, pp. 2–3.

—"Assad Treads Cautiously", *Middle East Economic Digest*, vol. 37, no. 40, 8 October 1993, pp. 2–3.

—"The Unstoppable Peace Train", *Middle East Economic Digest*, vol. 37, no. 38, 24 September 1993, pp. 2–3.

—"The Public-Sector Problem in Syria", *Middle East Economic Digest*, vol. 37, no. 22, 4 June 1993, pp. 2–4.

—"The Prospects for Islamism", *Middle East Economic Digest*, vol. 37, no. 2, 15 January 1993, pp. 2–3.

Buzan, B. "From International System to International Society: Structural Realism and Regime Theory Meet the English School", *International Organisation*, vol. 47, no. 3 (Summer 1993), pp. 327–52.

—"New Patterns of Global Security in the Twenty-First Century", *International Affairs*, vol. 67, no. 3 (July 1991), pp. 431–51.

Calvocoressi, P. "World Power 1920–1990", *International Affairs*, vol. 66, no. 4 (October 1990), pp. 663–74.

Chalala, E. "Syrian Policy in Lebanon, 1976–1984: Moderate Goals and Pragmatic Means", *Journal of Arab Affairs*, vol. 4, no. 1 (Spring 1985), pp. 67–87.

Church, G. "Why Assad Saw the Light: Syria Shrewdly Says Yes to Bush's Peace", *Time*, vol. 138, no. 4, 17 December 1990, p. 13.

Cochran, M. "The New World Order and International Political Theory", *Paradigms,* vol. 8, no. 1 (Summer 1994), pp. 106–22.

Cohen, S. "The Geopolitics of a Golan Heights Agreement", *Focus,* vol. 42, 1 June 1992, pp. 15–22.

—"The Geopolitical Aftermath of the Gulf War", *Focus,* vol. 41, 1 June 1991, pp. 23–7.

Cordahi, C. "Sticking to its Principles", *Middle East International,* no. 398, 19 April 1991, p. 16.

Dajani, L. "The Casablanca Conference – Winners and Losers", *Middle East International,* no. 488, 18 November 1994, pp. 18–19.

Dallal, S. "The Zionist Bureaucracy in the US Government", *Middle East International,* no. 381, 3 August 1990, pp. 16–17.

David, S. "Explaining Third World Alignment", *World Politics,* vol. 43, no. 2 (January 1991), pp. 233–56.

Dawisha, A. "Syria under Asad, 1970–78: The Centres of Power", *Government and Opposition,* vol. 13, no. 2 (1978), pp. 341–55.

Dergham, R. "Assessing Assad", *Middle East Insight,* vol. xii, no. 4&5 (May/August 1996), pp. 12–13.

Diab, M. "Have Syria and Israel Opted for Peace?", *Middle East Policy,* vol. iii, no. 2 (1994), pp. 77–90.

Dooley, B. "A Crisis of Confidence", *The Middle East,* no. 214 (August 1992), p. 17.

Drake, L. "A Netanyahu Prime Minister", *Journal of Palestine Studies,* vol. XXVI, no. 1 (Autumn 1996), pp. 58–69.

Drysdale, A. "The Asad Regime and its Troubles", *Middle East Report (MERIP),* no. 110 (November/December 1982), pp. 3–11.

Edge, S. "A Historic Deal?", *Middle East Economic Digest,* vol. 37, no. 36, 10 September 1993, p. 8.

Edge, S., and D. Butter. "Can the US Pull Peace from War?", *Middle East Economic Digest,* vol. 37, no. 32, 13 August 1993, pp. 2–3.

Ehteshami, A. "Defence and Security Policies of Syria in a Changing Regional Environment", *International Relations,* vol. XIII, no. 1 (April 1996), pp. 49–67.

Faksh, M. "Asad's Westward Turn: Implications for Syria", *Middle East Policy,* vol. ii, no. 3 (March 1993), pp. 49–61.

—"The 'Alawi Community of Syria: A New Dominant Political Force", *Middle Eastern Studies,* vol. 20, no. 2 (April 1984), pp. 133–53.

Falk, R. "State of Siege: Will Globalization Win Out?", *International Affairs,* vol. 73, no. 1 (January 1997), pp. 123–36.

Fisk, R. "'New World Order That Only Led to Tragedy", *The Independent,* 9 October 1996, p. 17.

—"Remaining Issues", *London Review of Books,* 23 February 1995, pp. 13–16.

Fletcher, M. "Clinton Hails Breakthrough: Assad Ready to Sign Peace with Israel", *The Times,* 17 January 1994, p. 1.

Freedman, L. "Syrian Initiative Increases Regional Risks for Assad", *The Times,* 17 January 1994, p. 10.

—"Order and Disorder in the New World", *Foreign Affairs,* vol. 71, no. 1 (1992), pp. 20–37.

Frost, M. "Constituting a New World Order: What States, Whose Will, What Territory?", *Paradigms,* vol. 8, no. 1 (Summer 1994), pp. 13–22.

Gaddis, J. "Toward the Post-Cold War World", *Foreign Affairs,* vol. 70, no. 2 (Spring 1991), pp. 102–22.

Gaffney, F. "The Radical Entente: New Threat to US – Collaboration of Anti-Western Radicals in North Korea, Iran, Iraq, Syria and Russia", *Insight,* vol. 9, no. 16, 19 April 1993, p. 18.

Galvani, J., P. Johnson and R. Theberge. "The October War: Egypt, Syria, Israel", *Middle East Report (MERIP),* no. 22 (November 1973), pp. 3–21.

Galvani, J. "Syria and the Baath Party", *Middle East Report (MERIP),* no. 25 (February 1974), pp. 3–16.

Gardner, D. "Syria Rejects Israeli Demand to Restart", *Financial Times,* 28 November 1996, p. 4.

Gause III, F. "The Illogic of Dual Containment", *Foreign Affairs,* vol. 73 (March 1994), pp. 56–61.

George, A. "Syria: No Hidden Agenda", *The Middle East,* no. 229 (December 1993), p. 10.

—"Remnants of an Ancient Community", *The Middle East,* no. 214 (August 1992), pp. 15–16.

Gereffi, G. "Power and Dependency in an Interdependent World: A Guide to Understanding the Contemporary Global Crisis", *International Journal of Comparative Sociology,* vol. 25, no. 1&2 (1984), pp. 91–113.

Ghilès, F. "Algeria again at the Crossroads", *Middle East International,* no. 417, 24 January 1992, pp. 3–4.

Gold, D. "The Syrian–Israeli Track – Taking the Final Step: What Sacrifices Will Assad Make to Get Back the Golan?", *Middle East Insight*, vol. x, no. 6 (September/October 1994), pp. 14–17.

Goodarzi, J. "The Syrian–Iranian Axis: An Enduring Entente?", *Middle East International*, no. 522, 29 November 1996, pp. 19–20.

Gordon, E., H. Kutler and S. Fishkoff. "Rabin Offers Syria 'Mutual' Cuts in Armed Forces", *The Jerusalem Post International Edition*, 15 October 1994, p. 1.

Graham, G. "Account Offers Credit to Countries in Economic Transition", *Financial Times*, 16 December 1994, p. 4.

Graz, L. "How it Looked Close up", *Middle East International*, no. 467, 21 January 1994, p. 6.

Guzzini, S. "Structural Power: The Limits of Neorealist Power Analysis", *International Organisation*, vol. 47, no. 3 (Summer 1993), pp. 443–78.

Hallaj, M. "The Seventh Round of the Bilateral Peace Talks", *Middle East International*, no. 437, 6 November 1992, pp. 5–6.

—"Peace Talks: The Illusion of Optimism Exposed", *Middle East International*, no. 434, 25 September 1992, pp. 3–4.

—"Round Six: Hope then Disappointment", *Middle East International*, no. 433, 11 September 1992, pp. 3–4.

Halliday, F. "A New World Myth", *New Statesman*, 4 April 1997, pp. 42–3.

—"International Relations and its Discontents", *International Affairs*, vol. 71, no. 4 (October 1995), pp. 733–46.

Hawatmeh, G. "Jordan's Dramatic Peace Gestures", *Middle East International*, no. 480, 22 July 1994, pp. 3–4.

—"Hussein Stands by the PLO", *Middle East International*, no. 466, 7 January 1994, p. 9.

—"The Pluses and the Minuses", *Middle East International*, no. 412, 8 November 1991, pp. 4–5.

—"Still in Two Minds", *Middle East International*, no. 409, 27 September 1991, p. 8.

—"Fissured Opinion", *Middle East International*, no. 395, 8 March 1991, pp. 14–15.

Heller, M. "The Middle East: Out of Step with History", *Foreign Affairs*, vol. 69, no. 1 (1990), pp. 152–71.

Hinnebusch, R., "Does Syria Want Peace? Syrian Policy in the Syrian–Israeli Peace Negotiations", *Journal of Palestine Studies,* vol. XXVI, no. 1 (Autumn 1996), pp. 42–57.

—"The Political Economy of Economic Liberalization in Syria", *International Journal of Middle East Studies,* vol. 27 (August 1995), pp. 305–20.

—"Syria: The Politics of Peace and Regime Survival", *Middle East Policy,* vol. iii, no. 4 (April 1995), pp. 74–87.

—"Asad's Syria and the New World Order: The Struggle for Regime Survival", *Middle East Policy,* vol. ii, no. 1 (May/June 1993), pp. 6–14.

—"State and Civil Society in Syria", *Middle East Journal,* vol. 47, no. 2 (Spring 1993), pp. 243–57.

—"The Politics of Economic Reform in Egypt", *Third World Quarterly,* vol. 14, no. 1 (1993), pp. 159–71.

—"Syrian Policy in Lebanon and the Palestinians", *Arab Studies Quarterly,* vol. 8, no. 1 (Winter 1986), pp. 1–20.

—"Syria under the Ba'th: State Formation in a Fragmented Society", *Arab Studies Quarterly,* vol. 4, no. 3 (Summer 1982), pp. 177–99.

—"Political Recruitment and Socialization in Syria: The Case of the Revolutionary Youth Federation", *International Journal of Middle Eastern Studies,* vol. 11, 1980, pp. 143–74.

Hiro, D. "Middle East: Twin Track Peace Process Increasingly Divergent", *Inter Press Service English News Wire,* 19 November 1996.

Hirst, D. "Shameless in Gaza", *The Guardian,* 21 April 1997, pp. 8–9.

Hoffman, S. "A New World and Its Troubles", *Foreign Affairs,* vol. 69, no. 4 (1990), pp. 115–22.

Huntington, S. "The Clash of Civilizations?", *Foreign Affairs,* vol. 72, no. 3 (Summer 1993), pp. 22–49.

Islam, S. "Hussein's Plea for Jordan", *Middle East International,* no. 409, 27 September 1991, p. 9.

Israelyan, V. "The October 1973 War: Kissinger in Moscow", *Middle East Journal,* vol. 49, no. 2 (Spring 1995), pp. 248–68.

Jansen, G. "South Africa Caves in on Arms", *Middle East International,* no. 543, 7 February 1997, pp. 11–12.

—"The Giant's Failure", *Middle East International,* no. 525, 10 May 1996, pp. 6–7.

—"Syria's Bottom Line", *Middle East International,* no. 434, 25 September 1992, pp. 4–5.

—"Talking Again", *Middle East International,* no. 389, 7 December 1990, p. 15.

—"The Ousting of 'Aoun", *Middle East International,* no. 386, 26 October 1990, pp. 8–10.

—"Unpopular U-Turn", *Middle East International,* no. 384, 28 September 1990, pp. 11–12.

Jansen, M. "Lebanon Cease-fire Terms", *Middle East International,* no. 525, 10 May 1996, pp. 5–6.

—"An Unusual Delegation", *Middle East International,* no. 471, 18 March 1994, p. 11.

Jerusalem Post Staff, "Poll Shows Majority Oppose Any Full Withdrawal from Golan", *The Jerusalem Post International Edition,* 15 October 1994, p. 1.

Kagian, J. "More of the Same at the UN", *Middle East International,* no. 544, 21 February 1997, p. 6.

—"Damning UN Report", *Middle East International,* no. 525, 10 May 1996, pp. 4–5.

—"Retreat from 799: Security Council Bends to US Pressure", *Middle East International,* no. 444, 19 February 1993, p. 3.

Kamal, S. "Hussein's Sorrow and Shame", *Middle East International,* no. 546, 21 March 1997, p. 9.

Kanaan, G. "Syria and the Peace Plan: Assad's Balancing Act", *Middle East Report (MERIP),* no. 65 (March 1978), pp. 10–11.

Karsh, E. "Peace in the Middle East", *The Oxford International Review,* vol. 5, no. 1 (Winter 1993), pp. 36–40.

Kessler, J. and T. Smerling. "Beyond Democratization: American Jewish Activists Cross the Divide to Syria", *Middle East Insight,* vol. x, no. 6 (September/October 1994), pp. 12–13.

Kidron, P. "Har Homa: The Price of Netanyahu's Showmanship", *Middle East International,* no. 545, 7 March 1997, pp. 3–5.

—"Yitzhak Rabin, 1922–1995", *Middle East International,* no. 513, 17 November 1995, p. 4.

—"Rabin Caves in on Land Confiscations", *Middle East International,* no. 501, 26 May 1995, p. 3.

—"Israel and Syria – A Deal in the Offing?", *Middle East International,* no. 484, 23 September 1994, pp. 3–4.

—"242 But Not An Inch", *Middle East International,* no. 433, 11 September 1992, pp. 4–6.

—"Sullen Acceptance", *Middle East International,* no. 411, 25 October 1991, pp. 9–11.

—"Consternation in Israel", *Middle East International,* no. 409, 27 September 1991, pp. 4–6.

Kienle, E. "Arab Unity Schemes Revisited: Interest, Identity, and Policy in Syria and Egypt", *International Journal of Middle East Studies,* vol. 27, no. 1 (February 1995), pp. 53–71.

Kirkpatrick, J. "We Shouldn't Risk U.S. Dollars on Unreliable Arafat and Assad", *Human Events,* vol. 51, 28 July 1995, pp. 10–11.

Kirkpatrick, J. *et al.* "The Modernizing Imperative: Tradition and Change", *Foreign Affairs,* vol. 72, no. 4 (September/October 1993), pp. 22–4.

Krause, K. "Insecurity and State Formation in the Global Military Order: The Middle Eastern Case", *European Journal of International Relations,* vol. 2, no. 3 (1996), pp. 319–54.

Krauthammer, C. "The Unipolar Moment", *Foreign Affairs,* vol. 70, no. 1 (Winter 1991), pp. 23–33.

Kubursi, A. and S. Mansur. "Oil and the Gulf War: An 'American Century' or a 'New World Order'", *Arab Studies Quarterly,* vol. 15, no. 4 (Fall 1993), pp. 1–17.

Lawson, F. "Domestic Transformation and Foreign Steadfastness in Contemporary Syria", *Middle East Journal,* vol. 48, no. 1 (Winter 1994), pp. 47–64.

—"Political–Economic Trends in Ba'thi Syria: A Reinterpretation", *Orient,* vol. 29 (December 1988), pp. 579–94.

Lewis, N. "The Isma'ilis of Syria Today", *Royal Central Asian Society Journal,* vol. 39, no. 1 (January 1952), pp. 69–77.

Lifton, R. "Talking with Assad: A Visit to a Middle East in Transition", *Middle East Insight,* vol. x, no. 6 (September/October 1994), pp. 8–11.

Little, R. "Neorealism and the English School: A Methodological, Ontological and Theoretical Reassessment", *European Journal of International Relations,* vol. 1, no. 1 (March 1995), pp. 9–34.

Lucas, I. "How Far Has Syria Changed Course?", *Middle East International,* no. 407, 30 August 1991, pp. 15–16.

Mahbubani, K. "The Dangers of Decadence: What the Rest Can Teach the West", *Foreign Affairs,* vol. 72, no. 4 (September/October 1993), pp. 10–14.

Makovsky, D. "In the Lion's Den: An Israeli Visits 'Forbidden' Palace", *The Jerusalem Post International Edition,* 5 November 1994, p. 2.

—"Clinton: 'Not Insignificant' Progress in Talks with Assad", *The Jerusalem Post International Edition,* 5 November 1994, p. 2.

—"Rabin Already Working on Golan Referendum", *The Jerusalem Post International Edition,* 15 October 1994, p. 2.

Marlowe, L. "Freer Economy Pays Syria Big Dividends: The Flow of Investment That Has Followed Reform", *Financial Times,* 5 November 1992, p. 4.

—"Syria Holds the Key to UK Hostages Release", *Financial Times,* 2 November 1990, p. 4.

Marschall, C. "Syria–Iran: A Strategic Alliance, 1979–1991", *Orient,* vol. 33, no. 2 (1992), pp. 433–44.

Martin, J. "International Patience Paid Off, Says FBI: Peaceful End to Montana Seige as Authorities Learn Lessons of WACO", *Financial Times,* 15 June 1996, p. 4.

—"Political Extremes Dance on Dark Side of the Moon: Revolutionary Left and Right in US Sometimes Share Anarchic Hatreds", *Financial Times,* 6 June 1996, p. 3.

McGuinn, B. "The Perils of Conventional Wisdom: A Reassessment of Syrian Options", *Global Affairs,* vol. 8, no. 1 (Winter 1993), pp. 148–60.

Miller, R. "The Golan Heights: An Obsolete Security Buffer", *Mediterranean Quarterly* (Spring 1993), pp. 123–8.

Moore, J. "An Israeli–Syrian Peace Treaty: So Close and Yet So Far", *Middle East Policy,* vol. iii, no. 3 (1994), pp. 61–79.

Muir, J. "Rabin's Revenge Exacts an Appalling Toll", *Middle East International,* no. 456, 6 August 1993, pp. 3–4.

—"Syrians Refuse the Bait", *Middle East International,* no. 413, 22 November 1991, pp. 5–6.

—"The Arabs Fall Into Line", *Middle East International,* no. 405, 26 July 1991, pp. 4–5.

—"The PLO, Syria, and Iran", *Middle East International,* no. 392, 25 January 1991, pp. 9–10.

—"Why Asad Turned to Cairo?", *Middle East International,* no. 366, 5 January 1990, pp. 3–4.

Muslih, M. "The Golan: Israel, Syria, and Strategic Calculations", *Middle East Journal,* vol. 47, no. 4 (Autumn 1993), pp. 611–32.

Nader, G. "Imagining Peace with Syria: Changes Show the Country and Regime Are Prepared for Peace", *Middle East Insight*, vol. xi, no. 1 (November/December 1994), pp. 10–13.

—"Syrian Foreign Minister Farouk al-Sharaa Reaffirms Peace for Golan Withdrawal", *Middle East Insight*, vol. xi, no. 1 (November/December 1994), pp. 14–23.

Nasrallah, F. "Syria's Post-war Gains and Liabilities", *Middle East International*, no. 396, 22 March 1991, pp. 20–1.

Neff, D. "Christopher's Final Goal", *Middle East International*, no. 518, 2 February 1996, pp. 7–8.

—"The 30th Veto to Shield Israel", *Middle East International*, no. 501, 26 May 1995, pp. 5–6.

—"Hussein and Rabin Make their Declaration", *Middle East International*, no. 481, 5 August 1994, pp. 3–4.

—"Syria is the Key Issue", *Middle East International*, no. 480, 22 July 1994, p. 4.

—"Clinton Dangles Carrots for the Palestinians", *Middle East International*, no. 448, 16 April 1993, pp. 3–4.

—"Clinton, Rabin, and a Deal with Syria", *Middle East International*, no. 446, 19 March 1993, p. 3.

—"The Make-or-Break Process Begins in Madrid", *Middle East International*, no. 411, 25 October 1991, p. 3.

—"Settlements and Guarantees: The US Threatens Linkage", *Middle East International*, no. 409, 27 September 1991, pp. 3–4.

—"The Bruising Battle between Bush and Shamir", *Middle East International*, no. 404, 13 September 1991, pp. 3–4.

Neriah, J. "Progress and Challenges on the Syrian Track: An Israeli Perspective on the Negotiations", *Middle East Insight*, vol. xi, no. 4 (May/June 1995), pp. 8–12.

North, A. "Southern Iraq: Flight from the Marshes", *Middle East International*, no. 458, 10 September 1993, p. 20.

Norton, A. "Lebanon after Ta'if: Is the Civil War Over?", *Middle East Journal*, vol. 45, no. 3 (Summer 1991), pp. 457–74.

Nye, J. "What New World Order?", *Foreign Affairs*, vol. 71, no. 2 (Spring 1992), pp. 83–97.

—"American Strategy after Bipolarity", *International Affairs*, vol. 66, no. 3 (July 1990), pp. 513–22.

Nye, J., W. Owens and E. Cohen. "A Technological Revolution Is Transforming the Nature of Power. And the United States Is Clearly in the Lead", *Foreign Affairs,* vol. 75, no. 2 (March/April 1996), pp. 20–36.

O'Sullivan, E. "Cementing Peace with Prosperity", *Middle East Economic Digest,* vol. 37, no. 38, 24 September 1993, pp. 4–5.

Ozanne, J. "Struggle to Hold it All Together: Shimon Peres, the Acting Israeli Leader Faces Formidable Challenges in Keeping the Peace Process Going", *Financial Times,* 11 November 1995, p. 6.

—"Police Sees Arms Stockpile at Home of Rabin's Assassin", *Financial Times,* 10 November 1995, p. 16.

—"Israel Cautious over Syrian Offer on Golan", *Financial Times,* 18 January 1994, p. 4.

—"'Peace Agreement Is a Recipe for Civil War': Jewish Settlers to Fight on as 'Vanguard Soldiers'", *Financial Times,* 8 December 1993, p. 7.

Parsons, A. "The United Nations Comes into its Own", *Middle East International,* no. 382, 31 August 1990, pp. 27–9.

Perera, J. "Syria and Russia: Reinforcing Old Ties", *Middle East International,* no. 489, 2 December 1994, pp. 11–12.

Perthes, V. "Syria's Parliamentary Elections: Remodelling Asad's Political Base", *Middle East Report* (*MERIP*), no. 174 (January/February 1992), pp. 15–18.

—"The Syrian Economy in the 1980s", *Middle East Journal,* vol. 46, no. 1 (Winter 1992), pp. 37–58.

Piel, G. "The West is Best", *Foreign Affairs,* vol. 72, no. 4 (September/October 1993), pp. 25–6.

Pipes, D. "Syria's People May Not Want Peace", *Jewish Exponent,* 25 November 1994, pp. 1–3.

—"Syria: The Post-Assad Era", *Politique Internationale,* vol. 59 (Spring 1993), pp. 97–110.

Rathmell, A. "Syria's Search for an 'Honourable Peace'", *Middle East International,* no. 480, 22 July 1994, pp. 16–17.

Ravenhill, J. "The North–South Balance of Power", *International Affairs,* vol. 66, no. 4 (October 1990), pp. 731–48.

Richards, C. "Assad Adds His Weight to Middle East Peace Talks", *The Independent,* 17 January 1994, p. 1.

—"Clinton Wooed by Syrian President", *The Independent,* 17 January 1994, p. 11.

Roberts, A. "A New Age in International Relations?", *International Affairs,* vol. 67, no. 3 (July 1991), pp. 509–26.

Robinson, L. "Rentierism and Foreign Policy in Syria", *Arab Studies Journal,* vol. iv, no. 1 (Spring 1996), pp. 34–54.

Rodan, S. "Of Two Minds at the Top: The Heads of Military Intelligence are at Loggerheads over whether Syria is Ready for Peace with Israel", *The Jerusalem Post International Edition,* 29 October 1994, pp. 11–12.

Rodenbeck, M. "Quiet Unease", *Middle East International,* no. 393, 8 February 1991, p. 15.

Roseau, J. "Normative Challenges in a Turbulent World", *Ethics and International Affairs,* vol. 3, no. 1 (1992), p. 16.

Rosecrance, R. "A New Concert of Powers", *Foreign Affairs,* vol. 71, no. 2 (Spring 1992), pp. 64–82.

Russett, B. and J. Sutterlin, "The UN in a New World Order", *Foreign Affairs,* vol. 70, no. 1 (1991), pp. 69–83.

Sadiki, L. "Al-Nidam: An Arab View of the New World (Dis)order", *Arab Studies Quarterly,* vol. 17, no. 3 (Summer 1995), pp. 1–18.

Sadowski, Y. "Arab Economies after the Gulf War: Power, Poverty, and Petrodollars", *Middle East Report (MERIP),* no. 170 (May/June 1991), pp. 4–8.

—"Cadres, Guns and Money: The Eighth Regional Congress of the Syrian Ba'th", *Middle East Report (MERIP),* no. 134 (July/August 1985), pp. 3–8.

Sakr, N. "Syria: Stability the Key to 1980 Targets", *Middle East Economic Digest,* vol. 19, no. 48, 28 November 1975, p. 3.

—"Oil and Aid Boost Syrian Recovery", *Middle East Economic Digest,* vol. 19, no. 28, 11 July 1975, p. 6.

Salloukh, B. "State Strength, Permeability, and Foreign Policy Behavior: Jordan in Theoretical Perspective", *Arab Studies Quarterly,* vol. 18, no. 2 (Spring 1996), pp. 39–59.

Sarkees, M. and S. Zunes, "Disenchantment with the 'New World Order': Syria's relations with the United States", *International Journal,* vol. XLIX, no. 2 (April 1994), pp. 356–77.

Sayigh, Y. "The Middle East Strategic Balance: Capabilities for Waging War", *Middle East International,* no. 378, 22 June 1990, pp. 15–16.

Schiff, Z. "Dealing with Syria", *Foreign Policy*, no. 55 (Summer 1984), pp. 92–112.

Seale, P. "Asad's Regional Strategy and the Challenge from Netanyahu", *Journal of Palestine Studies*, vol. XXVI, no. 1 (Autumn 1996), pp. 27–41.

—"Syria and the Peace Process", *Politique Etrangère*, vol. 57, no. 4 (Hiver 1992), pp. 785–96.

Seelye, T. "Syria and the Peace Process", *Middle East Policy*, vol. ii, no. 2 (February 1993), pp. 104–9.

Serrill, M. "A Radical Return to the Ranks; at Last Syria Joins the World in Condemning Iran", *Time*, vol. 130, no. 21, 23 November 1987, p. 35.

Shad, T., S. Boucher and J. Gray-Reddish. "Syrian Foreign Policy in the Post-Soviet Era", *Arab Studies Quarterly*, vol. 17, no. 1 & 2 (Winter/Spring 1995), pp. 77–94.

Shahak, I. "The Real Problem between Israel and Syria", *Middle East International*, no. 523, 12 April 1996, p. 19.

—"Israel and Syria: Peace through Strategic Parity?", *Middle East International*, no. 490, 16 December 1994, pp. 18–19.

Shoval, Z. "Does Damascus Want Peace?", *Jerusalem Post*, 2 December 1996, pp. 6–7.

Singer, J. "Under Pressure: Syrian Participation in the Peace Process", *Harvard International Review*, vol. 17, no. 4 (1995), pp. 58–61.

Special Correspondent, "Boundless Ambition", *The Middle East*, no. 229 (December 1993), pp. 18–19.

Special Correspondent, "Syria: The President, the Sheikh and Le Piano", *The Economist*, 17 April 1993, p. 68.

Stanely, B. "Drawing from the Well: Syria in the Persian Gulf", *Journal of South Asian and Middle Eastern Studies*, vol. XIV, no. 2 (Winter 1990), pp. 45–64.

Swann, R. "Trying Not to Gloat", *Middle East International*, no. 525, 10 May 1996, pp. 7–8.

—"Europe's Abortive Bridge-building", *Middle East International*, no. 391, 11 January 1991, pp. 5–7.

Syria – Country Profile, *The Economist Intelligence Unit*, several issues.

Torrey, G. "The Ba'th – Ideology and Practice", *Middle East Journal*, vol. 23, no. 4 (Autumn 1969), pp. 445–70.

Trendle, G. "Hizbollah Serves Its Purpose", *The Middle East*, no. 208 (February 1992), p. 13.

Usher, G. "Unfinished Struggle – Arafat after Hebron", *Middle East International,* no. 542, 24 January 1997, pp. 3–4.

—"Hizballah, Syria, and the Lebanese Elections", *Journal of Palestine Studies,* vol. XXVI, no. 2 (Winter 1997), pp. 59–67.

—"Picture of War", *Middle East International,* no. 535, 4 October 1996, pp. 3–5.

—"Hamas and the Bus Bomb", *Middle East International,* no. 506, 4 August 1995, pp. 4–5.

—"Land Confiscation in Arab Jerusalem", *Middle East International,* no. 500, 12 May 1995, pp. 3–4.

—"Why Gaza Mostly Says Yes", *Middle East International,* no. 459, 24 September 1993, pp. 19–20.

Van Dam, N. "Middle Eastern Political Clichés: 'Takriti' and 'Sunni' Rule in Syria, a Critical Appraisal", *Orient,* vol. 21, no. 1 (January 1980), pp. 42–57.

Van Dusen, M. "Political Integration and Regionalism in Syria", *Middle East Journal,* vol. 26, no. 3 (Spring 1972), pp. 123–36.

Wagner, R. "What was Bipolarity?", *International Organisation,* vol. 47, no. 1 (Winter 1993), pp. 77–106.

Waldner, D. "More than Meets the Eye: Economic Influence on Contemporary Syrian Foreign Policy", *Middle East Insight,* vol. xi, no. 4 (May/June 1995), pp. 34–7.

Walker, R. "Security, Sovereignty, and the Challenge of World Politics", *Alternatives,* vol. 15, pp. 3–27.

Walker, T. "No Queues from Outside Syria's Newly Opened Door: In Spite of Appearances, the Fundamentals of the Assad Regime Remain the Same", *Financial Times,* 18 March 1992, p. 4.

—"Syria and Iran Defence Link Up: A 'Strange Marriage' in the Gulf", *Financial Times,* 9 March 1992, p. 16.

Wallerstein, I. "The Rise and Future Demise of the World Capitalist System: Concepts for Comparative Analysis", *Comparative Studies in Society and History,* vol. 16, no. 4 (Autumn 1974), pp. 387–415.

Walsh, K. "George Bush's New Friends? The President May Move to Improve Ties to Syria and Iran", *US News and World Report,* vol. 111, no. 9, 26 August 1991, p. 24.

Waltz, K. "The Stability of a Bipolar World", *Daedalus,* vol. 93 (Summer 1964), pp. 881–909.

Washington Report, vol. xii, no. 2 (August 1993).

Weeks, A. "Do Civilizations Hold?", *Foreign Affairs*, vol. 72, no. 4 (September/October 1993), pp. 24–5.

Weinstein, F. "The Uses of Foreign Policy in Indonesia: Approach to the Analysis of Foreign Policy in the Less Developed Countries", *World Politics*, vol. 24, no. 3 (April 1972), pp. 356–81.

Whittington, J. "Syria's Economy Shackled by Old Institutions", *Financial Times*, 11 May 1993, p. 4.

Widlanski, M. "Assad Case: Bush's Favourite Drug Pusher", *The New Republic*, vol. 206, no. 5, 3 February 1992, p. 8.

Ya'ari, E. "Syria Next vs. Damascus Last", *Middle East Insight*, vol. xi, no. 1 (November/December 1994), pp. 20–3.

—"Syrian Foreign Minister Addresses Israeli Public", *Middle East Insight*, vol. xi, no. 1 (November/December 1994), p. 19.

Yorke, V. "Prospects for Peace: The Syrian Dimension", *Middle East International*, no. 414, 6 December 1991, pp. 16–17.

Ziarati, M. "The Regional Balance of Power in the Air", *Middle East International*, no. 463, 19 November 1993, pp. 20–1.

Zisser, E. "Asad of Syria – the Leader and the Image", *Orient*, vol. 35, no. 2 (June 1994), pp. 247–60.

Books and chapters in books

Abir, M. *Saudi Arabia: Government, Society and the Gulf Crisis*, London: Routledge, 1993.

Abu Jaber, K. *The Arab Ba'th Socialist Party: History, Ideology, and Organization*, Syracuse: Syracuse University Press, 1966.

Abukhalil, A. "Determinants and Characteristics of Syrian Policy in Lebanon" in D. Collings (ed.), *Peace for Lebanon? From War to Reconstruction*, Boulder: Lynne Rienner, 1994.

Agha, H. and A. Khalidi, *Syria and Iran: Rivalry and Cooperation*, London: Pinter, 1995.

Allison, G. *Essence of Decision: Explaining the Cuban Missile Crisis*, Boston: Little, Brown, 1971.

Althusser, L. (ed.), "Ideology and Ideological State Apparatuses" in *Lenin and Philosophy and Other Essays*, London: New Left, 1971.

Altoma, S. "The Emancipation of Women in Contemporary Syrian Literature" in R. Antoun and D. Quataert (eds.), *Syria: Society, Culture, and Polity*, Albany: State University of New York Press, 1991.

Ambrosius, L. *Wilsonian Statecraft: Theory and Practice of Liberal Internationalism during World War I*, Wilimmington: 1991.

Anon., "Druzes" in *Islamic Desk Reference compiled from E. Van Donzel (ed.), Encyclopaedia of Islam*, Leiden: E.J. Brill, 1994.

Antonius, G. *The Arab Awakening: The Story of the Arab National Movement*, London: Hamish Hamilton, 1961.

Antoun, R. "Ethnicity, Clientship, and Class: Their Changing Meaning" in R. Antoun and D. Quataert (eds.), *Syria: Society, Culture, and Polity*, Albany: State University of New York Press, 1991.

Ashrawi, H. *This Side of Peace : A Personal Account*, New York: Simon & Schuster, 1995.

Ayoob, M. "Unravelling the Concept: National Security in the Third World" in B. Korany, P. Noble and R. Brynen (eds.), *The Many Faces of National Security in the Arab World*, New York: Macmillan, 1993.

Ayubi, N. (ed.), "Farms, Factories . . . and Walls: Which Way for European/Middle Eastern Relations?" in *Distant Neighbours: The Political Economy of Relations between Europe and the Middle East/North Africa*, London: Ithaca, 1995.

Ayubi, N. *Over-stating the Arab State: Politics and Society in the Middle East*, London: I.B. Tauris, 1995.

Bahout, J. "The Syrian Business Community, its Politics and Prospects" in E. Kienle (ed.), *Contemporary Syria: Liberalization between Cold War and Cold Peace*, London: British Academic Press, 1994.

Baker, R. "Imagining Egypt in the New Age: Civil Society and the Leftist Critique" in T. Ismael and J. Ismael (eds.), *The Gulf War and the New World Order: International Relations of the Middle East*, Gainseville: University Press of Florida, 1994.

Ball, A. *Modern Politics and Government*, London: Macmillan, 1987.

Ballard, R. "Effects of Labour Migration from Pakistan" in H. Alavi and J. Harriss (eds.), *Sociology of 'Developing Societies': South Asia*, Basingstoke: Macmillan, 1989.

Bannerman, M. "Syrian Arab Republic" in D. Long and B. Reich (eds.), *The Government and Politics of the Middle East and North Africa*, Boulder: Westview Press, 1995.

Bar-Siman-Tov, Y. *Linkage Politics in the Middle East: Syria between Domestic and External Conflict, 1961–1970*, Boulder: Westview Press, 1983.

Bercovitch, J. "Introduction" in M. Efrat and J. Bercovitch (eds.), *Superpowers and Client States in the Middle East: The Imbalance of Influence*, London: Routledge, 1991.

—"Superpowers and Client States: Analysing Relations and Patterns of Influence" in M. Efrat, and J. Bercovitch (eds.), *Superpowers and Client States in the Middle East: The Imbalance of Influence*, London: Routledge, 1991.

Berger, H. "Senator Robert A. Taft Dissents from Military Escalation" in T. Paterson (ed.), *Cold War Critics: Alternatives to American Foreign Policy in the Truman Years*, Chicago: Quadrangle, 1971.

Bernstein, B. "Walter Lippman and the Early Cold War" in T. Paterson (ed.), *Cold War Critics: Alternatives to American Foreign Policy in the Truman Years*, Chicago: Quadrangle, 1971.

Beschloss, M., and S. Talbott, *At the Highest Levels: The Inside Story of the End of the Cold War*, London: Little, Brown, 1993.

Bienefeld, M. "Is a Strong National Economy a Utopian Goal at the End of the Twentieth Century" in R. Boyer and D. Drache (eds.), *States against Markets: The Limits of Globalization*, London: Routledge, 1996.

Bill, J. and R. Springborg, *Politics in the Middle East*, New York: HarperCollins, 1994.

Booth, K. "Dare Not to Know: International Relations Theory versus the Future" in K. Booth and S. Smith (eds.), *International Relations Theory Today*, Cambridge: Polity Press, 1995.

Brown, S. *International Relations in a Changing Global System: Toward a Theory of the World Polity*, Boulder: Westview Press, 1992.

Buettner, F. and M. Landgraf, "The European Community's Middle Eastern Policy: The New Order of Europe and the Gulf Crisis" in T. Ismael and J. Ismael (eds.), *The Gulf War and the New World Order: International Relations of the Middle East*, Gainseville: University Press of Florida, 1994.

Bull, H. "The Balance of Power and International Order" in R. Little and M. Smith (eds.), *Perspectives on World Politics*, London: Routledge, 1992.

Burrell, R. and A. Kelider, *Egypt: The Dilemmas of a Nation – 1970–1977*, *The Washington Papers*, vol. v, no. 48, London: Sage, 1977.

Burrows, R. and B. Spector, "The Strength and Direction of Relationships between Domestic and External Conflict and Cooperation" in J. Wilkenfeld (ed.), *Conflict Behavior and Linkage Politics,* New York: David McKay, 1973.

Butter, D. "Lebanon" in *The Cambridge Encyclopaedia of the Middle East and North Africa,* Cambridge: Cambridge University Press, 1988.

Buzan, B. *People, States and Fear: An Agenda for International Security Studies in the Post-Cold War Era,* Boulder: Lynne Rienner, 1991.

Cantori, L. "The Middle East in the New World Order: Political Trends" in T. Ismael and J. Ismael (eds.), *The Gulf War and the New World Order: International Relations of the Middle East,* Gainseville: University Press of Florida, 1994.

Carr, E. *The Twenty Years Crisis: 1919–1939,* London: Macmillan, 1939.

Cattan, H. *The Palestine Question,* London: Croom Helm, 1988.

Chase-Dunn, C. *Global Formation: Structures of the World-Economy,* Oxford: Blackwell, 1992.

Chomsky, N. *World Orders, Old and New,* London: Pluto Press, 1994.

—*Deterring Democracy,* London: Vintage, 1992.

—"The US in the Gulf Crisis" in H. Bresheeth and N. Yuval-Davis (eds.), *The Gulf War and the New World Order,* London: Zed, 1991.

—*The Fateful Triangle: The United States, Israel & the Palestinians,* Boston: South End Press, 1983.

Clapham, C. *Third World Politics: An Introduction,* London: Croom Helm, 1985.

Clavert, P. *The Foreign Policy of New States,* Sussex: Wheatsheaf, 1986.

Cobban, H. "The Nature of the Soviet–Syrian Link under Asad and under Gorbachev" in R. Antoun and D. Quataert (eds.), *Syria: Society, Culture, and Polity,* Albany: State University of New York Press, 1991.

—*The Superpowers and the Syrian–Israeli Conflict: Beyond Crisis Management?,* London: Praeger, 1991.

Cordesman, A. "Current Trends in Arms Sales in the Middle East" in S. Feldman, and A. Levite (eds.), *Arms Control and the New Middle East Security Environment,* Tel Aviv: Jaffee Center for Strategic Studies, 1994.

—"United States Power-projection Capabilities in the Gulf and South-West Asia: Changing Forces for a Changing World" in C. Davies (ed.), *Global Interests in the Arab Gulf,* Exeter: University of Exeter Press, 1992.

Couloumbis, T. and J. Wolfe, *Introduction to International Relations: Power and Justice,* Englewood Cliffs: Prentice-Hall, 1987.

Cox, R. "Social Forces, States and World Orders: Beyond International Relations Theory" in R. Keohane (ed.), *Neorealism and its Critics,* New York: Columbia University Press, 1986.

Curtiss, R. *Stealth PACs: How the Israeli–American Lobby Took Control of US Middle East Policy,* Washington: American Educational Trust, 1990.

Dahl, R. "Balance of Power and World War I" in J. Nye (ed.), *Understanding International Conflicts: An Introduction to Theory and History,* New York: HarperCollins, 1993.

Dawisha, A. *Syria and the Lebanese Crisis,* London: Macmillan, 1980.

Dessouki, A. and B. Korany (eds.), "A Literature Survey and a Framework for Analysis" in *The Foreign Policies of Arab States: The Challenge of Change,* Boulder: Westview Press, 1991.

—"The Primacy of Economics: The Foreign Policy of Egypt" in B. Korany and A. Dessouki (eds.), *The Foreign Policies of Arab States: The Challenge of Change,* Boulder: Westview Press, 1991.

Deutsch, K. *The Analysis of International Relations,* Englewood Cliffs: Prentice-Hall, 1988.

Dixon, S. "The Russians: The Dominant Nationality" in G. Smith (ed.), *The Nationalities Question in the Soviet Union,* London: Longman, 1992.

Drache, D. "From Keynes to K-Mart: Competitiveness in a Corporate Age" in R. Boyer and D. Drache (eds.), *States against Markets: The Limits of Globalization,* London: Routledge, 1996.

Drysdale, A. "The Syrian Armed Forces in National Politics: The Role of the Geographic and Ethnic Periphery" in R. Kolkowicz and A. Korbonski (eds.), *Soldiers, Peasants and Bureaucrats,* London: Allen & Unwin, 1982.

—"The 'Alawis of Syria" in G. Ashworth (ed.), *World Minorities,* vol. II, London: Quartermaine House/Minority Rights Group, 1978.

Drysdale, A. and R. Hinnebusch, *Syria and the Middle East Peace Process,* New York: Council on Foreign Relations, 1991.

Dunning, J. *The Globalization of Business,* London: Routledge, 1993.

Ehteshami, A. and R. Hinnebusch, *Syria and Iran: Middle Powers in a Penetrated Regional System,* London: Routledge, 1997.

Ehteshami, A. "The Rise and Convergence of the 'Middle' in the World Economy: The Case of the NICs and the Gulf" in C. Davies (ed.), *Global Interests in the Arab Gulf*, Exeter: Exeter University Press, 1992.

Ekins, P. *A New World Order: Grassroots Movement for Global Change*, London: Routledge, 1992.

Evans, P., D. Rueschemeyer and T. Skocpol (eds.), "On the Road toward a More Adequate Understanding of the State" in *Bringing the State Back In*, Cambridge: Cambridge University Press, 1990.

Evron, Y. *War and Intervention in Lebanon: The Syrian–Israeli Deterrence Dialogue*, Baltimore: Johns Hopkins University, 1987.

Falk, R. "Reflections on the Gulf Experience: Force and War in the UN System" in T. Ismael and J. Ismael (eds.), *The Gulf War and the New World Order: International Relations of the Middle East*, Gainseville: University Press of Florida, 1994.

Farques, P. "Demographic Explosion or Social Upheaval" in G. Salame (ed.), *Democracy without Democrats? The Revival of Politics in the Muslim World*, London: I.B. Tauris, 1994.

Finer, S. *Comparative Government*, Middlesex: Penguin, 1985.

Fisk, R. *Pity the Nation: Lebanon at War*, Oxford: Oxford University Press, 1991.

Freedman, L. and E. Karsh, *The Gulf Conflict 1990–1991: Diplomacy and War in the New World Order*, London: Faber & Faber, 1993.

Freedman, R. "The Soviet Union and Syria: A Case Study of Soviet Policy" in M. Efrat and J. Bercovitch (eds.), *Superpowers and Client States in the Middle East: The Imbalance of Influence*, London: Routledge, 1991.

Fukuyama, F. *The End of History and the Last Man*, London: Penguin, 1992.

Galtung, J. "A Structural Theory of Imperialism" in R. Little and M. Smith (eds.), *Perspectives on World Politics*, London: Routledge, 1992.

Garnett, J. "The Role of Military Power" in R. Little and M. Smith (eds.), *Perspectives on World Politics*, London: Routledge, 1992.

Gazit, S. *The Middle East Military Balance, 1988–1989*, Boulder: Westview Press, 1989.

Gereffi, G. "Power and Dependency in an Interdependent World: A Guide to Understanding" in R. Little and M. Smith (eds.), *Perspectives on World Politics*, London: Routledge, 1992.

Gerner, K. and S. Hedlund, *The Baltic States and the End of the Soviet Empire,* London: Routledge, 1993.

Gilpin, R. *The Political Economy of International Relations,* Princeton: Princeton University Press, 1987.

Glassé, C. "Isma'ilis" in *The Concise Encyclopaedia of Islam,* London: Glassé, 1989.

Golan, G. *Moscow and the Middle East: New Thinking on Regional Conflict,* London: Pinter, 1992.

—*The Soviet Union and the Palestine Liberation Organisation: An Uneasy Alliance,* New York: Praeger, 1980.

Goode, R. "State Building as a Determinant of Foreign Policy in the New States" in L. Martin (ed.), *Neutralism and Non-Alignment,* New York: Praeger, 1962.

Gorbachev, M. *Perestroika: New Thinking for Our Country and the World,* London: Fontana Press, 1987.

Graebner, N. (ed.), *The Cold War: A Conflict of Ideology and Power,* Lexington: Heath, 1976.

Gramsci, A. *Selections from the Prison Notebooks,* London: Lawrence & Wishart, 1971.

Haas, E. "Obscurities Enshrined: The Balance of Power As an Analytical Concept" in P. Viotti, and M. Kauppi (eds.), *International Relations Theory: Realism, Pluralism, and Globalism,* New York: Macmillan, 1987.

Hague, R. and M. Harrop, *Comparative Government and Politics: An Introduction,* London: Macmillan, 1987.

Halliday, F. "The End of the Cold War and International Relations: Some Analytic and Theoretical Conclusions" in K. Booth and S. Smith (eds.), *International Relations Theory Today,* Cambridge: Polity Press, 1995.

—"The Cold War as Inter-systemic Conflicts – Initial Theses" in M. Bowker and R. Brown (eds.), *From Cold War to Collapse: Theory and World Politics in the 1980s,* Cambridge: Cambridge University Press, 1992.

—"State and Society in International Relations: A Second Agenda" in H. Dyer and L. Mangasarian (eds.), *The Study of International Relations: The State of the Art,* London: Macmillan, 1988.

Hannah, J. *At Arms Length: Soviet–Syrian Relations in the Gorbachev Era,* Washington: Washington Institute for Near East Policy, 1989.

Haas, E. *Beyond the Nation-State*, Stanford: Stanford University Press, 1964.

Heeger, G. *The Politics of Underdevelopment*, London: St Martin's Press, 1974.

Heikal, M. *Sphinx and Commissar: The Rise and Fall of Soviet Influence in the Arab World*, London: Collins, 1978.

—*The Road to Ramadan*, London: Collins, 1975.

Held, C. *Middle East Patterns*, Boulder: Westview Press, 1994.

Hendrickson, D. "The End of American History: American Security, the National Purpose, and the New World Order" in G. Allison and G. Treverton (eds.), *Rethinking America's Security: Beyond Cold War to New World Order*, New York: Norton, 1992.

Heydemann, S. "The Political Logic of Economic Rationality: Selective Stabilization in Syria" in H. Barkey (ed.), *The Politics of Economic Reform in the Middle East*, New York: St Martin's Press, 1992.

Hilan, R. "Trade Relations between Syria and Europe in Historical Perspective" in N. Ayubi (ed.), *Distant Neighbours: The Political Economy of Relations between Europe and the Middle East/North Africa*, London: Ithaca, 1995.

Hill, E. "The New World Order and the Gulf War: Rhetoric, Policy, and Politics in the United States" in T. Ismael and J. Ismael (eds.), *The Gulf War and the New World Order: International Relations of the Middle East*, Gainesville: University Press of Florida, 1994.

Hindess, B. *Discourses of Power: From Hobbes to Foucault*, Oxford: Blackwell, 1996).

Hinnebusch, R. "Egypt, Syria, and the Arab State System in the New World Order" in H. Jawad (ed.), *The Middle East in the New World Order*, London: St. Martin's Press, 1994.

—"Liberalization in Syria: The Struggle of Economic and Political Rationality" in E. Kienle (ed.), *Contemporary Syria: Liberalization between Cold War and Cold Peace*, London: British Academic Press, 1994.

—*Asad's Syria and the New World Order: The Struggle for Regime Survival*, issue paper no. 9, Washington: Middle East Council, May/June 1993.

—"Revisionist Dreams, Realist Strategies: The Foreign Policy of Syria" in B. Korany and A. Dessouki (eds.), *The Foreign Policies of Arab States: The Challenge of Change*, Boulder: Westview Press, 1991.

—"Class and State in Ba'thist Syria" in R. Antoun and D. Quataert (eds.), *Syria: Society, Culture, and Polity,* Albany: State University of New York Press, 1991.

—*Authoritarian Power and State Formation in Ba'thist Syria: Army, Party, and Peasant,* Boulder: Westview Press, 1990.

—*Peasant and Bureaucracy in Ba'thist Syria: The Political Economy of Rural Development,* Boulder: Westview Press, 1989.

Hinsely, F. *Nationalism and the International System,* London: Hodder & Stoughton, 1973.

Hirschfeld, Y. "The Odd Couple: Ba'athist Syria and Khomeini's Iran" in M. Ma'oz and A. Yaniv (eds.), *Syria under Assad: Domestic Constraints and Regional Risks,* London: Croom Helm, 1986.

Hirst, D. *The Gun and the Olive Branch: The Roots of Violence in the Middle East,* London: Futura, 1983.

Hobbes, T. *Leviathan,* New York: Penguin, 1985.

Hoffman, M. "Critical Theory and the Inter-Paradigm Debate" in H. Dyer and L. Mangasarian (eds.), *The Study of International Relations: The State of the Art,* London: Macmillan, 1988.

Holsti, K. "International Theory and War in the Third World" in B. Job (ed.), *The Insecurity Dilemma: National Security of Third World States,* Boulder: Lynne Rienner, 1992.

Hopkins, K. and I. Wallerstein. "Patterns of Development of the Modern World-System" in K. Hopkins and I. Wallerstein (eds.), *World-System Analysis: Theory and Methodology,* Beverley Hills: Sage, 1982.

Hopwood, D. *Egypt: Politics and Society 1945–90,* London: HarperCollins, 1991.

—*Syria 1945–1986: Politics and Society,* London: HarperCollins, 1988.

Hourani, A. *Minorities in the Arab World,* London: Oxford University Press, 1947.

—*Syria and Lebanon: A Political Essay,* London: Oxford University Press, 1946.

Huntington, S. *Political Order in Changing Societies,* New Haven: Yale University Press, 1968.

Kant, I. *Immanuel Kant's Critique of Pure Reason,* tr. N. Smith, London: Macmillan, 1950.

Karkouti, M. "Syria" in Middle East Review 1993/94 *The World of Information,* London: Kojan Page and Walden, 1993.

Karsh, E. *The Soviet Union and Syria: The Asad Years,* London: Routledge, 1988.

Kennedy, P. *The Rise and Fall of Great Powers: Economic Change and Military Conflict,* London: Unwin Hyman, 1988.

Keohane, R. (ed.), "Realism, Neorealism and the Study of World Politics" in *Neorealism and Its Critics,* New York: Columbia University Press, 1986.

—"Theory of World Politics: Structural Realism and Beyond" in *Neorealism and Its Critics,* New York: Columbia University Press, 1986.

Keohane, R. and J. Nye, *Power and Interdependence: World Politics in Transition,* Boston: Little, Brown, 1977.

Keohane, R., J. Nye and S. Hoffman, *After the Cold War: International Institutions and State Strategies in Europe, 1989–1991,* London: Harvard University Press, 1994.

Kern, M., P. Levering and R. Levering, *The Kennedy Crisis: The Press, the Presidency, and Foreign Policy,* Chapel Hill: University of North Carolina Press, 1984.

Kerr, M. *America's Middle East Policy: Kissinger, Carter and the Future,* Beirut: Institute for Palestine Studies, 1980.

—*The Arab Cold War 1958–1964: A Study of Ideology in Politics,* London: Oxford University Press, 1965.

Kessler, M. *Syria: Fragile Mosaic of Power,* Washington: National Defense University Press, 1987.

Khalaf, S. "Land Reform and Class Structure in Rural Syria" in R. Antoun and D. Quataert (eds.), *Syria: Society, Culture, and Polity,* Albany: State University of New York Press, 1991.

Khalidi, A. and H. Agha, "The Syrian Doctrine of Strategic Parity" in J. Kipper and H. Saunders (eds.), *The Middle East in Global Perspective,* Boulder: Westview Press, 1991.

Khoury, P. "Syrian Political Culture: A Historical Perspective" in R. Antoun and D. Quataert (eds.), *Syria: Society, Culture, and Polity,* Albany: State University of New York Press, 1991.

—*Syria and the French Mandate: The Politics of Arab Nationalism 1920–1945,* Princeton: Princeton University Press, 1987.

Khuri, F. "The 'Alawis of Syria: Religious Ideology and Organization" in R. Antoun and D. Quataert (eds.), *Syria: Society, Culture, and Polity,* Albany: State University of New York Press, 1991.

Kienle, E. "Syria, the Kuwait War, and the New World Order" in T. Ismael and J. Ismael (eds.), *The Gulf War and the New World Order: International Relations of the Middle East,* Gainesville: University Press of Florida, 1994.

—*Ba'th v Ba'th: The Conflict between Syria and Iraq, 1968–1989,* London: I.B. Tauris, 1990.

Kienle, E. (ed.), "The Return of Politics? Scenarios for Syria's Second Infitah" in *Contemporary Syria: Liberalization between Cold War and Cold Peace,* London: British Academic Press, 1994.

King, N. "The Qualitative Research Interview" in C. Cassell and G. Symon (eds.), *Qualitative Methods in Organizational Research: A Practical Guide,* London: Sage, 1994.

Kissinger, H. "Balance of Power Sustained" in G. Allison and G. Treverton (eds.), *Rethinking America's Security: Beyond Cold War to New World Order,* New York: Norton, 1992.

Knorr, K. *On the Uses of Military Power in the Nuclear Age,* Princeton: Princeton University Press, 1966.

Korany, B. and A. Dessouki (eds.), "The Global System and Arab Foreign Policies: The Primacy of Constraints" in *The Foreign Policies of Arab States: The Challenge of Change,* Boulder: Westview Press, 1991).

Korany, B., P. Noble and R. Brynen (eds.), "The Analysis of National Security in the Arab Context: Restating the State of the Art" in *The Many Faces of National Security in the Arab World,* New York: Macmillan, 1993.

Kramer, M. (ed.), "Syria's 'Alawis and Shi'ism" in *Shi'ism, Resistance, and Revolution,* Boulder: Westview Press, 1987.

Krasner, S. "Power Politics, Institutions, and Transnational Relations" in T. Risse-Kappen (ed.), *Bringing Transnational Relations Back In: Non-State Actors, Domestic Structures and International Institutions,* Cambridge: Cambridge University Press, 1995.

—*Defending the National Interest: Raw Materials, Investments and US Foreign Policy,* Princeton: Princeton University Press, 1978.

Kuroda, M. "Economic Liberalization and the Suq in Syria" in T. Niblock and E. Murphy (eds.), *Economic and Political Liberalization in the Middle East,* London: British Academic Press, 1993.

Kuroda, Y. "Bush's New World Order: A Structural Analysis of Instability and Conflict in the Gulf" in T. Ismael and J. Ismael (eds.), *The Gulf War and the New World Order: International Relations of the Middle East,* Gainesville: University Press of Florida, 1994.

Lapidus, I. *A History of Islamic Societies,* Cambridge: Cambridge University Press, 1991.

Lassassi, A. *Non-alignment and Algerian Foreign Policy,* Aldershot: Avebury, 1988.

Lavy, V. and E. Sheffer, *Foreign Aid and Economic Development in the Middle East: Egypt, Syria, and Jordan,* New York: Praeger, 1991.

Lawrence, T. *Seven Pillars of Wisdom: A Triumph,* London: Cape, 1990.

Lawson, F. *Why Syria Goes to War? Thirty Years of Confrontation,* London: Cornell University Press, 1996.

—"Domestic Pressures and the Peace Process: Fillip or Hindrance?" in E. Kienle (ed.), *Contemporary Syria: Liberalization between Cold War and Cold Peace,* London: British Academic Press, 1994.

Leca, J. "Social Structure and Political Stability: Comparative Evidence from the Algerian, Syrian, and Iraqi Cases" in A. Dawisha and W. Zartman (eds.), *Beyond Coercion: The Durability of the Arab State,* London: Croom Helm, 1988.

Lerche, C. and A. Said, *Concepts of International Politics,* Englewood Cliffs: Prentice-Hall, 1970.

Linklater, A. "Neo-realism in Theory and Practice" in K. Booth and S. Smith (eds.), *International Relations Theory Today,* Cambridge: Polity Press, 1995.

Little, R. "International Relations and the Triumph of Capitalism" in K. Booth and S. Smith (eds.), *International Relations Theory Today,* Cambridge: Polity Press, 1995.

Longrigg, S. *Syria and Lebanon under French Mandate,* London: Oxford University Press, 1958.

Lorenz, J. *Egypt and the Arabs: Foreign Policy and the Search for National Identity,* Boulder: Westview Press, 1990.

Luard, E. *The Balance of Power: The System of International Relations 1648–1815,* New York: St Martin's Press, 1992.

—*The Globalization of Politics: The Changed Focus of Political Action in the Modern World,* Basingstoke: Macmillan, 1990.

Ma'oz, M. *Syria and Israel: From War to Peace-making,* Oxford: Clarendon Press, 1995.

—*Assad: The Sphinx of Damascus,* London: Weidenfeld and Nicolson, 1988.

—"The Emergence of Modern Syria" in M. Ma'oz and A. Yaniv (eds.), *Syria under Assad: Domestic Constraints and Regional Risks,* London: Croom Helm, 1986.

Ma'oz, M. and A. Yaniv (eds.), "The Syrian Paradox" in *Syria under Assad: Domestic Constraints and Regional Risks,* London: Croom Helm, 1986.

Ma'oz, Z. "The Evolution of Syrian Power 1948–1984" in M. Ma'oz and A. Yaniv (eds.), *Syria under Assad: Domestic Constraints and Regional Risks,* London: Croom Helm, 1986.

MacFarlane, S. *Superpower Rivalry and Third World Radicalism: The Idea of National Liberation,* London: Croom Helm, 1985.

Machiavelli, N. *The Prince,* Oxford: Oxford University Press, 1986 (first published in 1532).

Magraw, R. *France 1815–1914: The Bourgeoisie Century,* London: Fontana Press, 1987.

Mandel, E. *Long Waves of Capitalist Movement: A Marxist Interpretation,* London: Verso, 1995.

Mangold, P. *National Security and International Relations,* London: Routledge, 1990.

Marcuse, H. *One Dimensional Man,* London: Routledge, 1964.

Marx, K. and F. Engels, *The Communist Manifesto,* London: Penguin, 1985 (first published in 1848).

Masterman, M. "The Nature of a Paradigm" in I. Lakatos and M. Musgrave (eds.), *Criticism and the Growth of Knowledge,* Cambridge: Cambridge University Press, 1970.

McGowan, P. and H. Shapiro, *The Comparative Study of Foreign Policy: A Survey of Scientific Findings,* London: Sage, 1973.

McQuail, D. *Mass Communication Theory: An Introduction,* London: Sage, 1989.

Mearsheimer, J. "Disorder Restored" in G. Allison and G. Treverton (eds.), *Rethinking America's Security: Beyond Cold War to New World Order,* New York: Norton, 1992.

Mendenhall, K. "Asad's Syria: Into the Nineties" in S. Dorr and N. Slater (eds.), *Security Perspectives and Policies: Lebanon, Syria, Israel, and the Palestinians (Conference Papers),* Defense Academic Research Support Program, May 1991.

Merle, M. *The Sociology of International Relations,* Leamington Spa: Berg, 1987.

Migdal, J. "Strong States, Weak States: Power and Accommodation" in M. Weiner, S. Huntington, *et al.* (eds.), *Understanding Political Development,* London: Little, Brown, 1987.

Mishra, R. "The Welfare of Nations" in R. Boyer and D. Drache (eds.), *States Against Markets: The Limits of Globalization,* London: Routledge, 1996.

Morgenthau, H. *Politics Among Nations: The Struggle for Power and Peace,* New York: Knopf, 1968.

Morse, E. "The Transformation of Foreign Policies: Modernization, Interdependence and Externalization" in R. Little and M. Smith (eds.), *Perspectives on World Politics,* London: Routledge, 1992.

Mouffe, C. (ed.) "Hegemony and Ideology in Gramsci" in *Gramsci and Marxist Theory,* London: Routledge, 1979.

Munro, A. *An Arabian Affair: Politics and Diplomacy behind the Gulf War,* London: Brassey's, 1996.

Nasrallah, F. "Syria after Ta'if: Lebanon and the Lebanese in Syrian Politics" in E. Kienle (ed.), *Contemporary Syria: Liberalization between Cold War and Cold Peace,* London: British Academic Press, 1994.

—"The Treaty of Brotherhood, Co-operation and Co-ordination" in Y. Choueiri (ed.), *State and Society in Syria and Lebanon,* Exeter: Exeter University Press, 1993.

Nevo, J. "Syria and Jordan: The Politics of Subversion" in M. Ma'oz and A. Yaniv (eds.), *Syria under Assad: Domestic Constraints and Regional Risks,* London: Croom Helm, 1986.

Niblock, T. "International and Domestic Factors in the Economic Liberalization Process in Arab Countries" in T. Niblock and E. Murphy (eds.), *Economic and Political Liberalization in the Middle East,* London: British Academic Press, 1993.

Nicholson, M. *Causes and Consequences in International Relations: A Conceptual Study,* London: Pinter, 1996.

Noble, P. "The Arab System: Pressures, Constraints, and Opportunities" in B. Korany and A. Dessouki (eds.), *The Foreign Policies of Arab States: The Challenge of Change,* Boulder: Westview Press, 1991.

Nogaard, O., D. Hindsgaul, L. Johannsen and H. Willumsen (eds.), *The Baltic States after Independence,* Cheltenham: Edward Elgar, 1996.

Nordlinger, E. "Taking the State Seriously" in M. Weiner, S. Huntington, *et al.* (eds.), *Understanding Political Development*, London: Little, Brown, 1987.

Nye, J. and R. Keohane, *Understanding International Conflicts: Origins of the Great Twentieth Conflicts*, Harvard: HarperCollins, 1993.

Nye, J. and R. Smith, *After the Storm: Lessons from the Gulf War*, London: Aspen Institute, 1992.

Owen, R. *State, Power, and Politics in the Making of the Modern Middle East*, London: Routledge, 1992.

Paterson, T. "Introduction: American Critics of the Cold War and Their Alternatives" in T. Patterson (ed.), *Cold War Critics: Alternatives to American Foreign Policy in the Truman Years*, Chicago: Quadrangle, 1971.

Penrose, E. "From Economic Liberalization to International Integration: The Role of the State" in T. Niblock and E. Murphy (eds.), *Economic and Political Liberalization in the Middle East*, London: British Academic Press, 1993.

Perthes, V. *The Political Economy of Syria under Asad*, London: I.B. Tauris, 1995.

—"Stages of Economic and Political Liberalization" in E. Kienle (ed.), *Contemporary Syria: Liberalization between Cold War and Cold Peace*, London: British Academic Press, 1994.

—"The Private Sector, Economic Liberalization, and the Prospects of Democratization: The Case of Syria and Some Other Arab Countries" in G. Salame (ed.), *Democracy without Democrats? The Renewal of Politics in the Muslim World*, London: I.B. Tauris, 1994.

Petran, T. *Syria*, New York: Praeger, 1972.

Petrella, R. "Globalization and Internationalization: The Dynamics of the Emerging World Order" in R. Boyer and D. Drache (eds.), *States Against Markets: The Limits of Globalization*, London: Routledge, 1996.

Pipes, D. *Greater Syria: The History of an Ambition*, Oxford: Oxford University Press, 1990.

Potter, D. "The Autonomy of Third World States within the Global Economy" in A. McGrew and P. G. Lewis, *et al.*, *Global Politics: Globalisation and the Nation-State*, Cambridge: Polity Press, 1992.

Rabinovich, I. "The Changing Prism: Syrian Policy in Lebanon as a Mirror, an Issue and an Instrument" in M. Ma'oz and A. Yaniv (eds.), *Syria Under Asad: Domestic Constraints and Regional Risks,* London: Croom Helm, 1986.

—"The Foreign Policy of Syria: Goals, Capabilities, Constraints and Options" in C. Tripp (ed.), *Regional Security in the Middle East,* New York: St Martin's Press, 1984.

—*Syria under the Ba'th 1963–66: The Army–Party Symbiosis,* Jerusalem: Israel University Press, 1972.

Radosh, R. and L. Liggio, "Henry A. Wallace and the Open Door" in T. Paterson (ed.), *Cold War Critics: Alternatives to American Foreign Policy in the Truman Years,* Chicago: Quadrangle, 1971.

Ramet, P. *The Soviet–Syrian Relationship Since 1955: A Troubled Alliance,* Boulder: Westview Press, 1990.

Randle, R. *Issues in the History of International Relations: The Role of Issues in the Evolution of the State System,* New York: Praeger, 1987.

Rathmell, A. *Secret War in the Middle East: The Covert Struggle for Syria, 1949–1961,* London: I.B. Tauris, 1995.

Richards, A. and J. Waterbury, *A Political Economy of the Middle East: State, Class, and Economic Development,* Boulder: Westview Press, 1990.

Rodinson, M. *Israel and the Arabs,* Middlesex: Penguin, 1969.

Rosenau, J. *The Scientific Study of Foreign Policy,* New York: The Free Press, 1971.

Rousseau, J. J. *The Social Contract,* London: Penguin, 1987.

Rubenburg, C. *Israel and the American National Interest,* Urbana: University of Illinois Press, 1986.

Rugh, W. *The Arab Press: News, Media, and Political Process in the Arab World,* London: Croom Helm, 1979.

Sa'ad, M. *Regional System and Inter-Arab Conflicts: The Iraqi–Kuwaiti Crises of 1961 and 1990,* Matsushita: International Middle Eastern Studies, September 1992.

Sadowski, Y. *Scuds or Butter?: The Political Economy of Arms Control in the Middle East,* Washington: Brookings Institute, 1993.

Saunders, B. *The United States and Arab Nationalism: The Syrian Case, 1953–1960,* London: Praeger, 1996.

Schapiro, L. *Totalitarianism,* London: PallMall, 1977.

Schilcher, L. *Families in Politics,* Stuttgart: Franz Steiner Verlag, Wiesbaden, 1985.

Scruton, R. *A Dictionary of Political Thought,* London: Pan, 1983.

Seale, P. "Asad: Between Institutions and Autocracy" in R. Antoun and D. Quataert (eds.), *Syria: Society, Culture, and Polity,* Albany: State University of New York Press, 1991.

—*Asad of Syria: The Struggle for the Middle East,* London: I.B. Tauris, 1988.

—*The Struggle for Syria: A Study of Post-War Arab Politics, 1945–1958,* London: Oxford University Press, 1965.

Sheehan, M. *The Balance of Power, History and Theory,* London: Routledge, 1996.

Shevardnadze, E. *The Future Belongs to Freedom,* London: Sinclair-Stevenson, 1991.

Simpson, J. *Despatches from the Barricades: An Eye-Witness Account of the Revolutions That Shook the World 1989–90,* London: Hutchinson, 1998.

Skinner, Q. *Machiavelli,* Oxford: Oxford University Press, 1981.

Skocpol, T. "Bringing the State Back In: Strategies of Analysis in Current Research" in P. Evans, D. Rueschemeyer and T. Skocpol (eds.), *Bringing the State Back In,* Cambridge: Cambridge University Press, 1990.

—*States and Social Revolutions,* Cambridge: Cambridge University Press, 1979.

Smith, B. *Understanding Third World Politics: Theories of Political Change and Development,* Bloomington: Indiana University Press, 1996.

Smith, G. (ed.), "Nationalities Policy from Lenin to Gorbachev" in *The Nationalities Question in the Soviet Union,* London: Longman, 1992.

Smith, S. "The Self-Images of a Discipline: A Genealogy of International Relations Theory" in K. Booth and S. Smith (eds.), *International Relations Theory Today,* Cambridge: Polity Press, 1995.

—"Paradigm Dominance in International Relations: The Development of International Relations as a Social Science" in H. Dyer and L. Mangasarian (eds.), *The Study of International Relations: The State of the Art,* Basingstoke: Macmillan, 1988.

—"Foreign Policy Analysis and International Relations" in H. Dyer and L. Mangasarian (eds.), *The Study of International Relations: The State of the Art,* London: Macmillan, 1988.

Snow, D. *Distant Thunder: Third World Conflict and the New International Order,* New York: St Martin's Press, 1993.

Springborg, R. "The United Nations in the Gulf War" in T. Ismael and J. Ismael (eds.), *The Gulf War and the New World Order: International Relations of the Middle East,* Gainesville: University Press of Florida, 1994.

Stoessinger, J. "The Anatomy of the Nation-State and the Nature of Power" in R. Little and M. Smith (eds.), *Perspectives on World Politics,* London: Routledge, 1992.

Stone, M. "Syria" in Middle East Review 1995 *The World of Information,* London: Kogan Page and Walden, 1994.

Strange, S. "Political Economy and International Relations" in K. Booth and S. Smith (eds.), *International Relations Theory Today,* Cambridge: Polity Press, 1995.

Streeck, W. "Public Power beyond the Nation-State: The Case Study of the European Community" in R. Boyer and D. Drache (eds.), *States Against Markets: The Limits of Globalization,* London: Routledge, 1996.

Sukkar, N. "The Crisis of 1986 and Syria's Plan for Reform" in E. Kienle (ed.), *Contemporary Syria: Liberalization between Cold War and Cold Peace,* London: British Academic Press, 1994.

Tadié, B. "The Movement of the Non-Aligned and its Dilemmas Today" in M. Selim (ed.), *Non-Alignment in a Changing World,* Cairo: American University Press, 1983.

Taheri, A. *The Inside Story of Islamic Terrorism: Holy Terror,* London: Sphere, 1987.

Thompson, K. *Cold War Theories: Volume I, World Polarization 1943–1953,* Baton Rouge: Louisiana State University Press, 1981.

Tibawi, A. *A Modern History of Syria including Lebanon and Palestine,* London: Macmillan, 1969.

Tickner, J. "Re-visioning Security" in K. Booth and S. Smith (eds.), *International Relations Theory Today,* Cambridge: Polity Press, 1995.

Tillman, S. *The United States in the Middle East,* Bloomington: Indiana University Press, 1982.

Tilly, C. "War Making and State Making as Organized Crime" in P. Evans, D. Rueschemeyer and T. Skocpol (eds.), *Bringing the State Back In,* Cambridge: Cambridge University Press, 1990.

Torrey, G. *Syrian Politics and the Military*, Columbus: Ohio State University Press, 1964.

Tucker, R. *Stalin in Power: The Revolution from Above 1928–1941*, New York: Norton, 1992.

Van Dam, N. *The Struggle for Power in Syria: Politics and Society under Asad and the Ba'th Party*, London: I.B. Tauris, 1996.

Viotti, P. and M. Kauppi. *International Relations Theory: Realism, Pluralism, Globalism*, London: Macmillan, 1987.

Wallerstein, I. *Historical Capitalism with Capitalist Civilization*, London: Verso, 1996.

—"The World System versus World-Systems: A Critique" in A. Gunder Frank and B. Gills (eds.), *The World System: Five Hundred Years or Five Thousand?*, London: Routledge, 1993.

—*Geopolitics and Geoculture: Essays on the Changing World-System*, Cambridge: Cambridge University Press, 1991.

—"The Art of the Possible, or the Politics of Radical Transformation" in K. Hadjor (ed.), *New Perspectives in North–South Dialogue: Essays in Honour of Olaf Palme*, London: I.B. Tauris, 1988.

—"Crisis as Transition" in S. Amin, G. Arrighi, A. Frank and I. Wallerstein (eds.), *Dynamics of Global Crisis*, London: Macmillan, 1982.

Waltz, K. "Anarchic Order and Balances of Power" in R. Keohane (ed.), *Neorealism and Its Critics*, New York: Columbia University Press, 1986.

—"Toward Nuclear Peace" in R. Art and K. Waltz (eds.), *The Use of Force: International Politics and Foreign Policy*, Lanham: University Press of America, 1983.

—*Theory of International Relations*, Reading, Mass.: Addison-Wesley, 1979.

—*Man, the State and War: A Theoretical Analysis*, New York: Columbia University Press, 1968.

Watson, A. *The Evolution of International Society*, London: Routledge, 1992.

Weber, M. *The Theory of Social and Economic Organisation*, New York: The Free Press, 1968.

Windson, P. "Superpowers and Client States: Perceptions and Interactions" in M. Efrat and J. Bercovitch (eds.), *Superpowers and Client States in the Middle East: The Imbalance of Influence,* London: Routledge, 1991.

Yamak, L. *The Syrian Social National Party: An Ideological Analysis,* Cambridge: Harvard University Press, 1966.

Yaniv, A. "Alliance Politics in the Middle East" in A. Braun (ed.), *The Middle East in Global Strategy,* London: Westview Press, 1987.

Yorke, V. *Domestic Politics and Regional Security: Jordan, Syria, and Israel. The End of an Era?,* Aldershot: Gower, 1988.

Young, J. *Cold War Europe 1945–1989: A Political History,* London: Hodder & Stoughton, 1991.

Zaalouk, M. *Power, Class and Foreign Capital in Egypt: The Rise of the New Bourgeoisie,* London: Zed, 1989.

Ziadeh, N. *Syria and Lebanon,* London: Ernest Benn, 1957.

Official publications

Statistical Abstract, (Damascus: Central Bureau of Statistics, 1993).

Conference papers and Ph.D. theses

Bahout, J. "The Syrian Business Community and Prospects for Political Change", Conference papers, School of Oriental and African Studies, University of London, May 1993.

Betz, D. "Conflict of Principle and Policy: A Case Study of the Arab Baath Socialist Party in Power in Syria, 8 March 1963–23 February 1966" (Ph.D. thesis, Ann Arbor), Ann Arbor: Xerox University Microfilms, 1976.

Daneels, I., R. Hinnebusch and N. Quilliam. "Omni-Balancing Revisited: Syrian Foreign Policy between Rational Actor and Regime Legitimacy", Paper presented at British Society of Middle Eastern Studies Conference, 1995.

El-Attrache, M. "The Political Philosophy of Michel 'Aflaq and the Ba'ath party in Syria" (Ph.D. thesis, Ann Arbor), Ann Arbor: Xerox University Microfilms, 1976.

Makdisi, N. "The Syrian National Party: A Case Study of the First Inroads of National Socialism in the Arab World" (Ph.D. thesis, Ann Arbor), Ann Arbor: Xerox University Microfilms, 1977.

Najem, T. and N. Quilliam. "Issues in Political Economy of the Middle East: The Assimilation of Pariah States into the Hegemonic World Order: A Case Study of Syria and Lebanon", Paper presented at the University of Coventry, April 1996.

Picard, E. "Espace de référence et espace d'intervention du mouvement rectificatif au pouvoir en Syrie 1970–1982" (Paris: thèse de III cycle, 1985).

Poelling, S. "The Role of the Private Sector in the Syrian Economy", Paper presented at University of Exeter conference, 19–20 March 1994.

Torrey, G. "Independent Syria, 1946–54" (Ph.D. thesis, Ann Arbor), Ann Arbor: University of Michigan, 1961.

Index